THE FIELD OF THE STAR

Nicholas Luard is the author of numerous non-fiction books, including *Andalucia: A Portrait of Southern Spain* and *The Last Wilderness*, an account of his expeditions across the Kalahari; he has also written twelve novels. He is chairman of the John Muir Trust, Scotland's foremost wild-land conservation trust, and a Member of Council of the World Wildlife Fund. He lives on a farm in Wales with his wife Elisabeth, the eminent cookery writer.

Also by Nicholas Luard

Non-fiction

THE WILDLIFE PARKS OF AFRICA
THE LAST WILDERNESS
LANDSCAPE IN SPAIN (with Michael Busselle)
ANDALUCIA: A PORTRAIT OF SOUTHERN SPAIN

Fiction

THE WARM AND GOLDEN WAR
THE ROBESPIERRE SERIAL
TRAVELLING HORSEMAN
THE ORION LINE
THE DIRTY AREA
GONDAR
KALA
HIMALAYA
SANCTUARY
SILVERBACK

THE FIELD OF
THE STAR

*A Pilgrim's Journey
to Santiago de Compostela*

Nicholas Luard

PENGUIN BOOKS

PENGUIN BOOKS

Published by the Penguin Group
Penguin Books Ltd, 27 Wrights Lane, London w8 5tz, England
Penguin Putnam Inc., 375 Hudson Street, New York, New York 10014, USA
Penguin Books Australia Ltd, Ringwood, Victoria, Australia
Penguin Books Canada Ltd, 10 Alcorn Avenue, Toronto, Ontario, Canada m4v 3b2
Penguin Books (NZ) Ltd, Private Bag 102902, NSMC, Auckland, New Zealand

Penguin Books Ltd, Registered Offices: Harmondsworth, Middlesex, England

First published by Michael Joseph 1998
Published in Penguin Books 1999
1 3 5 7 9 10 8 6 4 2

Set in Postscript Monotype Fournier
Printed in England by Clays Ltd, St Ives plc

For Francesca Susan Luz de Beauregard Baron Luard.

*And her mother, Elisabeth, her brother, Caspar,
her sisters, Poppy and Honey, and her multitude of friends.*

*And for my sister, Priscilla, my chief companion on
the long journey.*

*And also for all the scoundrels, scroungers, scholars, vintners,
pickpockets, poets, priests, soldiers and songmakers, fellow-
pilgrims, robber monks, thieving innkeepers, farmers' wives,
evil-smelling and penny-pinching landladies, the fine and warm
and generous folk — overwhelmingly the vast majority — we met
along the route. They were all part of the caravan. They were all
in their different ways on the same road. Bless the lot of them.*

'The moon and sun are eternal travellers. Even the years wander on. A lifetime adrift in a boat, or in old age leading a tired horse into the years, every day is a journey, and the journey itself is home. From the earliest times there have always been some who have perished along the road. Still I have always been drawn by windblown clouds into dreams of a lifetime of wandering.'

Narrow Road to the Interior, Matsuo Bashō (1644–94).

Foreword

This is the story of a pilgrim's journey on foot to Santiago de Compostela, the cathedral town and shrine of St James close to the Atlantic shore in north-western Spain.

In French the ancient pilgrim path to Santiago is called the *Chemin*, in Spanish the *Camino*. Both terms have a double meaning: the physical route on the ground through the mountains and across the plains, and the reflective internal journey the pilgrim makes in his mind as he travels. I have done what most English writers do and used the word 'Way'. It's simple and yet has the resonance of both the French and Spanish equivalents.

I travelled with two companions, one of whom, Hilary Hugh-Jones, had planned the journey over several years. The other was my sister, Priscilla Wintringham-White who helped with the organization and subsequently invited me to join them.

We made the journey in stages over the course of four years, starting each stage where we'd left off before. The time may sound long but for good reasons many of today's pilgrims take much longer. Our total time on the Way was perhaps three months. Like many others, we had family or work commitments, or both, and it was difficult to be away for more than a few weeks at a time. Now I'm glad it was so. Instead of a hurried one-season tramp with our heads to the ground, we travelled and experienced the Way at almost every time of the year – spring, summer, autumn, even in the approaches of winter.

We saw the flowers and falling leaves, saw the arriving and departing migrant birds, picked the fruits, waded through the floods, took shelter from the storms, were chilled by the frosts and snows, burned by the Castilian sun. We got, I think, the true flavour of the journey – harsh in the winter cold, green and golden and gentle in spring and summer.

The story of our travels makes no attempt to be a gazetteer or historical guide. The literature of the Santiago pilgrimage is vast. Many others, scholars better qualified than I, have recorded its history, the

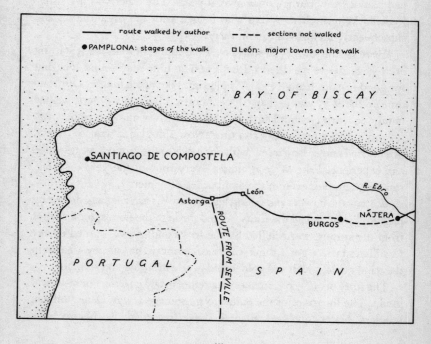

route walked by author ----- sections not walked
●PAMPLONA: stages of the walk ▫León: major towns on the walk

BAY OF BISCAY

●SANTIAGO DE COMPOSTELA

R. Ebro

Astorga ▫ ▫León

NÁJERA

ROUTE FROM SEVILLE

BURGOS

PORTUGAL

S P A I N

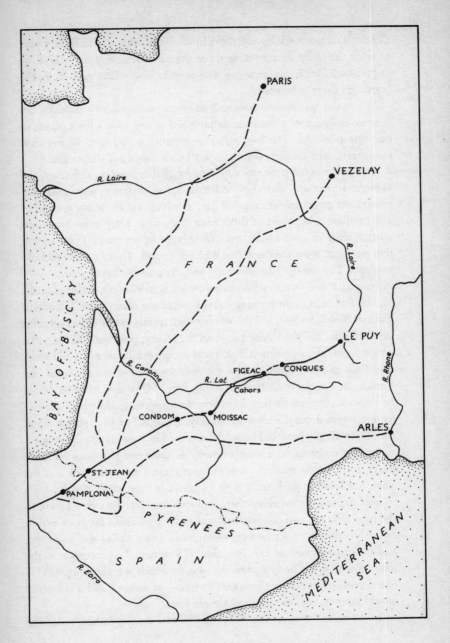

Camino's architectural legacy, the cultural, religious and economic impact of what the Way became over more than a thousand years – and the impact on Europe was immense. For anyone who wants to study it, the books are there to be read.

When she was sent to Switzerland as our ambassador's consort, my mother-in-law sent a memorable postcard to my wife with a plaintive one-line message: 'Darling, mountains really aren't me.' In my case mountains, like deserts, *are* me, but I know just what she meant.

The fragmented procession of buildings that borders the Way, the abbeys, fortresses, churches, cathedrals, monasteries, convents and towers, are often magnificent but they aren't me either. Many are empty and desolate now, most of them decaying ruins. They were brick and mortar tents thrown up by man for a specific purpose. They served that purpose. Now they are wasting back to soil. There's a melancholy to them. The energy, the vibrancy and the passion have gone.

Instead, I'm drawn to what exultantly lives: wilderness, skeins of birds, orchids and bees, night-hunting animals, wind and rain, the fall of sunlight and cast cloud-shadow, and the whole rough untidy tangle of engagement between man and the landscape – and the poetry, painting and song that comes from their interaction. Spirit and people exhilarate me. Cold stone says little to me – given always the seductive exceptions of places like Venice, the mosque in Córdoba and the glory of Chartres. All of us should be allowed a few contradictions in how we view things. In what follows I have just noted, maybe idiosyncratically, a handful of what struck me as the outstandingly beautiful built relics of medieval and later pilgrimage.

No one embarks on a long journey, let alone one that lasts for three years, for a single reason. I was no exception. I was aware of it at the start, but looking back on it now I can see it even more clearly. Of a myriad of motives involved there was one in chief. The year I took to the road with my two companions was 1993. Two and a bit years earlier my eldest daughter, Francesca, twenty-five years old as she was then, had been diagnosed as carrying the HIV virus, the precursor to the breakdown of the body's immune system which we know as AIDS. She'd been given about two years to live – as fortune and a fair wind would have it, she was granted almost four.

In the end, I took to the Way simply as a man, a father, reflecting on his daughter's approaching death, and trying to make sense both of the coming event and what there was between the two of us. It didn't work out like that as perhaps the story tells. I think now it doesn't matter a jot or tittle. Francesca won. She defied analysis and reconciliation. She was too brave and bold, too intelligent, too perceptive, too private in what she wanted to guard. In the poet Robert Frost's words:*

> While the customs slept
> I crossed to safety,
> And what I would not part with,
> I have kept.

I can do nothing about her, now or then. Father and daughter did not make their peace. Maybe it was of no account. Maybe I had the whole thing at widdershins and peace existed anyway and I simply didn't recognize it, although sometimes peace between us seemed to rage like one of the forest fires that intermittently threatened our house in Andalucía.

Francesca kept her own counsel.

She stared me down and she stared down death. My only conclusion at the end was that I was lucky, I was blessed to have known her. A good fairy may not have attended her birth, good fairies shouldn't allow what was visited on her, but the fairy certainly attended mine in allowing me to be with her and grow up with her. That was riches beyond measure. She was impossible, dangerous and glorious. Many have heard of her. Her story has been told often, and strangers now visit her grave.

Parents so often believe they form their children and their lives. In part it's clearly true. What they can overlook is how much a child can change and shape *them*. There's an interaction, it's a two-way process, I am certainly not the person I would have been if I hadn't known her. Francesca took a kindly pruning-axe to me, chopped away many of the obscuring branches, and let me look at affairs through different and perhaps more clear-seeing eyes.

Apart from my companions, Priscilla and Hilary, I owe thanks to

---

* Reproduced from *The Poetry of Robert Frost*, edited by Edward Connery Lathem, by kind permission of the Estate of Robert Frost and Jonathan Cape Ltd.

many, notably the girl's friends. The word most often used to describe Francesca on television and in the press after her death was 'iconic'. I'm never quite sure what the word means. If it indicates she was a magnet, a focus for her generation, that she attracted the best and boldest to her, and that her destiny turned out to be one that threatened all of them, then I see a measure of truth in it. She lived life with passion, at the edge and to the full, but without any of the narcotics so many of us use as props.

Francesca saw too clearly. She had too much self-discipline. She thought life was funny and strange and rich enough to be experienced without any ultimately dulling crutches. Her friends acknowledged her vision and clustered around her. For them she was the standard-bearer. She carried their banner high.

Together with her family, her travels, her work and her art, they were her life. They gave her everything and she returned it in hearts, spades, diamonds and clubs. She could be a tempest, a whirlwind, a hurricane, but meanness never found a place in the vocabulary of her emotions. With open hands she gave everything back and often threw in the intellectual equivalent of the kitchen-sink for good measure too.

Francesca redefined the meaning of the generosity of the heart.

I refer at times to her journal. It is a remarkable document, a description of a young woman contemplating her approaching death which has, in my experience, no precedent. Parts of it have been published in Elisabeth Luard's book *Family Life*. Among the many tributes paid to it one, by James le Fanu writing in the *Telegraph*, described it as: 'An account with not a hint of self-pity, but rather filled with moments of such extraordinary insight that they take your breath away.' He, like other commentators who said the same, was right. The girl was rare. True to herself to the last, she went down leading the way as she'd always done, clear-eyed and unafraid, with every gun blazing and all her flags flying.

She led me what her old Scots nurse called a fine dance, but she unwrapped fear and in the worst of the terrible days showed the rest of us what it was – nothing.

Here, unvarnished but crafted as best I can, scratchy and stretched out across time, full of bumps and flaws – in other words, not at all neat and seamless as so many other accounts of the Pilgrim Way have been – is one man's tale of his strange daughter and his walk to the Field of the Star.

PART I

The Beginning

Le Puy is a small provincial town in the south-eastern quarter of France, not that far from the great industrial city of Lyon.

I sat on my bed in the Hôtel du Terminus.

The springs creaked, there were patches of damp on the walls, I could smell the rank discharge from the kitchen vents mingled with garlic and the stale smoke from the Gauloises cigarettes I used to smoke as a student in Paris. I heard the chatter and pacing footsteps of the prostitutes under the lamps in the street below.

It was almost midnight.

The hotel was exactly what Georges Simenon evoked so vividly in his Maigret novels. Shabby and down at heel with humpbacked corridors carpeted in stained and moth-eaten felt, little garret-like rooms, dim lights, the frequent shuddering rumble of trains beyond the flaking plaster.

Travelling salesmen in ball bearings and ladies' underwear slept here. So did lovers on furtive assignations. So too the occasional farmer from the countryside, out for a rare night's boozing and, with any luck, a quick reeling grope at the barmaid's breasts, the periodic provincial politician distributing a satchel of folding money from his party boss. They had all left their shadowy print on the place.

I stood up and walked down to the floor below.

I knocked on another cheap door – stained plywood coated with fading and yellowing varnish – and went in.

My two companions, the two women, were lying in twin beds, reading. I reached into my pocket and gave them the presents I had bought for them. Not so much presents, rather insignia, seals, emblems. I had thought for a long while what they should be before a close friend, Elspeth, decided for me. She chose ancient Ethiopian silver crosses.

Elspeth's judgement was right – it invariably is – the choice proper

3

and appropriate. The two got out of bed in their nightgowns, smiling happily, and kissed me. I went back to my room.

I had very little idea of what the three of us had embarked on, its course, its consequences, its effect on all our lives. We had set out on a journey which was to take us in stages four years to complete. We were about to walk the one-thousand-mile Pilgrim Way, the *Camino* to Santiago de Compostela – to the shrine of St James in the Field of the Star.

Letters to Francesca: 1

Dear Francesca: As a child, like children everywhere and in all ages, you loved stories.

For a professional story-teller, the man who puts his hat on the ground and hopes pennies will be tossed into it in exchange for a tale, I wasn't much good at telling them, at least not to you.

I was away far too often. It's often the case with young fathers, in mine more than most. I can't even now plead necessity. It was simply an urge to travel, explore and write. Not much of an excuse. Reviewing your mother's book Family Life *and noting she'd brought up the four of you almost on her own, one critic said I always seemed to be in 'another room or more often another country'.*

Another room, another country. I winced.

Your mother is charitable. When we married, far wiser than her years — she was barely twenty-one — she observed even then that strong male breeding stock is likely to come laced with the blood of the lion-killing moran, the adventurer and wanderer. She staked out her ground, ring-fenced it, and reared the clan behind the thorn. She made her place a citadel. And she let me go off. She tolerated much, but there were limits I went beyond at my peril. I was just about wise enough not to set foot outside them.

It took me years to find out but in the end, like most saddle-weary crusaders, I discovered that the funniest stories, the best songs, the warmest fires, and the sweetest stews — preferably simmered with barley and lean smoked bacon — were those available at the home hearth.

I put on my boots. I roamed and returned. I tugged off the by-then-sodden leather, and sat with my head bowed on the settle by the door.

'How are the girls?' was always my first question.

'Whatever your shortcomings as a father,' Elisabeth used to say, 'you'll make a wonderful grandfather. I can already see your grey beard shining in the sunset over the lakeside fire, while you carve another hickory owl-whistle as you pass on words of wisdom to the little ones.'

I eyed her speculatively.

Her face was smiling, teasing, inscrutable. I have a feeling it may have been a joke at my expense — perish the possibility — but there might have been a kernel of truth under the laughter. I'd learnt how to read lion spoor with the best, to measure the timing of the big cats' tracks from frost-hardening and sun breakdown, and I wasn't so bad with a flintstone and a Sheffield blade.

Oh, my God, Francesca, I wish I'd been able to be grandfather to the children you so much wanted to have.

Perhaps I could have settled the score, paid off the debts, taught them the things that, modestly, I'm not bad at like the ones I've mentioned. Also casting flies over trout streams, reading poems, shooting straight through a V-sight with a rifle, knowing good honest wines like those from Chateauneuf's stony pastures, navigating not by compass but stars and sunlight, whittling and pewter-polishing, fire-making and pitching tents.

Tiny skills but vital for us all to learn. A cask of treasure to be passed down which defines us, equips us for living, and makes us safe. I missed the chance with you. And you, of course, in the urgency of your youth had no more awareness of what we were both missing than I did.

You simply raged at what you, understandably, saw as my inadequacies. Absent father. Another room, another country. On one occasion, when I did come back home to write, you came into my study, a little raggedy rapscallion of a girl, and stared at me in what's appropriately called stony silence. After a few bleak and chilling minutes you whirled away, slamming the door as you went out.

I quailed. You could only have been six or seven, but it was an hour or more before I could compose myself enough to go on writing. You had the force of a hurricane even then.

Once on my birthday, you must have been about thirteen at the time, you gave me an envelope. Inside was my birthday present — a worn £1 note. I looked up and saw you watching me steadily with your damson-dark eyes, so dark they were almost black. I was humiliated and embarrassed, but I said nothing. There was nothing I could say. We should all, and parents in particular, give thoughtfully chosen individual presents to each other on days of celebration. Cavalier and careless I'd taken to reaching for my wallet and tossing you impersonal anonymous money.

Money's useful, but it's not what a father should give his eldest daughter on the anniversary of her birth. That calls for something splendid and special and personal. Damn you, Fran, for that characteristically sharp reminder. You wanted something from me and I hadn't measured up.

I did bring you back stories from my travels.

Mainly they were tales of Africa, of old white hunters and elephant and lion and my adventures on my expeditions across the great stone plateau of the Kalahari Desert. I think you enjoyed them, although with your extraordinary self-containment and enigmatic gaze it wasn't easy to tell. Perhaps they fell more into the category of news and anecdote rather than proper stories.

I dedicated one book to you, a story inspired by the climb you and I and your beloved big brother, that man of poetry and iron, made up through the Himalayan snows towards the Tibetan border. There was another story I wanted to give you, a 'true' one, although what, in that famous quote of jesting Pilate's question, is truth? He didn't stay for an answer, but I'll try as best as I can to give you the truth.

It's the story of my long journey, my pilgrimage, to Santiago de Compostela. The walk was made for you and my pilgrimage was dedicated to you. If I claimed you were my only reason for setting out, you'd have laughed and called me, not for the first time, a liar. And of course you'd have been right. Most writers are liars. I'm no exception. I went because it was an adventure, because I was restless, because I love Europe and its peoples and the wild landscapes of the pilgrim road as it crosses France and Spain.

And yet – I will hold to this – I went first and foremost because of you. I set out in 1993, some two years after you'd been diagnosed as HIV-positive. I didn't for one moment think that God or the stars or pagan Ceres in spring would make you well in recognition of what I was doing. They were all benign but they were remote. Their powers were suspended for they knew, as you and I did, you'd entered what the Spanish call a camino sin salida *– a road with no way out.*

The best I could do was light candles for you along the path, and to reflect not just on you but on the two of us. Wayward distant father and brilliant turbulent daughter. Matters were seldom easy between us, were they? We collided again and again. Jostling angrily, we spat like cats at each other. Yet your mother always said you were more like me than any of the others, and frayed and strained as it often was, the bond was deep and it lasted. I alone was with you when the last of those damnable tests were done, when the final sentence was handed down, and we both realized from then on we were measuring time in weeks. We held hands then. Absurdly I needed comforting far more than you did, and you knew it — your spirit so much larger than mine — and you gave it to me.

You had the first part of the story, but missed out on the end. A story with no ending is always unsatisfactory. Here's the whole business. Here, too, is my search for you.

For you and myself and what there was between us.

I

As the so-called Dark Ages gave way to the medieval times, three great pilgrimages emerged to haunt, almost to dominate, the consciousness of Europe.

They were respectively to Rome, Jerusalem and Santiago, the Spanish name for St James, St Jacques as the French know him, after whom the city was called.

From a crusader-nobleman to the peasant-farmer at the gates of his lord's castle, it was virtually incumbent on everyone to complete one of the pilgrimages. The most favoured of the three great journeys, outranking even Jerusalem, was to Santiago in north-western Spain.

It has been estimated that in certain years one-tenth of Europe's population was either on pilgrimage, or engaged in servicing the pilgrim trade. The medieval Church was, in effect, the first global travel agency – the known western edge of the world finished then, of course, at Cape Finisterre, literally the 'end of the earth'.

The essence of Santiago's story, St James's story, is simply told. James, a disciple of Christ, one of the twelve apostles and the first of the Christian disciples, was murdered by Herod either in Palestine or in Rome. His body was removed by his followers from the place of execution, taken in a stone boat to Spain where he'd earlier been preaching the gospel, and secretly buried in a field – Compostela, the field of the star. 'Stela' needs no explanation. 'Compo', or *campo* in today's spelling, is the Castilian word for meadow or more generally the countryside.

Why the boat was made of stone, as all the early accounts insist it was, no one has really explained. My own guess is that stone heightened the drama and momentousness of what was in itself an epic voyage. The body of an ordinary mortal would have been lucky to complete it in a sturdily built orthodox craft. Only a saint of extraordinary powers could have ridden through the Mediterranean storms in a skiff fashioned from rock.

Whatever the reason for the boat's strange making, James came back to the Iberian peninsula.

Eight centuries later, a Galician priest had a dream in which a star's beam pointed to where James's body lay. He obtained the permission of his bishop to dig the ground, and found the saint's remains. A shrine was built above the spot and later the great cathedral.

So much for the Roman Church's version of the truth or the story or the legend, or a strange tangled blend of all three. Whatever, matters grew more fierce and complicated in the aftermath of the priest's discovery. In AD 711 the *moros*, the Moors, the Arabs, invaded and conquered the Iberian peninsula in one of the fastest *blitzkriegs* in the history of warfare. Those Christians who survived the invasion retreated, gathering in a fragile rim of resistance behind their northern castles – 'Castilian' is the name the Spaniards give to the language that evolved there – and set about trying to drive the heathens out.

The job took them almost eight hundred years, but from the start they knew they needed a banner to fly above their armies, an icon to enthuse and inspire them. They chose James as their inspiration. The gentle disciple was transformed into bloody sword-wielding Santiago *matamoros* – St James the blackamoor killer as the phrase translates today, unacceptably, perhaps, in our politically correct times.

Whenever the Christian armies were facing defeat at the hands of the murderous Arab hordes, a ghostly horseman appeared in their ranks and changed the course of the battle – once he scythed down fifty thousand of the enemy. Finally the *reyes católicos*, the Christian monarchs Isabella and Ferdinand, won back the country.

The year was 1492. Before the monarchs entered the last Moorish citadel to fall, the magical water-filled city of Granada, Isabella knelt and prayed. After eight hundred years Spain was free. The Genovese Jewish navigator, the compulsively ambitious, red-haired, and probably deranged Columbus, was impatiently waiting a few miles away for permission to sail – and money to charter his ships. Isabel had a more important matter on her mind. She had already committed herself to pawning her jewels to finance the adventurer – she wanted spices and her travelling store-cupboard was empty – but there was something she had to do before she sent him on his way.

She had to thank St James for deliverance.

By then the saint's shrine was long since established as the focus for Europe's greatest pilgrimage.

There were many ways of approaching Santiago. Hundreds of thousands from Britain, like the medieval divine, Blessed Julian of Norwich, came by boat. Often they perished, their ships foundering in storms in the Bay of Biscay or being attacked and sunk by pirates. Others, St Francis of Assisi was one, chose their own circuitous routes – in his case, it seems to have taken him over much of southern Europe.

The vast majority gathered at four major assembly points in France and left from there. The meeting places were at Paris, Vézelay, some 130 miles south-east of the capital, Le Puy and Arles in Provence, all four of them important regional trading-posts and logical centres for the pilgrim caravans to congregate and provision themselves before they set off. The pilgrim roads led south-west. The first three came together shortly before the great snow-flanked wall of the Pyrénées, the fourth shortly afterwards. After winding up the mountains through the pass of Roncesvalles, where Roland blew his horn in his desperate call for help against what for centuries was thought to be a pursuing Arab army but what was probably a renegade guerrilla force of Basque bandits, they continued in a single stream across Spain to the pilgrims' destination.

We chose the curious, rock-pinnacled town of Le Puy as our departure point.

The reason was simple. The ancient pilgrim roads from Paris, Vézelay and Arles, although still used, have largely been covered with concrete and turned into modern highways. From Le Puy, the path – and for much of the way it is hardly even a path – winds silent and undisturbed through the mountains of the Massif Central and down onto the Gascon plain. Man has largely abandoned his settlements there. The country is desolate, empty.

To the rare walker, the pilgrim, it is a wilderness paradise.

*

What created the dynamic of pilgrimage, particularly the pilgrimage to Santiago, what made it so essential for so many to set out on the Way in spite of all its hazards?

There was no clear answer a thousand years ago, nor is there now. The Church would claim faith and the honouring, through a contemporary disciple and saint, of God materializing as man, the carpenter's son – probably a carpenter too – Jesus Christ. I like people who work in wood. I count among my good friends shipwrights, carpenters, bodgers, carvers and cabinet-makers. They're among the best people I know. They fashion things in the oldest living material man has used. I have no difficulty in seeing Jesus as part of their company. And I have little trouble with the idea of faith, of something outwith proof or logic, difficult and elusive as the concept may be.

Yet I hold to it and that's faith, and faith is undefinable. It has so many shapes, forms and contours, and all of them are beyond reason or logic. It is still not enough, not enough to explain pilgrimage and least of all to explain Santiago.

So what does?

I think the seventeenth-century Japanese poet Matsuo Bashō, whom I quoted at the start, gives the first clue in his words: 'the journey itself is home.' My old friend, the late Laurens van der Post, visionary and wilderness philosopher, would almost certainly nod in agreement. In his chronicles of the wanderings of the hunter-gatherer Kalahari clans of Bushmen, the San peoples, Sir Laurens suggests the same: journey and home are indivisible. We are not by nature, by evolution and genetic inheritance, rooted dwellers in a single place. We are instinctive nomads. We have an urge to roam – it takes us out on the roads. That's where, even if the roads are unmarked, we belong.

Until we made our first permanent settlements as farmers and herders, perhaps in the Jordan valley 25,000 years ago, we'd been travellers. Twenty-five thousand years may sound a long time. Compared to the three to five million years of our evolving existence before those settlements, those early camps, fires and stockades, the span is nothing – barely even a drop on time's nose. Patterns and habits, strategies for survival, don't just breed out. They're enduring, they last.

So we wander.

And because of the message, the remote inheritance, we need the roads, we need the stars above them, we need to reflect on both. It still leaves us with Santiago. Why did Europe, why does it still, anchor its journeyings around the man in the stone boat? The explanation may lie in someone we know as John the Baptist.

Very odd and very troubling to the orthodox, the Baptist is. He had a long beard, he emerged from the woods, and he was dangerous. Disturbingly, he dealt in waters. He baptized Christ in the river Jordan and vanished. Woods, rivers and waters are both vital and menacing. Diana the huntress came from them. The harvest goddess Ceres walks in the forest glades; Leda met her swan there. To this day almost every Spanish village *romería*, a pilgrimage celebration, starts in a wood or, even more often, at the headwaters of a stream.

The wild with its trees and rivers may be essential to life, but it is a place best avoided by civilized modern man.

The Christ considered it for forty days and sensibly returned home. Soon afterwards a gang of thugs, servants of the imperial occupying power, nailed the young man to a cross with a couple of known thieving bandits on either side, so the three of them should die.

That should show the locals their place, was the message Pilate intended. Be a subversive, a criminal, a thief, and we'll pin you to a cross-bar of your country's good native cedar.

The so-called Baptist linked the old and the new, the pagan past and modern Christianity. He passed the torch of belief — superstition, religion, sheer self-evident good sense, call it what one will — to the young man. The two communities of Stonehenge and Bethlehem, with their city fathers of druids and priests, were twinned as closely as London and Paris are today, but a new voice carried faith's message now. The past had stolen its way into the future. The trouble was the past wouldn't surrender its own immensely ancient inheritance and identity so easily.

John the Baptist was the green man, piping Pan, Johnny Appleseed, Robin Hood, the giant of the glens and forests and mountains. The Gawain poet wrote about him, Piers the Ploughman touched on him, Rabelais chronicled some of his adventures, he keeps nudging into Shakespeare's plays — who on earth is Puck if not the Baptist's child, his skittering wayward shadow? The Baptist, the green man, had his constituency. The Church tried to deprive him of it by claiming he'd joined their party but the electorate, humanity, kept turning out to vote for him as their original and preferred candidate.

In Spain the people amalgamated the Baptist with the apostle James, and reincarnated him as Santiago, their inspiration and saviour, the giant *matamoros*. The Church had little choice except to connive and try to turn it to its advantage. At least the green man had a Christian name and the patina of sanctity. The Celtic tribes invoked him in their battles with the Moors, the Church used him with remarkable skill and cunning to extend its empire, the land was freed and Isabella gave him thanks.

Nothing in human affairs is ever neat and tidy. Gold leaf makes a fine cosmetic plaster, but invariably blood and semen come leaking out to corrode it. Lift the rug and there are always spiders scuttling everywhere in different directions. All manner of other considerations must have been involved in the Jamesian cult, from blind obsessional faith to the cynical settling of blood feuds and land disputes – even Isabella's hunger for spices for her table gets caught up in the equation. Santiago, St James, St Jacques, was used in all his guises from green man to Christian saint to justify every one of them.

What I sensed before we set out became a conviction as the journey went on. We were certainly wanderers because it was natural for us to roam. But we weren't just wanderers on a Christian road. We were walking far older tracks. Tracing the way to James's grave, we were treading in the steps of Puck and Robin Hood. We stepped over hidden arrangements of the bones of slaughtered bears, compositions of dried buttercups and meadowsweet, rings of stones piled to protect them. In the cathedral at Compostela the two, the pagan and the Christian, the old and the new, came together.

That came much later. Compostela was miles, months, years ahead. It is a fearfully long way from Le Puy to the city named after the man in the stone boat.

2

'I can't ever sleep at the start of a big safari,' old Syd used to say, adding gloomily, 'can't bloody "go" either.'

I knew just what Syd meant.

He was a retired white hunter I adopted as camp boss and general organizer of my expeditions across southern Africa's Kalahari Desert. Each time we set out, for the first few days he'd appear blearily and red-eyed in the dawn light, trudge away into the bush with a roll of toilet paper, and return frustrated and cursing. Half a dozen early morning beers did wonders for his temper, but nothing for his bowels.

Then, as we began to make our way across the ancient stone plateau, everything would suddenly change. He'd return beaming from his dawn foray with the toilet roll noticeably thinner. The beers would be drunk with pleasure, not medicinally and vengefully, and I'd know we were truly on our way.

Like Syd I slept little that first night. Like him too I got up early, haggard and fretful, to join my companions for breakfast. I inspected them warily over a steaming bowl of *café au lait*.

One could apply many descriptions to Priscilla and Hilary. Shrinking violets wouldn't be one of them. I boxed as a welter-weight for the army and in the American Golden Gloves tournament. Even thirty years on I was still well muscled and running marathons. Compared to the two of them, I was a whey-faced little scrap of a figure – a pallid rake-thin chimney sweep from the wilder shores of Dickens's imagination.

They were and are formidable.

In their early forties both are close to six feet in height with broad-boned, finely honed, finely balanced bodies. There is something majestic and dangerous about their presence. A brutal drug-crazed mugger meeting either of them in a darkened alleyway would be well advised to run like a stag for the bright lights of the high street, and ask for police protection.

Yet both, too, in quite distinct ways, are beautiful and alluring. Priscilla, second of my sisters, has sleepy eyes, boyishly cropped hair – to her irritation she was sometimes taken for a man on the road to Santiago – and a temperament and will of sheet-beaten, kiln-forged steel. Since she was my sister, I'd obviously known her all my life. I knew nothing about her friend Hilary at all, I'd never even met her until the pilgrimage began.

'You're going to walk a thousand miles with a woman you've never seen?' a friend said to me in bewilderment before we started. 'You're mad! She may be illiterate, have bad breath, an evil temper and hate men.'

I asked Priscilla.

'Forget about it,' she said crisply. 'You'll love her.'

And I did from the moment I saw her.

Hilary's breath was sweet, her temper was calm, even if rocking occasionally with the tides of her exuberant personality, she had a boundless love of people – including men – and she was wonderfully, interestingly learned and literate. Not just in works of words, where as a writer I'm naturally comfortable, but in music where I am often at a loss.

Her hair was long and auburn and she tossed it wildly, extravagantly, like a tumultuous mane on a cantering horse. Her eyes flashed. She was and is a beauty. And if her height is about six feet, her spirit, her energy, her enthusiasm, the span of her inquiring mind, could only be measured in furlongs.

'You'll love her,' the words returned often.

Of course.

A pilgrim on the Santiago road traditionally carries a staff, a scrip and a scallop shell, the emblem of St James.

The staff, a vital piece of equipment for repelling dogs and helping heave oneself up mountains or keeping one's balance fording rivers, speaks for itself. I managed to leave mine behind at the first night's hotel, but I found a replacement a couple of days later. The scrip is the leather satchel in which the pilgrim carries his few and most valued possessions.

Hilary and I had their modern equivalent, well-worn canvas backpacks. They were large, well designed, and held everything we'd need for three weeks on the road. What they weren't, after being crammed with books, binoculars, waterproofs, a change of clothes and so on, was light. Each of them weighed well over twenty pounds. Twenty pounds is a fairly sturdy burden in itself. At the end of a twenty-five-mile tramp, scaling hills and trudging through rain or snow, it becomes a leaden load.

Compared to what Priscilla set out with, however, our packs were bagatelles, trifles.

Not only had she taken enough to service an entire nomadic caravan – from abseiling ropes to medicine boxes to three-volume reference works – she'd packed it all in a true scrip, a vast leather pannier which needed the combined efforts of the other two of us to heave onto her shoulders. Being leather, the pannier also, of course, absorbed water. When it rained – and it rained often – the weight seemed almost to double.

Somehow, in spite of swollen knees and aching shoulders, Priscilla struggled through the first part of the journey. On later stages she compromised. She switched to a canvas backpack, and reluctantly left out the ropes, oxygen cylinders and emergency bags of coal, but to the very end she carried a mighty load. If we'd been hit by a snow-and-ice avalanche on our summer crossing of the Castilian plain, she'd still have been equipped to deal with it.

Snow-and-ice avalanches aren't common in the searing August heat of central Spain. I never told her that. Nor will I now.

The third of the pilgrim's badges, the scallop shell, was a matter of debate between the three of us. The scallop is a strange and interesting creature, a sea-travelling migrant – most appropriate for the pilgrim's emblem. When the stone boat carrying St James's body beached on the Spanish shore, the horse of a passing rider panicked. The horse plunged into the sea, and both it and its rider vanished beneath the waves. When they appeared again from the surf, both were covered with scallop shells.

The awed attendants of the saint, dragging his body ashore, realized it was a sign. The scallop was James's chosen insignia.

I close my eyes and try to visualize the scene.

The black rocky inlets below Cape Finisterre, the turbulent waves and ochre-white Atlantic spume that cascades over them, the chill sting of the wind and the screaming gulls and wheeling roseate terns. The horseman passing, like Yeats's horseman with his cold eye, and his mount, maddened, terrified by the stone boat, bridling and rearing and racing uncontrollably for the sea.

The two vanish. The rider, choking, fights with the reins and bit beneath the surface to check and turn the animal. They clamber back through the spray onto the shore. They emerge soaked, glistening, salty, draped with dark banners of seaweed – and starred from shoulder to haunch to fetlock with scallop shells.

The rider gazes at the little group who form the boat's crew. As frightened as he is, they stare back at him. Then he kicks his spurs into the horse's flanks. As they gallop away into the hills, one by one the scallop shells drop from them. The saint's escort know it is a portent. One of them picks up a shell and places it on James's naked shrunken chest. Then they carry him up the cliff path and bury the shell with him.

I'd been vaguely aware of the scallop as a recurring motif in European art, architecture and sculpture from the Middle Ages onwards, but I'd never appreciated its significance – it had seemed simply an elegant decorative embellishment to works in paint or stone. Within days of setting out for Santiago, I realized why the shell was used so often and how important it was. More than anything else it was the pilgrim's passport, talisman, almost his identity.

The question was: should we wear the shell along the way as the badge of the journey or did we, as Hilary insisted, have to earn the right to wear it by completing the pilgrimage – in which case, of course, we couldn't pin it on ourselves until we reached Santiago?

Later each of us arrived at separate decisions in our own time. That first morning we agreed to postpone the debate and start as we were – without the scallop shell.

*

We left the hotel at 8.00 a.m. It was 23 April, St George's Day, a good omen, I thought, for a trio of English pilgrims to set out. The spring morning was bright and clear and chill. The skies over the town shone the pale translucent blue of a clutch of eggs in a blackbird's nest and the early sun was golden, but there was the promise of rain in the damp air. We climbed upwards to the traditonal departure point, Le Puy's cathedral, our boots and staffs tapping on the cobblestones.

Small children waiting for school to open, the girls in neat pinafores, the boys in carefully pressed shorts, each of them clutching a little metal canteen holding the hot midday meal. They perched like swallows on the walls on either side of the school gates, chattering and giggling. We stopped and spoke to them.

What were we doing, they asked, and where were we going?

We were pilgrims, we said, we were following the Chemin de St Jacques to the city of Santiago in Spain. Did they know about St Jacques? They shook their heads. They had never heard of the Pilgrim Way or the city at its end. Five centuries earlier, when hundreds of pilgrims left Le Puy every week, they'd have known about little else. Today it was a mystery.

A bell rang, the gates rattled open, and the children vanished as abruptly as the tiny migrant birds they so much resembled.

We went into the cathedral. Above the altar is an exquisite black madonna, thoughtful and serene and clothed in an alabaster cloak decorated with gold flowers. I studied her. She reminded me of the black St Sara in the little fortress church of Saintes-Maries-de-la-Mer in the Camargue, but somehow gentler and more generous – the Camargue lady's features and no doubt her spirit, too, are as tough as teak.

Le Puy's lady, I discovered, isn't the original. She was hacked to pieces and then burned in the obscene and infamous event known as the French Revolution. By great good luck, just before the carnage erupted and left its lasting brutalizing stain on France's soul, a geologist, who was also an artist, happened to be in Le Puy studying volcanoes – the region is a famous volcanic area. He fell in love with the madonna, and got the church's permission to make detailed drawings of her.

After a measure of sanity returned to the country, his drawings were used to recreate her. Whether the peace in her face comes from him or from her first incarnation no one now knows and it doesn't matter. I committed Le Puy's black virgin to my memory. She looked like a good companion for the journey – and I needed good companions.

I lit a candle and looked round for the other two. Priscilla and Hilary had vanished. I went outside, sat down on one of the walls where the swallows had gathered, and waited for them. I knew what they were doing.

They had gone to have their passports stamped.

It's often cynically claimed there's no such thing as a free lunch. In fact, as human nature is capable of being infinitely benign and generous as well as infinitely malign, there are not only free lunches available in life but free shelter and medical care too – to the wayfarer, the destitute, the beggar, the holy man and, above all, the pilgrim.

If we read the formidable intelligence of dolphins correctly, we're not unlike them – social creatures programmed not just to look after and nurture each other, including utter strangers, but different species too. We also know, and here dolphins seem to be more innocent and trusting than we are, that our freely given bounty, our generosity, is a magnet for exploitation by rogues, thieves and ruffians.

When the pilgrim roads began to thread across Europe, a vast support system evolved to help and care for the traveller. Religious faith played a major part but the motive for much of it was bluntly commercial. There was money to be made, large sums of money, out of the pilgrim trade; from ferries, inns, shops, vineyards, waggon hire, candle-selling, prostitution, blacksmithery and cobbling, so much more. Yet there was altruism too.

Pilgrims travelling the Way were on God's business. People on God's business deserved to be looked after. Military orders developed to protect them. The problem was to distinguish the charlatan determined to dig his shovel into the stores of generosity available to the true pilgrim, from the true pilgrim himself.

The answer was the pilgrim's passport.

The original passports were blank rolls of parchment. At every staging-post along the way, the pilgrim would have it stamped and dated by the local priest. Arriving at his next destination, the traveller produced it as proof he was a genuine pilgrim and not some feckless rogue scrounging a bowl of stew and a free night's lodging. It would be stamped again the following morning and the pilgrim would continue on his journey – to use it again the next evening.

The practice is centuries old and still continues, although today the passport takes the form of a booklet rather than a parchment scroll. The stamp is carved from a wooden block which is applied to an ink-soaked pad before being pressed down on the paper, much like the John Bull children's printing kits I remember being given just after the war. Each stamp has a different design, usually incorporating some heraldic device of the town or village it belongs to, and many are remarkably elaborate and beautiful. The one at Le Puy pre-dates the French Revolution since it was hidden by the priests during the mindless slaughter; some are much older.

Unlike Priscilla and Hilary, I set off without a passport. I treated the whole idea rather cavalierly as some sort of sentimental relic from the past.

'I don't need one of those,' I said loftily to them both. 'Only God stamps my passport.'

'I just hope God personally vouches for you each night when we get to Spain,' Hilary said. 'Otherwise you'll be sleeping in the street.'

She was right. The pilgrim passport – which also gives the pilgrim unconditional passage across the French–Spanish border – wasn't needed in France. So few people now visit the ancient pilgrim refuges north of the Pyrénées, its use as proof of entitlement to shelter has largely been abandoned. Once we reached Spain everything changed. There it was essential.

Hard-eyed priests and guardians of hostels examined the dates and stamps as suspiciously as if they'd been dubious markings on a forged £20 note. Without proof of my journey I would indeed have been sleeping in the street. Luckily by then I had a passport. Hilary hadn't trusted me to get one on my own, and had sent off for one for me.

'Just in case,' she said, 'like the French customs, God is working an overtime ban.'

3

'There!' Priscilla said.

We had walked down from the cathedral through the winding alleys of Le Puy and out onto the narrow road that leads towards the west, passing on the way a small wooden carving of St Jacques. Now we were standing beside a stone cross that marked the start of the Pilgrim Way.

I looked at where Priscilla was pointing. Painted on a lamp post was a double band, one red, one white, with a small arrow below and the legend 'GR65' above.

Forlorn and wistful Mary, Queen of England, declared that when she died the word 'Calais' would be found engraved on her heart. When I die, the coloured square and the number 65 will be engraved on mine. We saw them first that morning. Over the weeks, the months, the years that followed, we were to see them again and again, hour after hour – at sunrise, through rain and snowstorms, in the midday heat, at night by starlight or in an anxiously searching lamp's beam. From fifty yards to a mile or more apart, we saw them on mountain boulders, on posts marking river fords, on storm-felled trees, on farm gates, in streets and on taverns, churches and brothels at the heart of great cities.

Two short stripes of red and white, with '65' often, although not always, scrawled above them.

The 'GR' stands for Grandes Randonnées, the extraordinarily efficient French system of classifying the recommended routes for long-distance walkers. 65 is the number given to the Way of St James. The red and white symbol is the way-mark, the sign and confirmation on the ground that the traveller is on course and heading in the right direction. Naturally, the system isn't infallible. Rain and sleet scour off paint. Trees aren't only blown down by storms, the winter gales can roll the trunks away. Farm gates can rot and crumble. Rivers in spate can rise and drown the way-marks. Brothels can be closed and their walls scrubbed clean.

We encountered all those hazards but, by and large, the system works. In the course of almost a thousand miles – much of it through some of the most remote and uninhabited countryside in Europe – we lost our way on only a handful of occasions. The red and the white of the French GR65, and the yellow way-marks in Spain – where pillar-mounted brass or glazed ceramic pilgrim shells are often used as additional pointers – and the dedicated local bands of the pilgrimage supporters who keep the Way signposted, did us proud.

As we stood by the stone cross checking our maps for the day ahead, we heard the clump of boots on the road behind. We glanced round. A man with a large metal-framed pack on his back and a rangy friendly-looking dog trotting at his side was approaching us.

'Good morning,' he said as he stopped. 'I am Dutch Robert from Gouda in Holland and this is Fanny. You go to Santiago, too? Yes? Excellent.'

He beamed. Fanny sat down, scratched her ear thoughtfully, and then wagged her tail. Robert, like so many of the Dutch, spoke fluent English, and we started to talk.

Although almost half of the traditional Pilgrim Way runs through France, very few of today's pilgrims follow it. The vast majority, even among the most dedicated spiritual travellers, start at the foot of the pass of Roncesvalles in the Pyrénées and walk only the Spanish part of the journey. After Roncesvalles the trickle of pilgrims, particularly in high summer, becomes a stream, but by the time we eventually reached the pass, we'd probably met fewer than twenty companions on the road.

Robert was the first. He was a master-printer of about fifty, tanned and cheerful, cynical about the ways of mankind and the honesty of innkeepers, but as friendly as Fanny.

Starting from Gouda he'd already been walking for six weeks – or he should have been. In fact, for two of the weeks he'd been laid up with a kidney complaint which had swollen his feet grotesquely and made walking impossible. The cause was dehydration. Like many novice long-distance walkers, he hadn't realized how much moisture the human body loses through sweat and the simple activity of breathing.

'Now I've learnt to drink three litres of water every day,' he said, tapping the large container hanging from his waist. 'Now I go well.'

While it wasn't a lesson the three of us needed to learn, it was still a sharp and useful reminder. Even in ice and snow, the human organism requires liquid far more than food. We made it a rule to drink at minimum every two hours, and more often when the temperature rose.

Robert's life was complicated. We learnt about it over the days that followed. The reason for his story coming to us in bits and pieces lay in the structured pattern of a pilgrimage journey.

Early in the now thousand years' experience of pilgrimage travel, the pilgrim discovered he or she, whether walking, riding, or being carried in a waggon, could only cover so much distance in a day – the average being roughly somewhere between twelve and twenty miles. Less than twelve miles was an unsatisfactory hop; more than twenty was a marathon that ran into night, darkness and all the attendant dangers of wolves, robbers and cold.

Way-marks charted the path. Way-stations provided the night's sanctuary. Geography and history dictated to a large extent where the way-stations were set – fords and mountain passes, the crossing points of trade routes, old market sites, garrison forts, church and monastic settlements. They all had to accommodate the natural rhythm of the journey. Twelve to twenty miles apart. Not less, not more.

Now, as then, the pilgrim gets locked into a cycle. The companions he meets at one way-station, he'll almost certainly meet again at the next the following night. Sometimes people break the journey and leave the road for a rest, to meet friends, or simply to reflect on what they're doing. In general they trudge on together, not necessarily encountering each other during the day's walk, but almost invariably joining up in a common refuge as darkness falls.

So it was with Robert and the amiable, scrounging Fanny. We met them, we parted, we found them again, and so it went on.

The tangle in Robert's life, the difficulties he had to deal with, stemmed from his relationships with three different women: his wife, whom he treated with loving romantic care as his mistress; his secretary, who was also his mistress; and his mistress who, needless to say, was his mistress too. None of the three was aware of the roles the others played in his existence.

As he'd promised to keep all three in daily touch with his journey, this led to problems. We'd find him sitting frowning in a pilgrimage hostel above a pile of postcards, frantically trying to puzzle out what he'd said to whom, when he'd said it, and whether it contradicted something he might have written before.

Priscilla and Hilary tried to help him, drawing up information flow charts and cut-off points. They did their best, but when Robert introduced a fourth lady who wasn't yet a member of the harem but whom he'd been speculatively eyeing as a candidate, they gave up.

'Never mind,' Robert said philosophically as he shuffled the postcards at random. 'I am a friend of many ladies. Better a friend to many than an enemy to one.'

'Robert,' I asked, 'why on earth have you come on pilgrimage?'

He laughed. 'To get away from the women. Why else? They are the curse and delight of my life. Yes, sir. Why else?'

He patted Fanny who joggled her rump and switched her tail in apparent agreement.

We strolled along all morning.

The sun was warm, the air fresh and benign, the fields on either side were covered in violets, hellebores and cowslips. We passed through gently rolling meadows and came to a humpbacked bridge over a stream. We stopped and looked down into the quietly running water with the reflections of kingcups cascading across the surface. The tight strong clusters of petals flickered gold in the run-off from the spring rains.

At one o'clock we reached the little hamlet of St-Christophe-sur-Dolaison and found a restaurant which gave us a fine four-course lunch with wine and coffee for a small sum of francs a head. We savoured the meal and took our time — we had all the time in the world — and then set off again.

Although none of us said so to each other, all three of us had discovered in a single morning that the way to Santiago was nothing more than a carefree saunter, a ramble in sunlight through some of the loveliest countryside in Europe punctuated only by stops to enjoy excellent and extraordinarily cheap meals.

None of us, after those first few hours, could begin to imagine why the pilgrimage was considered one of the hardest and most arduous journeys in the world.

We went on from St-Christophe.

The sky clouded as we left the village, the sun disappeared, and a fierce chill wind rose from the north. To our surprise, we found we still had more than fifteen kilometres to cover before nightfall and our next destination. The distance wasn't all that great and we were fit. However, we were carrying our heavy packs, the route – one of the rare sections where it was badly way-marked – wound upwards through dense pine forests, and the temperature dropped by the minute.

We heaved ourselves on.

We took breaks to shelter against the cold and the now-raging wind in the lee of crumbling farm walls, the legacy of long-deserted settlements. We struggled to our feet and set out again. Ice-laden rain started to fall and swirled across our faces. We lost our way in the trees, back-tracked, cast round, and eventually found the path again.

As dusk fell, we wearily tramped down through the forest and arrived at the tiny village of St-Privat-d'Allier. The plan had been to spend the night at the *gîte* there. The Gîtes d'Etape are travellers' rest-houses, run on similar principles to Youth Hostels. Mercifully this *gîte* – a gaunt forbidding shed – was closed. Instead, we took rooms at the Vieille Auberge, the village inn.

In our journal that night before she collapsed with cold and exhaustion, my sister Priscilla wrote:

'I may not live to see the dawn as I have never been so physically tired in my whole life. I can hardly move, let alone walk. It took me ten minutes to creep downstairs to the restaurant. And there's only another thousand miles to go.'

I know just what Priscilla meant.

Tall, confident and determined, strong as an ox, agile and sinewy as a wild Barra goat – she walks and stalks the red deer on the icy Highland tops of Knoydart – the Santiago Way had made demands on her that even on that first day taxed her almost to the limits.

We had had the seductive experience of the sunlight, the spring-flushed river, the cowslips, marsh marigolds and violets.

The path of St James, however, asks more demanding questions of its travellers than the ones posed by a stroll through early springtime meadows.

Letters to Francesca: 2

So that was how it all started.

Sometimes sheer exhaustion paradoxically delays one falling asleep. I was almost as tired as Priscilla but it happened to me that night. Lying awake in my little bed and listening to the rain in St-Privat's Vieille Auberge, I thought about you as I'd do so often over the days and nights ahead.

There was something strange about you from the start.

According to the conventional medical wisdom of the time, you should never have survived your birth. You were what was known as a 'blue' or rhesus negative baby, the product of two parents whose blood groups are incompatible. The first child, in your case your brother, is unaffected. All the later children are, or were, under threat, and at the time relatively few rhesus negative infants lived for more than a short while. Today, the problem has been solved. Not then. Then you should have died as your mother's transferred antibodies swept through your bloodstream.

Within an hour of your birth it was clear you were failing fast. There was only one chance of survival in the view of the gynaecologist who'd delivered you, and a leaf-slim one at that – to take you from the central London nursing home where you'd been born to the one hospital in Britain which specialized in pioneering blood transfusion techniques for rhesus negative babies.

It was a bitterly cold January night, the coldest I remember. The doctor loved antique cars, and he had a magnificent vintage Daimler which had once belonged to the royal family. I held you, a swaddled scrap of a child, in my arms as we drove, often sliding on the black ice of the London streets, to Queen Charlotte's in west London.

After you died many people wrote commenting on the style, panache and elegance with which you'd lived your life. In retrospect, it seems entirely appropriate that, at barely an hour old, your first journey should have been made in a car built and furnished with mahogany and gold for Queen Mary.

But, my goodness, it was characteristic of you too that within sixty minutes of your arrival on the planet you were already causing havoc.

Inside the hospital we had to wait briefly while the first transfusion was prepared. As I sat holding you — by now you were barely breathing — I noticed a framed photograph of a strong-faced but benignly smiling old man hanging in the place of honour on the wall opposite me. Lifting you, not really sure you were still alive but needing something to take my mind off the appalling possibility that you might have died in my arms, I got up and studied it.

The caption below the photograph told me he was called Bernard Baron.

Your full name, when you were eventually christened, was Francesca Susan Luz de Beauregard Baron. Luz commemorated your Andalusian upbringing; the Republican mothers in the Spanish Civil War called their daughters Luz and Paz, 'Light' and 'Peace'. de Beauregard was one of our family's Huguenot names. Baron came from your great-great-grandfather, the old man in the photograph.

A multi-millionaire philanthropist whose munificence rivalled that of his American contemporaries of the first part of the century, the Rockefellers and Carnegies, among Bernard Baron's gifts to London — they included the Baron Housing Trusts in the East End, the Lindo wing at St Mary's Hospital in Paddington, and many more — were the blood laboratories at Queen Charlotte's.

That night the gift saved your life.

You received your transfusion, the first of many. For hours you hovered between life and death. Towards dawn, the sturdy and formidable matron of the premature babies unit and its rows of oxygen tents, Sister Penrhys — I came to know her well when our succeeding children were born, sometimes living, sometimes dying — came out to speak to me.

'The child's going to live.'

It was all she said.

She said exactly the same when your younger sisters, Poppy and Honey, went through the same perilous transfusions and she was satisfied they'd survived them. A good thrifty Welshwoman, Sister Penrhys was never one to waste words.

I went back to central London as day broke in flurries of snow and a bitter wind to give the news to the exhausted Elisabeth.

Your mother said, 'You didn't have to tell me. I could see it in your smile as you came in.'

I wish it had always been like that.

Letters to Francesca: 3

It wasn't, of course.

Like prison fugitives, Poppy and Honey somehow slipped under the wire although, particularly in Honey's case, their escapes still baffle the surgeons and doctors. Like you they lived. Your small brothers weren't so lucky. Both Peter Astrolabe and the last, Boychild Luard, only survived a matter of days. Perhaps they lacked the tenacity, the ferocious desire for life, the clenched grip on existence you three girls had. Maybe the daughters of Eve, as biologists believe, are simply stronger than her sons.

When I saw the dead Boychild I decided in a frenzy of grief to bury him at sea.

He was our sixth child and I already knew he'd be the last. His loss was no greater than Peter Astrolabe's — to most parents all their children, be there two or twelve of them, stand equally shoulder-to-shoulder in the love they command and the grief they leave in their going — but the finality of the last-born's departure needed marking with a gesture that combined tears for his loss with defiance and celebration. For him, for his dead brother, for his surviving siblings, for the whole clan. He wasn't going to vanish in anonymity. He was going to leave to the sound of trumpets, well, to a ship's sirens and the crash of breaking waves.

I chartered a British Railways tug and its five-man crew, hired a whisky priest for the service, and the family set off for Newhaven.

It was a bitterly cold and windy March day. As we careered along the harbour-front, your grandmother's chauffeur at the wheel, the five of us — your mother was still in hospital — the scarlet-eyed priest surreptitiously swigging from the bottle hidden under his cassock, I could see the white-capped waves rearing and boiling beyond the mole.

The tug was old, rusting and salt-caked. So was its skipper. A storm was coming and he was understandably reluctant to set out. A fistful of bonus money settled his disquiet. We collected the tiny coffin from the boot, stumbled aboard, and headed out into the Channel. There, just beyond the three-mile limit, we put Boychild to rest beneath the angry waters.

The deck was heaving and we had to cling for dear life to the rails. The skipper wrestled with the wheel. The priest had abandoned any pretence of trying to hide the whisky. He held the bottle in one hand, the prayer book in the other and he bellowed out the litany, but the austere and magnificent words were lost in the wind. He managed to get to the end and then tumbled down and vomited in the scuppers.

I and a couple of deckhands slid the coffin overboard. When Edwina Mountbatten was buried at sea it was reported that even the great Admiral, Lord Mountbatten, had forgotten sealed wooden boxes float in water. She had bobbed embarrassingly around on the surface until she was sunk by volleys of machine-gun fire. I was more careful. I'd made the undertakers drill holes in the coffin.

All four of you had beautiful little posies of wild spring flowers — primroses, bluebells, cowslips and violets — to throw into the sea. You three eldest did it impeccably. The trouble was your youngest sister, the anarchic Honey. Honey thought the flowers were much too pretty to be thrown away. Sliding backwards and forwards across the deck, half-blinded with spray, I shouted at her, I cajoled, pleaded, and swore. Nothing made any difference. She hung on to them grimly and stubbornly.

Finally, I lost my temper. The tug's keel was momentarily level, I hurled myself at Honey, wrestled the flowers from her, and threw them overboard in the wake of the other posies. It was a mistake. The tug reared up again, I lost my balance and tumbled into the scuppers alongside the priest. I wallowed choking beside him, soaked and with my face full of whisky fumes.

I remember you, your brother and Poppy gazing down at me in astonishment as I washed round like a landed mackerel, belly-up and tangled with the priest and his bottle, and Honey scowling bitterly and accusingly behind you.

We drove back to London in silence. Honey stared at me reproachfully all the way.

I sat shivering in my sodden clothes. Elisabeth had said to me in Spanish after Boychild's death: Se acabó la cosa — *the matter is ended. She meant she wouldn't try for any more children. She had had six. As a rhesus negative blood group mother she had, against all odds at the time, given birth to four healthy living people. She had been a pioneer, a human laboratory, a testing ground for medical progress — intra-uterine transfusions, ultrasound scans, periscope investigations of her most private parts.*

She had done her bit. For science, research and herself. It was enough. Four children were enough. Boychild's burial beneath the grey waves of a Channel storm had ended that part of the story.

If a child's death, let alone the deaths of two children, is the worst that can befall a parent, then the worst was over. We were free now, free to get on and live.

To all four of you, Boychild's burial was an adventure, a solemn but unforgettable adventure; how could it be otherwise at your ages?

Yes, there was theatre and unintentional farce — me and the priest threshing around with the whisky bottle bobbing between us — inextricably mingled with the grief and the tears your mother and I had shed. Thirty years later I regret nothing. Your younger brother had died. He didn't slip away anonymously into the darkness. He went with spring blossom and thundering waves and the wheezing hooter I made the salt-caked skipper blow all the way as we butted back to harbour.

He was my son and your brother and he had a given name, christened even if only as Boychild in a draughty corridor in Queen Charlotte's Hospital by another equally dodgy vagrant member of the clergy. Whisky priests, starting with the one who married your mother and me at Westminster, have been a constant feature in our family life. I had to give him a backhander too which no doubt was invested in the local pub and the 2.30 chase at Aintree moments after the baptism finished. I wanted you to know that. To know it with passion and interest. Boychild had the same ancestors, he shared the same genes and bloodline. He was part of your past and part of your future — your own children would carry the same odds and ends of wisdom and folly as he did in his briefly toted luggage.

You belonged to each other.

And, as you told me afterwards, you realized it. You said you never forgot that day, nor your infant brother. You added that when I skidded on the deck and plunged into the bilge drains, you thought that, like the priest, I was as drunk as a lord.

Give us a break, Francesca, to use one of your favourite phrases. I was enraged, consumed with grief for the lost boy, determined to wrest the spring flowers from your sister as the last tribute, but that day I was as sober as a judge.

Well, more or less.

4

Back on the Santiago road, it was chill and grey again next morning after our night in St-Privat.

Over breakfast we held an O group, an 'Orders' gathering, a planning and discussion meeting. Taking its name from the endless O groups I'd attended in my military past, the sessions soon became one of the rituals of the journey.

'The packs,' I said. 'We're all carrying about twenty pounds and you, Priscilla, much more. We're starting to climb up into the mountains of the Massif Central. Let's find some way of moving the baggage ahead of us.'

There was a farmer in the bar having his morning *pastis*. He was on his way to market and his route took him through the village of that evening's stopping-point. For the cost of his petrol, he agreed to take our packs and leave them there.

From then on we used this system whenever we could. Sometimes it was a farmer, like that day, sometimes the farmer's son, sometimes the local bus, occasionally a taxi. But often, when there was neither farmer, taxi nor bus, we carried the packs ourselves. Priscilla and Hilary took a certain grim delight in the penance – they felt the burden was an appropriate tribute to pilgrimage.

I didn't.

From the Himalaya to the Kalahari Desert I'd toted enough packs to last me a lifetime and more. I just wanted to be rid of the debilitating weight on my shoulders and hips, and enjoy the unfolding landscape without laboriously shrugging off a hefty backpack each time I knelt down to study a wild flower.

St Francis travelled our way. Would he, I demanded, have had time for the birds of the air or the beasts of the field if he'd been humping a massive canvas sack up dale and down glen? He'd have had at least one servant to porter his belongings, I argued, and probably an ox-waggon in support. And as for St Teresa of Avila, it was well documented she never travelled anywhere except in a coach-and-four.

'If this is the way You treat your friends,' she once furiously shouted up at the sky from the muddy ditch where the overturned coach had spilled her out on to the road to Santiago, 'it's no wonder You have so few of them!'

Priscilla and Hilary coughed and shuffled.

They had no answer. They were just defiant and stubborn. Pain, I sensed, was to them an essential part of the Pilgrim Way. I cursed them roundly. Whenever I could, I took it on myself to arrange for our packs to be carried ahead of us. They never took exception.

We left St-Privat at 9.00 am and headed on.

The day was blustery, showery and cold. We climbed up to the tiny mountain hamlet of Rochegude, where a chapel barely larger than a swallow's nest and just as precarious in its setting had somehow been attached to the rocky peak. It was built of anciently hewn granite blocks, but it looked as if the birds had made it, carrying mud in their beaks as the flickering hirundines did up from the river so far, so distantly, below.

I stared down at the valley.

It was a mist-strewn doll's-house landscape, remote and still winter-coloured. The fields were furred with the night's silver frost and the slate roofs of the village houses shone darkly like mussel shells bulging from a Hebridean fisherman's creel. High up above it on the chapel's ledge I felt giddy, afraid, plagued with the vertigo that occasionally comes on me in mountains.

I'm no real climber, a scree and rock scramble to a Scottish high top is about as much as my wary approach to mountains can tolerate, but I know vertigo can plague even the greatest of the mountain men. It got to Don Whillans high on the south-west face of Everest. His climbing partner, Dougal Haston, perhaps the finest mountaineer of all, once told me the story.

He and Whillans had hauled themselves up to 25,000 feet when Whillans was overtaken by vertigo's plunging dizziness. They roped themselves into the snow and ice, bivouacked, and sat it out for eighteen hours as the Himalayan storms mauled the mountain. When the sickness passed, they headed on and reached the peak.

I passed the story on to Francesca when she, I and her brother climbed in the Himalaya up towards the Tibetan plateau. It became part of her own mythology.

'If Dougal Haston could handle this one,' she'd say at some particularly difficult moment on some challenging col or cwm, 'so can I.'

She never knew Dougal Haston. He died in an avalanche while she was still a child. But he was still, through the strange conduits by which comparable experiences are passed on, a witness to her life. In her mind she climbed where he had climbed. She laughed affectionately about him and took encouragement, spirit, from what he'd done.

They were both witnesses to each other in the snows.

From the swallow's nest of the shrine on the Rochegude summit, a goat's track plunges precipitously to the valley below.

We slid and stumbled down its zig-zagging curves through the forest until we reached the valley's floor and the grim little town of Monistrol-d'Allier. Monistrol was deserted and almost echoed with silence. The only sound was the distant murmur of its hydro-electric station. Where the town's inhabitants were we couldn't discover – there was no one on the few windy streets to ask. Someone must have lived there because after roaming disconsolately for a while, we found a small shop which sold us a baguette and a couple of slices of cheese for our lunch.

We headed on. Within minutes of leaving the town we were climbing again. Sheltering in the lee of a rock against the once more rising wind, I consulted the French pilgrim's vademecum, the slim *Topo-Guide* booklet. It said we had a steep 3,000-ft ascent to the Col of Montaure in front of us.

The guide was right. The climb was very steep and it was the second 3,000-ft ascent we were making that day.

We tramped upwards. On one of the narrow track's bends we passed a graceful iron cross bearing the scallop-shell emblem of St James. Blisters and shards of rust were breaking through the faded green paint that must have been applied to preserve it a century earlier. Many other pilgrims would have struggled up there before us. We stood aside to let a mountain shepherd and his flock pass on their way down to the valley.

The shepherd had a drawn weathered face and an oiled sheepskin cape over his shoulders. He raised his hand in greeting, but he didn't stop. It was cold and getting colder by the moment, and he was about his business. He had the sheep to tend to and they were a vital source of money-revenue that could be exchanged for other goods through the munificence of the EC farming subsidies. Far more important, the sheep remained what they had always been to peasant hill farmers — food.

The men in grey suits in Brussels might vanish. It had happened before through fire or flood, revolution or war. If the EC went pear-shaped and then belly-up, as all good pilgrims pray each night it will, he, his family and the village would still need to eat — and mutton was good meat protein. He had a wary eye. Country memories are long.

We saluted him in return. His thin sinuous dogs leapt silently from boulder to boulder, circling and guiding the flock. We climbed on.

The rain set in.

It cut into our faces carried by an easterly wind that must have risen in the Urals, tormented the Massif Central, and now was scouring the Auvergne mountains on its race westwards. We reached the top of the col and huddled under a pine tree in the shelter of a half-ruined stone wall to eat the baguette and the cheese. The sky was dark under deep-bellied cumulus clouds, rolling above us as part of the caravan of turbulence the wind drew with it. There was lightning, too, sudden golden-yellow flashes crackling through the sodden drifting air.

'Look!' Priscilla said.

I turned as she raised her arm and pointed.

A goldfinch had perched on a thorn bush just outside the circle of half-shelter the tree and the wall gave us. Its feathers were the same colour as the lightning and, as we watched it, the bird began to sing.

The song only lasted for a moment — it was early spring and in biological terms the bird was only staking out its territory for the breeding season. Then it flew off. Somehow in the rain and chill and greyness it provided the encouragement we all needed. As Christ anticipated in a childhood dream, a goldfinch was to swoop down and pluck a thorn from His brow on the road to Calvary. In his wonderful *tondo* carving, Michelangelo records the child Christ recoiling in terror when He first sees the bird.

The goldfinch reminded the carpenter's son of what was to come. Later, I'm sure, the Palestinian insurgent, reeling under the weight of the cross, was grateful to the bird – the thorny crown must have been marginally less painful for the removal of even one of the barbs it had driven into His skin. For us, certainly, the golden breast and the fluting scrap of song were omens of good cheer.

As we stood up and went on again, chilled, aching and sodden, we badly needed encouragement.

Our destination for the night was the village of Saugues. We got there in the early evening. By then the afternoon's rain had become a deluge, an unending cataract of swirling wind-tossed water, the temperature had dropped sharply, and the sky was darker still. The rain had turned the track into an ankle-high ditch of red-brown mud. The mud welled over our boots and saturated their insides. It also spat up as we trudged along and coated our faces.

We finally reached the little hotel where we'd booked in for the night, and rang the bell.

'Good evening,' Hilary said, giving one of her most engaging, her most irresistible smiles. 'We have a booking. I trust you are expecting us. We are pilgrims on the way to Santiago.'

'Of course, madame,' the young man who answered her said. 'Please may I assist you.'

His name was Denis.

Denis was courteous, efficient and imperturbable.

The arrival at dusk of three strangers drenched and shivering might have been an every evening event. He scooped up the puddled heaps of boots and clothes we hastily discarded, took them to the boiler-room to be hung up to dry, and returned to escort us upstairs. Dinner, he told us, would be ready in an hour.

In our room I perched on the old grey radiator – massive with iron grilles which throbbed throughout the night – until I'd thawed out.

Then, leaving the other two to bathe in the almost boiling hot water that unexpectedly cascaded from the leaking brass taps in the bathroom along the corridor, I went downstairs. I borrowed an umbrella from the willing Denis and stepped out onto the street in the continually pouring rain.

I wanted to buy a shirt.

Quite unconsciously, as I discovered later from books about the Santiago Way, all three of us had already adopted one of the practices, almost rituals, of the early pilgrims. The day's journey was completed in whatever clothes one had and in whatever way one could – on horseback, in a waggon, by boat where necessary, most often on foot. Given the frequent storms, rain and mud, like those we'd encountered that day, the rougher and sturdier the clothing the better, even if it made for a scarecrow arrival.

When darkness fell, when the pilgrim reached the night's refuge, it was almost a matter of honour that he presented himself clean and decent for the evening meal to his host – whether a surly innkeeper at a little fordside tavern or a group of learned monks gathered round the refectory table of some magnificent medieval monastery. To be neat and well clad wasn't only a courtesy to them, but a nightly gesture of respect to the Seigneur who had seen one safely through the day – and on whose benison one depended for next morning's journey.

From the beginning to the end the two women, Priscilla and Hilary, somehow managed to present themselves freshly and elegantly each night. They had nothing to draw on except the contents of their packs. Mixing and matching, exchanging a shirt, a blouse, a shawl – all of silk, anything else (as pilgrim records from the Middle Ages confirm) would have been too heavy – they looked impeccable.

I didn't. I was used to desert and mountain treks in the company of rough professional soldiers, beer-swilling white hunters, and hell's-brew-guzzling sherpas. Those expeditions were joyous, lovely, but they weren't elegant; they hadn't been made on God's way, on the path of St James. Now I was here and I felt grubby.

Pilgrimage isn't elegant, but there's a comforting shine to its old conventions and I was letting down my companions in not matching up to the required nightly polish. I needed a shirt. I found one. It was

Constable hayfield yellow, pure cotton, made in Taiwan, and fitted as if it had been tailored for me.

'*Te luce, ça te va*, it suits you,' Hilary said, pouring me out a glass of wine as we sat down to dinner. 'Probably because it's the colour of your liver.'

5

We made a late start. In spite of the night in the boiler-room, our boots were still damp.

The amiable Denis offered to put them in a low kitchen oven for an hour. After that, he said, they would at least be wearable. We accepted gratefully. While the other two went off to find the curé to stamp their pilgrim passports, I read *L'Equipe*, France's daily sporting journal and the only paper available in the hotel. The Basque Indurrain, I saw in a long profile on the centre pages, was once again favourite to win the Tour de France. We'd come across him again when we reached Pamplona and the Basque country.

The women came back.

They'd been led to the curé's house by an elderly local. Normally, the local said, he'd have had to charge for the service – a matter of escorting them along a couple of streets. However, as the *Papa* had decreed Protestants could be considered at least country members of the true faith, he would waive his fee. The curé had been old and grumpy and he would have charged them too until he discovered that Priscilla, like himself, read the Brother Cadfael detective novels. Then he smiled and they discussed fiction.

A sympathetic Polish Pope and a knowledge of popular literature, we decided, might not get one everywhere, but they were useful cost-cutting tools on pilgrimage.

The day started well.

The sky was gunmetal-grey and stormy, but for a while the rain held off. We crossed the river and climbed slowly away from Saugues through old water meadows carpeted with wild daffodils and marsh marigolds. At the top of the first long rise we walked through a pasture of pansies, a dense medieval tapestry of blue, violet and gold that might have been taken from a Cluny abbey and pinned across the ground for our delight, as if we'd been kings and queens advancing to sign a peace treaty in some hidden pavilion beyond.

Soon afterwards we lost our way and the rain set in.

Searching like foxhounds in pursuit of lost scent, we separated and cast backwards and forwards until we picked up the way-marks again. The red and white signals were forlorn, abandoned, faded and washed away. One of us eventually spotted one and shouted. We gathered and sheltered in a half-ruined hen-coop to eat our baguette and sliced *saucisson* lunch.

Propped against the coop's wall was a stout birch staff. The absent farmer – if he were sensible, he was no doubt warm inside his little flat in one of the nearby towns – must have left it there at the end of the autumn's herding the year before. I picked it up, hefted it, decided it was just what I wanted to replace a staff I'd left behind at Le Puy.

'It's called theft,' Priscilla said.

'The carpenter died with thieves on either side,' I replied. 'He even offered them lodging in His Father's house.'

She scowled at me, but she didn't object when I set off into the rain with the staff in my hand.

The day grew worse, far worse.

As we moved on, slowly climbing into the mountains of the Massif Central, the rain turned first to hail, then to sleet, then to snow. The temperature dropped every fifteen minutes, I was measuring it on my wrist-band thermometer, and the air was bitter. Within a couple of hours we were trudging through a snowstorm.

Priscilla's feet were badly blistered and she was limping. Hilary had a back problem, one that recurred at intervals throughout the journey, but she was walking faster. Both of them decided they could only go on at their own pace. Priscilla couldn't hurry to keep up, Hilary couldn't slow down – the cold was too harsh and she was concerned she'd lose the rhythm of her stride.

The falling snow thickened until it was almost impossible to see the track in front of us. We began to wade through drifts. All we knew was that we were still climbing with the occasional frosted way-mark pointing us along the path. The gap between the two women increased with every step. Like a sheepdog I doubled backwards and forwards between them, checking first on one, then on the other, and then turning again.

Hypothermia can be fast and brutal in its effects. I doubt we were in any real danger that day, but the snowstorm showed us how narrow the margins were between safety and disaster. We were in the lonely wilds of the Auvergne. A few more inches of the icily settling flakes, a northerly wind raging to build the drifts in front of us, another plunge in the temperature, and it could have been a close-run thing. Next day's local newspaper told us an elderly farmer and a child had died in the storm.

We would of course have emerged alive. We were travelling in an age of telephones and four-wheel-drive vehicles, not that there were many of either in the desolate valleys we'd been climbing. And it's in the nature of pilgrimage that most pilgrims survive. We were after all travellers on one of the roads the carpenter's son had mapped out, and surely His Father would have seen we completed it in safety. One can never be too sure. The Way of St James was reminding us of another lesson all good mountain men know: listen to the messages of the winds and the weather and ready yourself for what they're warning you that they're going to throw at you.

Hilary eventually struggled up to the road that was marked on our maps.

I joined her with the stumbling Priscilla at my side. We'd climbed another 4,000 feet. We sheltered for a while in a pilgrimage refuge beside the lofty little Chapelle St-Roch, our teeth chattering as we beat our arms and clung to each other for warmth. Then we forced ourselves out into the driving snow again.

An hour later in the dusk we reached our destination for the night, a farmhouse in the hamlet of La Roche.

The workaday farm was run by a sturdy but somewhat dour and toothless Auvergne lady named Mme Astruc. She helped us strip off our snow-drenched clothes, and showed us into the Astruc parlour while she went through to cook dinner. We huddled shivering over the flames of a wood fire. Then dinner came. It was one of the best, the richest, the most handsome and resplendent meals I have ever eaten.

It started with a clean and herb-scented winter vegetable soup. A chive omelette followed, the eggs golden-brown from the chickens in the yard outside. At the dinner's centre was an *aligot*, a magnificent tangled Auvergne cheese and potato fondue accompanied by sausages from the region. Then a platter of French cheeses. Finally, and like almost everything else home-made, a *tarte aux mûres* — preserved mulberries in a bed of cream and wafer-thin pastry.

It wasn't a meal, it wasn't a dinner, it was a feast — gruffly but cordially offered to the pilgrims who'd appeared out of the dusk and the snow. Bloated but smiling — there'd been good country wine to go with the food too — we climbed the stairs to bed.

The warmth generated by the parlour fire and the meal didn't last long. We were sleeping in the farmhouse attic. The few grey blankets on our beds were thin and worn. Outside, the snow was still falling and the temperature dropped steadily. The icy air swirled through the badly fitting uncurtained windows and by midnight the water in my bedside glass was frozen.

Priscilla somehow managed to sleep.

Hilary and I couldn't. We lay awake, tossing, huddling our arms against our legs, occasionally eyeing each other. If we'd had any sense, as we agreed afterwards, we'd have tossed away all the conventions of propriety and lain together with our arms bound round each other. It might have led to all manner of things, but at least we'd have created a little mutual island of warmth.

We didn't. We'd only known each other for a few days. We were simply and ridiculously too shy. The married former soldier and the consultant's wife stayed apart, at a fearsome cold- and energy-cost to them both. Never again. In future in the snows I will sleep with anyone, although I doubt whether I'll find such a lovely companion to hold in my arms.

In the middle of the night, chilled to the bone, I put on all the pairs of socks I could find and then my boots on top of them. I clambered back into bed and dozed under the star-bright skylight. It was the first time I'd attempted to sleep in my boots since I was a young special forces soldier in a savage winter in the Brecon Beacons thirty years earlier.

The snow was still falling next morning.

I looked through the window as we drank our breakfast coffee. It was obviously going to be another wild and bitterly cold Auvergne day. Mme Astruc's son, Bernard, came into sight through the frosted panes, herding some cows across the yard. He was a burly stocky young man, roughly my size and shape, and he was wearing an Auvergne farmer's winter over-clothing – a heavy oilskin tunic and oilskin trousers.

'Madame,' I said, 'I'd like Bernard's clothes. I'll buy them off his back.'

Mme Astruc opened the door and called her son in from the tempest outside.

The transaction took only minutes. Bernard undressed and I put on the tunic and the trousers. They fitted perfectly. Mme Astruc telephoned the travelling salesman who'd sold her the garments. The salesman said that if he could get through the snow, he'd bring a replacement set for Bernard that evening. Bernard settled himself down by the kitchen fire smiling happily. I'd done him an enormous favour. Without proper protection, there was no question of his going out for the rest of the day.

We headed off into the storm again.

It was another day of raging snow, sleet and rain. We crossed the river Truyère which had burst its banks and flooded all the surrounding fields; we waded through the ice-crusted water, climbed mist-veiled hills, and eventually reached another little town, Aumont-Aubrac, towards dusk. We tramped, far apart because of our own individual weariness, down the long main street to our lodging for the night.

Hilary had booked us into what sounded like an attractive auberge. It turned out to be – and it was no fault of Hilary's – a jerry-built little modern motor inn. The owner was a young man with a dark dangling moustache belonging to a cad from an Ealing Comedies' film of the early fifties, and a manner that was both odious and obsequious. Hilary took one glance at him and suggested we looked for somewhere else.

Priscilla was too wet and tired.

'We're here,' she said, 'there's a deluge outside, let's stay.' Her blisters were fearful. We stayed. The auberge offered a bath, but the owner had cunningly removed the bath plug so we couldn't use it. The evening meal was coarse and meagre. The only consolation was the appearance of Robert-from-Gouda with the friendly, tail-wagging Fanny.

We invited them to join us. I pulled up chairs for them both.

'I do not allow dogs in the restaurant,' the owner said from behind his moustache.

'Well, I always have dogs at my table,' I replied. 'Shall we go outside and discuss it? I've no doubt my companions will want to talk about it, too.'

I stood up. The others stood up. We all looked down at him.

We were tired and angry and hungry. I was unshaven and my steel bowie hunting knife gleamed at my belt. The ladies squared their shoulders, as broad as barn doors in their quilted parkas, and Hilary's eyes flashed murderously. All three of us had our heavy staffs with us. We probably looked like the SAS assault squad moments before the attack on the Iranian embassy.

The monsieur of the weeping moustache, in his breeze-block lodging house with its greedy prices and its missing bath plugs, was small and furtive. He was hopelessly outgunned. He turned and ran like a frightened rabbit.

We sat down and ate. Fanny wagged her tail happily.

6

The rain was still pouring down the following morning.

In revenge for our confrontation with him the night before, the hostel's owner had gone one further than removing the plugs from the basin and bath — he'd locked the bathroom door and departed for market with the key in his pocket. We made our ablutions, a wonderful word whose exact meaning I've never been sure about, in the restaurant's tiny lavatory.

We were joined by thirteen Swiss ladies who formed up in an orderly queue behind us. They were members of a ladies' cycling club from Grenoble, and their handsome multi-geared machines were padlocked in a line to the lamp post outside. They'd spent the night with Robert-from-Gouda and Fanny in the *gîte* below the hostel, a warren of foul-smelling dark passages like a dead badger's sett.

Hilary looked at them with approval. Their biceps bulged, their thigh muscles were like tree trunks, their moustaches — almost all of them sported one — were dark and pearled with the dawn rain. They were clearly not a tribe to be trifled with, and women after Hilary's heart.

They joined us for breakfast.

Then we all set off, Robert and Fanny striding ahead, the Swiss ladies pedalling furiously, the three of us tramping behind. If there had been any dust to shake from our heels, we'd have shaken it scornfully as we left the sorry lodging. There wasn't. Only mud which the chill gusting wind lifted from the gutters and threw against our legs.

We stopped briefly at a gun shop on the outskirts of the town for Hilary to buy a Lagioule knife. I had had one for years. Bone-handled, perfectly balanced, and with a blade cast from the finest tempered steel, they're among the best knives in the world. It served Hilary well over the weeks ahead, just as mine had done for so long.

We headed out into the countryside where the snow, the sleet and the rain had flooded the fields. Although the sky had partly cleared and there were fitful shafts of sunlight, there was no point in trying to follow the pilgrim track. We'd have found ourselves at best wading, at worst swimming. For as long as we could we stuck to the road. Eventually we struck away from it and headed back into the wilds of the Auvergne.

Wild daffodils were just coming into flower, but the trees were still leafless and bare, the turf frost-bitten and barren yellow, and the constant streams were foam-flecked with the winter's water-rush. We found a little mountain café where the owner sold us some beer and carefully measured bags of dried wild mushrooms — cèpes, faux morilles and chanterelles.

'Make sure you boil them first,' was her parting injunction. 'The best mushrooms grow in cowpats and that's where we gather them.'

It was early afternoon and slightly warmer. We were approaching the highest flanks of the Massif Central, and travelling along part of the ancient Roman Agrippan Way. The track dipped. We climbed a small hummock and looked down.

There was nothing in front of us except broad shining sheets of water with a range of violet peaks beyond. The winter floods had filled the upland meadows. We could either turn back and rejoin the road, hours behind us now, or we could try to make our way through the floods.

'What's the group's decision?' I asked.

The question was unnecessary.

When I turned round the two women were already stripping down. They tied up their clothes into neat bundles, placed them on their heads like Indian coolies, and waded forward in their knickers. I followed them, at intervals supporting Priscilla who was still stumbling with her wounded feet.

It was a strange and lovely passage in the journey. The sun came out and the wild flowers glowed on the banks. Cumulus clouds raced and tumbled overhead. Birds sang for us. We crossed ford after ford, sometimes up to our chests in the flow. The water was bitterly cold, racing past us, laced with the strange bronze flecks I remembered from the Hebridean burns of my childhood. I kept scooping it up and drinking it.

I was remembering not just the past, I realized afterwards, I was celebrating Francesca. I had taken her down to the pool below Eas Fors, the great waterfall on the Isle of Mull, and we'd drunk the same chill mountain water there, too.

Finally we climbed up from the flooded meadows. We dried ourselves as best we could and walked on, climbing higher and higher. On the highest ridge, as we approached the village of Rieutort in the dusk, we came on a towering heap of silvery elephant-grey boulders. They were utterly incongruous, unlike anything we'd seen all day, a bleak and haunting natural monument, a bold and defiant sculpture that Henry Moore might have positioned against the evening sky with a flowered skirt of gay wild narcissus rippling away for acres all round it, as bright and flamboyant as a *flamenco* dancer's dress.

We stepped gently through the wild garden of flowers. We walked down into Rieutort, drank from the well in the lonely little hamlet, and finally made our way in darkness to the pilgrim *gîte* at Montgros. We were billeted in the *gîte*'s dormitory. It had sixteen beds. Thirteen of them were occupied by our morning friends, the Grenoble lady cyclists — it turned out they worked for the Swiss Inland Revenue. We took the other three beds.

We showered and slopped through the mud to the *gîte*'s restaurant. We had another superb meal in front of a blazing log fire: local charcuterie, tripe prepared by Mme Rosalie, the farmhouse *gîte*'s owner, a wonderful selection of country cheeses, and a *tarte aux framboises* laced with redcurrants. Then filled with the sturdy black wine of Cahors we stumbled to bed.

The Grenoble ladies, utterly unconcerned by my presence, were undressing. They stripped naked and climbed into their sensible woolly pyjamas, so stiff and thick the trouser legs clattered together like chain-mail. For the first time in my life I, a solitary male, slept with fifteen women, thirteen of them Swiss tax inspectors with muscles, moustaches and steel-framed mountain bicycles.

I'm not normally a nervous man but I reached out in the darkness and held Hilary's hand for comfort and protection. Somewhere, I knew, Fran was laughing.

7

There seemed to be no end to the rain.

It cascaded down and drummed over the shingle roof all night. When we got up at dawn it was sweeping in great dark sheets across the landscape. We ran for our bowls of *café au lait* in the farmhouse dining-room and returned soaked. Not that it made any difference. Our boots and walking clothes were still sodden from the day before. Damp and shivering, we set off, casting a quick and affectionate look back at the farm.

French *gîte* lodgings are only suitable for former penal prisoners, the rough soldiery, or hardened inmates of British boarding-schools. If one's been tempered by any of the three, then the Montgros farm was a palace. It was a safe-house, a lonely but robust and cheerful corner on the journey, a place we all agreed we'd return to without hesitation.

Beyond were the upland wilds.

I felt strong and fit. I strode out beyond the other two across the rising planes of moorland. There was nothing except the harsh cold wind in my face, a few ruined walls, the still bare yellow grass with the snow-melt only just gone from the high pastures, the occasional cluster of leafless beech trees, and a sky, a sky that reached for ever. I had never seen anything like that sky.

It reminded me of the immensity of the star-strewn Kalahari skies. I'd lie beneath them at night in the desert and stare at them until the whole bright splendour of the Southern Cross and the Milky Way, tumbling and turning with constellations that stretched beyond distance, sent me giddily to sleep. The Auvergne sky was just as large, but it was much closer – a great dark and luminous lake of racing whirling clouds and bird skeins and threads of wandering sun.

Even on the high tops of the Hebrides in a Scottish winter, I had seldom felt such a sense of freedom, of exhilaration.

I went on faster and faster.

I walked through a high transhumance meadow where a great black bull bellowed at me. Transhumance — moving herds and flocks from their winter quarters in the valleys below to the upland pastures when the spring grass begins to grow — was an ancient agricultural practice I'd known all my life. I'd seen it everywhere from the Scottish Highlands, where the sheilings, the primitive summer quarters of the young shepherds, feature in so many songs and poems, to Romania, Spain and Switzerland. The bull and his cows could only have been there for a matter of days. I barely noticed the angry animal, although Priscilla and Hilary far behind had spotted it and were sure it was going to charge and scythe me down.

The creature would have been very unwise to try. That day in the air and the clouds and the drifting light, I was invulnerable.

I eventually sat down to shelter against the wind in the lee of one of the pasture's old stone walls. The other two caught up with me. We ate our 'pieces', as the Highland Scots would call our simple meal, and then headed on. We reached the top of a col, one of the highest points on the French stage of the journey, and began to descend. Three hours later the landscape had changed utterly.

The great open uplands of the Massif Central, the high gale-scoured roof of the mountains, were behind us. We were in the benign valleys below.

Protected from the wind by shelves of rock, we made our way downwards. The weather's windy turbulence was still battering the peaks above us, but below it was calm and still. The narrow path had been worn smooth by a thousand years of pilgrims' feet. It was green and fern-strewn, grassy and starred with flowers.

Hilary and I walked together.

There were wild orchids everywhere. Hilary is a knowledgeable botanist, I'm a keen but inexperienced one. We identified as many of the seemingly endless species as we could, while Priscilla, an ornithologist, scanned the sky for birds through the great arching vaults of the branches. Kites flew over us, the resident red and the migrating black, both with their forked tails and glistening feathers; the occasional plunging booted eagle, the dagger-winged silhouette of a solitary peregrine falcon.

It was a quiet and golden descent.

The air was still and sweet. We were thronged all about with the murmured sounds and rich scents of an ancient landscape. Waters tumbled over the rocks in the valley's river beside us. Halfway down we came on a deserted farmhouse, nestling in the woods like an abandoned bird's nest. Priscilla and Hilary explored it.

'It's a place of dreams,' Priscilla said. 'We could live here for ever.'

She was right.

The whole valley was a place of dreams, and all of us could have lived there for ever among the wheeling birds and the orchids, the towering trees and the rushing foaming waters. The problem was we were pilgrims, and pilgrims embark on a journey, a journey which has to be concluded. Reluctantly we headed on.

We reached our night's destination, the little village of St-Chély-d'Aubrac. The pilgrim *gîte* was one of the best we'd found, neat and clean and with a fireplace already stacked with logs. Wonderfully, too, there was no one else there. We inspected the crisp tartan-blanketed beds, lit the fire, and settled down. Then we heard footsteps on the stairs outside.

The door opened and a figure appeared. He was a young Frenchman named Jean-Paul, a fellow-pilgrim on the Way. He was bowed down under the largest pack I have ever seen, dwarfing even Priscilla's house-on-her-back. I was uncharitably enraged. I thought we'd got the *gîte* to ourselves. Now I was faced with sharing it with this garlic-smelling foreigner who undoubtedly had filthy personal habits.

'My sister and her companion are missionaries,' I told him. 'They have just returned from Africa, and are in quarantine for both black and yellow fever. For your health's sake, you should sleep downstairs.'

'I'm a volunteer missionary, too, monsieur,' Jean-Paul said. 'I've just come back from Africa. I've been inoculated against fevers.'

He beamed at me. I gave up. I parked him in the back bedroom, and we went out to eat.

Jean-Paul turned out to be a solemn but attractive and interesting young man. We walked together the following day and discussed theology, life, the meaning of the universe, and the exchange rates on the international money markets. When he wasn't on voluntary missionary work, he was a stockbroker who was toying with the idea of changing his profession for that of a Cistercian monk.

'I wish I was like you,' he said. 'I wish I could speak languages. Then the world would be open to me.'

'The world is full of language schools,' I replied. 'Enrol, learn, and enjoy.'

'How would God feel?'

'God speaks in many tongues. He'd approve. But to get on the right side of Him, start with Palestinian. It was the language His son spoke.'

Jean-Paul considered the proposition and nodded. 'You are very wise.'

'Indeed I am,' I said. 'I just wish my children thought the same.'

The rain had slid away from us and for once the day was warm. We climbed to a hamlet high in the mountains, and stopped to rest on a stone bench. A farmer and his wife appeared, herding their cattle to a nearby upland pasture. They penned the animals and stopped to talk to us.

The hamlet was called Lestrade. Not long ago it had a school and at least fifty *foyers*. In rural France, *foyers*, hearthplaces round which a family gathers to warm themselves, cook their meals, talk and conduct the business of living, are the traditional measure of population. In Lestrade the school had gone and there were only two *foyers* left.

The farmer said he scraped a living but would have little left for his children, who had long since left for the neighbouring towns. Until twenty years ago he'd worked the land with oxen. Now he used a tractor. He had nothing against the modern world and its technology, but he found it a lonely and trivial place compared to the world he'd grown up in. His wife agreed. She missed the school, the children, the companionship of the vanished community.

But what could they do? They had their land. No one was going to buy it, an upland farm was unsaleable. They could only soldier on and try to make a livelihood out of what was left.

It was a melancholy story, redeemed only by the stubborn good cheer of the ageing couple who told it to us, and one we heard again and again. The French countryside, like all the so-called marginal rural areas of Europe, is being abandoned. We walked through village after deserted village. The houses and cottages were empty and crumbling. There was rarely anyone about, not even a forlorn cat.

Prairie farms, cropped and harvested by massive machines, provide Europe with its food now. Supermarket chains distribute the produce and ruthlessly control and dictate the prices. The old patchwork peasant culture, a culture of sustainable self-sufficiency with a few surplus crops being exchanged for trade items like cotton and salt, has been swept away.

A few resilient pockets remain but the fun's gone, the ceremonies and festivals have gone, the laughter and the songs are out of it, the link between man and the living land has been broken. We either live in urban conglomerations, or we're in the agri-business, the one consuming what the other produces.

For years it's been fashionable to scorn and decry the past, to argue the benefits of state paternalism, of pensions and nationalized medicine, of metalled highways carrying streams of cars and trucks, of the deterrent wonders of nuclear weapons and the glories of satellite television creating a global village.

As I listened to the farmer and his wife, I wondered.

I wondered if humanity needed a global village, or rather the vast concrete sprawls which the euphemism stands for. I wondered if we needed broad-spectrum antibiotics and hip-replacement operations and state-guaranteed pensions. I wondered if we needed prairie farms and even tractors as simple and cheap as the one on the cobbled street before us. I wondered if the dispersal of families and the migration of children to towns really suited the future.

They were seditious, almost Luddite, thoughts. Expressed aloud, even speculatively, I might have sounded as if I were advocating the return of child chimney sweeps and child prostitution. I kept them to myself — although it did remind me that the chimneys at my Welsh farmhouse, Brynmeheryn, needed cleaning. My daughter Honey is slender and agile. Perhaps for a fiver I could persuade her to climb up and get to work.

'You've got a dreamy look,' Hilary said as the farmer and his wife left us. 'What are you thinking about?'

'Chimney sweeps,' I said. 'Let's head on.'

We did. We were heading down now into the valley of the river Lot. In the evening we reached the pleasant little market town of Espalion which straddles that lovely river, its waters now swollen by the rain and the snow-melt from the mountain.

8

We'd planned a short stop in Espalion.

It was a brief break-point in the journey, almost a rest, at least somewhere we could sleep between sheets, have a bath in the hotel Hilary found, and get our hair dealt with – in my case, a quick razored trim which unintentionally left me almost scalped and looking like a US marine recruit on indoctrination day. The ladies roamed the town and visited its churches, while I toured its exuberant street market and then sat drinking beer on a terrace overlooking the river.

Late in the morning we continued, following the course of the river. Like a Scottish salmon river, the Lot was in spate. The deep clay-brown waters, flecked with foam and carrying rafts of old leaves from the previous autumn, ran westwards in a great surging torrent that occasionally spilled over the banks and flooded the track. The riverside trees were still ragged and bare, but the fishing season had started and we passed the occasional huddled angler casting his line onto the rippling racing water.

The rain came and went, although when it drenched us now it was warm and soft with the feel of spring. We stopped to eat our midday picnic outside the lonely red sandstone church of St-Pierre-de-Bessuéjouls. Unlike my two companions, as I wrote at the start, I have little interest in the built environment. When you've seen one Romanesque church, in my view, you've seen them all. The places are lost and foundering at best, at worst cold and dead.

St-Pierre was different.

The sun came out, the light caught its crimson tower, the building glowed like a beacon. We went inside and climbed the winding stairs to the belfry. The beams that ran between the bells were decorated with extraordinary sinuous carvings of demons and dragons, grain and fruit, mermaids and centaurs. It was an extravagant cornucopia mingling the pagan and the Christian, and it felt warm and comforting.

'We must press on,' I said. The phrase had become something of a running joke between us. 'Press on. We've miles still to go.'

I thought of Robert Frost's poem about a winter in Vermont which ends with the lines: 'And I have miles to go before I sleep, Miles to go before I sleep.' The poem could have been written for us — and on every day, every stage of the journey.

The rain returned.

Under a grey drizzle we scrambled uphill in mud, through thick woodland patched with the occasional pasture. The pastures were guarded by electric fences and when I accidentally touched one strand of wire I received a shock that almost threw me to the ground. We came across a farm, the holiday home of a Parisian family, and the two women stopped to drink from their well. Then once more we started to descend.

We were coming down into the valley that carried the river Lot towards the sea. The weather cleared. The sky wasn't bright, it was still strewn with tossing storm clouds, but at least the rain had stopped and we had occasional glimpses of a sickle moon in the gathering dusk. Homing birds flew over us, rooks, a wandering eagle, pairs of burnished red kites. Owls were starting to call and I heard the distant barking of a fox.

An old farmer appeared on the track. He was carrying a pail of creamy milk. It had just been drawn from his cow and was warm and fresh, with a little haze of steam rising from it in the cooling air. Pilgrims have been sources of entertainment for centuries, the street-theatre of the wilds, and he stopped and interrogated us.

'Only thirty kilometres today?' He gave a scornful toothless chuckle. 'When I was young and we moved the herds, we did that before midday. You need feeding up.'

He produced a ladle, plunged it into the pail, and insisted we all drank.

By the time we reached the little town of Estaing, once a medieval trading post with an ancient bridge across the Lot, it was almost dark. Our quarters for the night were in a vast barrel-vaulted chapel that had been deconsecrated and turned into a pilgrim hostel. It had powdery sky-blue walls and some sixty or seventy neatly regimented metal beds. Although far more attractive, it reminded me of the cavernous barrack-huts I'd slept in as a young soldier. No one else was there and we had the place to ourselves.

We ate in one of the town's restaurants in the company of forty folk-singers celebrating their return from Catalonia where they'd been performing the old songs of the region. It had clearly been a demanding experience, and they were letting their hair down with a vengeance having returned to their home town. One of the group's matrons, unsteadily carrying a tumbler of Armagnac, weaved up to Priscilla, sat down, embraced her, and gave her a sample of their repertoire.

The woman's voice was magnificent. It would have silenced all the foghorns of the shipping in the English Channel on the worst of winter nights. Priscilla sat there grimly polite with her head ringing. The lady swung away to call for more Armagnac.

As she searched for the waiter, we stole away.

In the morning, Jean-Paul, our pilgrim companion from St-Chély with his world and its belongings on his back, was waiting at the hostel door. He insisted we visited his night's lodgings. We went there with him.

He'd slept in a multi-discipline, ecumenical, singing-and-dancing, hand-clapping, vegan, all-Christians-joyously-together retreat. The staff wore beards and ankle-length dirndl skirts. They were kind and welcoming, but there was something lonely, melancholy, about them. They were thin people, a bloodless group, strangers from other countries and other cultures. They lacked passion, conviction, the God-driven — or devil-driven — hardness that sends people out on crusades to rebuild or ruin the world. I looked at their little garden. It wasn't well tended. People who can't manage plants are unlikely to be good stewards of souls.

They gave us caffeine-free coffee and they were smilingly eager for us to sign their visitors' book. For some reason, perhaps because they thought it conferred approval and support, it seemed more important to have our names written down than actually to have us there.

We wrote in the book and went on our way.

That day took us, after another lovely green and flowery walk up and down through gently folding countryside, to a small village named

Espeyrac. There was a comfortable little hotel with a menu offering a good simple dinner at tables covered with clean red and white chequered cloths.

We settled in contentedly.

As I took my boots off in my room – the rooms were so small we had to sleep apart – I had seldom felt happier. In spite of the snow and the rain, the journey so far had been wonderful, a physically taxing but joyous tramp through some of the loveliest landscapes in Europe. Both Priscilla and Hilary had had problems with backs, blisters and swollen feet, but nothing had happened to me.

I felt strong and confident. There were only a couple of days to go on this particular stage. All was well with the world, and in the sunset outside the window it looked the best possible of all worlds.

In the early hours I fell ill.

Blessed with a robust constitution – as my wife Elisabeth used to remark, 'You'd make the average young mountain bullock look fragile' – I've almost never been ill in my life, certainly not with the infection I got then. I woke choking, with my chest heaving and my lungs struggling for air. By morning I was panting and coughing up mucus, while constant stabs of piercing pain were rattling my ribs.

There was another mountain road ahead of us. Hilary, the consultant's wife, had prudently brought some broad-spectrum antibiotics with her. I swallowed a handful and sent the two women on their way, saying I'd stay behind for a few hours and follow them if I felt better. By midday I felt worse. I could barely breathe. Angry and humiliated – it had been drummed into me as a young officer that foot soldiers aren't paid to become ill – I called for the local taxi.

Our destination for the night was the extraordinary and beautiful village of Conques. One of the oldest and best-known stops on the Pilgrim Way, it clings to the ridge that anchors its steep winding streets and clustered buildings like a mountain bird's nest. It is filled with medieval treasures and ghosts, dreams and bells, and clouds of circling, darting, air-skimming swifts. Sadly I saw little of it. The taxi delivered me to the Abbaye where I found a bed in a little white-washed cell, and threw myself down.

Hilary and Priscilla arrived in the late afternoon, damp but, to my sullen irritation, buoyant and invigorated by their walk through the hills. We cobbled together a meal in the Abbaye kitchen. I couldn't eat it. Nor could I sleep that night and tossed restlessly, often panting for breath. Finally, towards dawn, I dozed.

When I woke I found Hilary and Priscilla in the kitchen, packing. It was obvious they were going to have to go on without me while I made arrangements to take myself and my chest infection back to England. They headed on to complete the stage with overnight stops at Livinhac-le-Haut and Figeac.

I swallowed another handful of antibiotics – they seemed to be having no effect at all – bade farewell to the girls, and returned to my bed.

When I woke at midday, my lungs still weren't functioning and my legs were as weak as a new-born kitten's. That evening I found a logger in one of Conques' bars. For the price of his petrol, he agreed to drive me to the town of Figeac. From there I made my way to Toulouse, and flew back to London. I coughed and panted throughout the flight. What had started so optimistically, what had been so full of energy and delights, had ended for me in something close to disaster.

My wife met me at the airport.

She took me straight to our doctor. He quickly diagnosed the problem as a severe pulmonary infection. That wasn't too difficult; I'd already worked it out for myself. He prescribed targeted antibiotics at a much higher level than I'd been taking, and sent me away with the encouragement that I should have shaken off the infection within a week.

His parting comment was: 'In a way you're lucky. What you've got is very similar to the new strains of TB. You'll toss this one away without a problem, but they can be deadly.'

I brooded on his remark as we drove back to our farm in Wales. Illnesses, infections, aren't very interesting. They interrupt life. They cause a waste of time and energy. On the rare occasions I've been sick, I've resented it deeply. There was something different about this one. It wasn't just that I felt worse than I'd ever felt before, it was that the virus had attacked my lungs.

The first indication something was wrong with Francesca's health came on our return from the Himalaya four years before she died, when it emerged she'd contracted TB. Like me she was treated with antibiotics and like me recovered – or so it seemed. In her case, the TB puzzlingly recurred a few months later. After exhausting all the other tests to trace why it might have come back, a young doctor finally decided on impulse to check her for the HIV virus.

It was an inspired – tragically inspired might be a better phrase – guess. There was nothing at all in her past or her austere life-style to indicate she might ever be an HIV possibility. The test was positive. Francesca, as she wrote so clearly and forthrightly of herself in her journal, was harbouring the genesis of AIDS.

Until quite recently, it was common medical practice to suggest that close relatives of someone who'd tested positive were checked for the virus themselves. It was a blunt instrument, believed in some way to indicate due diligence by the doctors and so protect them. It's since proved totally unnecessary and as far as I know the practice has been dropped. Except in the most extraordinary, in fact almost unimaginable, circumstances, it's virtually impossible for relatives to pass on the virus to each other. The likelihood is about the same as acquiring it in the process of buying a ticket from a bus conductor.

Six years ago, with so little known about the disease, medicine's defensive perceptions were different. It was recommended that I and all the family were tested. We agreed. We were of course all negative, completely free of this modern plague. The test results took a couple of days to come through and while we waited all of us felt acute anxiety. We knew even less about the disease or its transmission than the doctors did. Thankfully, relatives today will not have to go through this experience but it did give me an insight into what Francesca had gone through with, miserably, a different result.

Yet there was something extraordinary in the coincidence of the infections that attacked us both, different as their causes were. It would be easy and convenient to say I'd picked up the TB strain from, say, the body of a dead sheep which had contaminated one of the Auvergne rivers we'd waded through.

Elisabeth, a pragmatist and utterly unsentimental, hadn't the slightest doubt about it.

'You're walking with Fran, she's walking with you,' she said crisply. 'You're shadowing each other. In a sense you *are* each other, you always have been. Of course you'll contract her illnesses on the Way, although, God willing, not the fatal one.'

I managed a smile. I remembered the injunction Elisabeth had so often given me when I set out on my wanderings.

'Bring me back something I can eat, and nothing I can catch.'

Of course.

Except that Francesca wasn't actually walking with me to Santiago, she was only a constant presence in my mind. Maybe there was no difference. Maybe it came to the same. Maybe she really was there after all, and part of our contract on the Way was to share similar strains of these damnable infections.

Maybe I and my fearsome eldest daughter, often hostile, frequently challenging and defying me, had more in common than either of us thought.

Letters to Francesca: 4

Queen Charlotte's Hospital all those years ago, with the doughty Sister Penrhys, her white hair sheen-metalled like a helmet and the dust-grey Rhondda valley cadences in her voice, and your long-dead but munificent great-great-grandfather, did you proud.

You survived the transfusions, the rinsing out of the bad blood and the topping up with the good, and you began to grow.

We were living in London. You went off to infant school, jaunty and confident in your smart new uniform. There was nothing special about you. You were just another little schoolgirl among thousands, the classic ugly duckling. Gawky, sassy, rather plain, hopping, skipping and jumping, and then erupting jubilantly with a trail of followers behind you when classes ended.

Except even then there were two things that separated you from the throng that followed. When you stopped scampering and shouting and settled into your natural rhythm, you exhibited a grace of movement such as I have never seen before or since. You spun, you floated, you glided. Even at five, everything in you carried the true sure stamp of a dancer.

Then occasionally I would see something in your eyes that startled me.

Like your hair, your eyes, as I have written, were very dark, almost black. From time to time they glazed over. They stilled and froze. Ice seemed to coat them, and they would study someone with a terrible impenetrable intensity. To the onlooker — I wasn't the only one who noticed it — it was chilling. It was impossible to tell what you were thinking, although I sensed you were looking far and deep beyond the surface, beyond any façade and through all the evasions and deceptions so many of us use, through and beyond them to the heart of things.

You scared the wits out of me then as you did so often later.

By the time you were five, our London flat was bulging and straining under the pressure of the six of us. We moved to southern Spain, to Andalucía, to the large rambling house I built in a valley in a cork forest

*above the Straits of Gibraltar. The house was named El Huerto Perdido,
the lost orchard, but the locals named it 'the great white bird in the trees'.*

The forest became the landscape of your childhood.

*It was a strange and wild landscape. When the cork bark was cropped,
as it was every nine years, the exposed naked trunks of the oaks were a
deep ox-blood red. You swung on their branches and played among them.
We had occasional infestations of gypsy hawk-moths, stripping the vegetation
for miles around and cocooning the house in filmy grey webs that glittered
with dew in the mornings. The nights were filled with stars and owl calls.
Mongoose and the lithe black and white striped wildcat, the genet, haunted
the glades. Terrapins nudged their way through our stream.*

*There was an old Moorish mill down the valley. I took you there once.
The mill's owner, the ninety-year-old, massively built, dreaming Fernando,
a famous smuggler and womanizer, told us stories of the brigands and
wolves who'd inhabited the crests when he was young.*

*'Beware, little senorita,' he pointed his finger at you, 'their ghosts are
there still.'*

*You gazed back at him, steadfast as always but saucer-eyed, and you
gripped my hand for comfort. Just as you did on the tiny, wheezing and
rattling ghost train at the annual fair in nearby Tarifa, the southernmost
point of Europe and our local town. The single coach ran so slowly, a wizard
in a mask could scamper alongside beating us over the head with his broom
as he brayed out fiendish laughter.*

*The great white bird of the house was set, appropriately, beneath one of
the two great bird migration paths from Africa to Europe. The dazzling
bronze-capped and emerald-winged bee-eaters were always among the first
to pass over us each spring. You used to alert me when you heard their
whistling calls as they swooped up the valley. You told me when eagles
were passing, and you helped me feed the wounded owls and honey buzzards
that were brought to us.*

We fed the most magnificent of them all, Bubo bubo, *the eagle owl,
the giant golden-eyed, talon-stamping, beak-snapping — the crack it made
with the black blades of its bill was as loud as a slamming door — as
darkness came.*

Do you remember the kitchen table, Fran?

Certainly you will. It is massive, made for us by an Andalusian shipwright, inlaid with old tiles from Sevilla so your mother could put down her peasant beans-and-bones stews without burning the wood. There's no metal in it, only oaken dowling. You must have had countless meals at it. Often you'd sit there hunched and glowering with your head lowered over your folded arms.

Then something would catch your attention, your imagination. A story, a fragment of poetry, the unexpected arrival of one of your family's rude and raucous chums — my friend David Towill with his bawdy stories that would have silenced the Wife of Bath, or that wonderful raconteur, Dominic Elwes, or the heron-shaped jester, Peter Cook, who could outmatch them both with anecdote for outrageous catherine-wheel-spinning ancecdote, the sparks flying with every word.

They've gone. They destroyed themselves in various ways as many of the best do. But they were there for you and when they came, you'd look up and the menacing fierceness would vanish. Your eyes would glow and your face would be irradiated with laughter. Child or woman, it was always the same. As a child, the defiant bristle-feathered duckling changed instantly into a serene and beautiful cygnet. Then one knew a swan was waiting to emerge. The trouble with swans is that they're dangerous. You need to approach them with caution, they've been known to break people's arms and legs with a beat of their wings.

The swan's appearance began in Spain. I don't think it was an accident it happened there. I think that when you went to live in Andalucía you came home.

Letters to Francesca: 5

We acquired a donkey named Bernardo for the house in the forest.

With our gardener, José, leading him by the halter and your brother trudging alongside, Bernardo carried you and your sisters on your daily journeys to school to learn about trapping and skinning rabbits, planting vegetables, mending mule-drawn threshing sleds, all the vital skills of an Andalusian country child, with, thrown in almost as an afterthought, a rough grounding in reading, writing and adding up figures.

Ostensibly Bernardo the donkey belonged to the whole family, but soon after his arrival a strange thing happened. He became yours. We didn't make the choice, nor did José who'd worked with donkeys all his life, nor did you. Bernardo made it for himself. He'd ignore the rest of us but whenever you appeared, he'd bray for you. He wouldn't stop until you'd gone to him, stroked him, and given him whatever it was he wanted.

It was the first time I'd noticed your effect on animals, although I was to see it repeated with all sorts of creatures. One of your last unrealized ambitions was to swim with dolphins. Like everything you did, you were a wonderful swimmer, supple and silvery in the water. If you had joined them in the waves I wonder what you would have made of them and they of you. I have a feeling neither of you, girl or dolphins, would have noticed you weren't of the same animal nation.

And in Spain you really began to dance.

Whenever I go back to the south, to Andalucía and the pueblos *where you're remembered, invariably I hear the same comment: she was the best dancer of all. What* gracia *the girl has,* gracia *far and beyond any of us.*

Gracia, grace, style, elegance, a certain splendour in one's presentation, is perhaps the highest accolade in the Castilian language. The term belonged to you, you deserved it, but you were always shy, too wary to accept it fully.

For God's sake, girl, will you please accept it now.

I've been lucky enough to have known and watched a number of great dancers — Fonteyn, Beriosova (at a party I once even danced rather ineptly with her myself), several more. Let's not make extravagant claims for you. You had no formal training, no acquired professional technique. You were an amateur — although I increasingly wonder quite what that means in almost any context. You mastered the patterns of the sevillana with its four formal sequences, you could snap the castanets to the changing rhythms as if you'd been born with the little wooden cups in your hands, you could improvise on the basic structures of flamenco for hour after hour, and people would gather to watch and clap in time as you did.

Some of it you were taught. More came from your own intense watching of other fine Andalusian dancers. The greatest part of all was your own. Feeling, instinct, a love of music, your body's natural delicate balance — you were incapable of a graceless move or gesture. All ancient peoples dance — the Kalahari San, the canoe-borne Maoris, the desert Berbers, the Zulus, the native American Indians. You'd have found yourself at home if you'd been born among any of them.

I shall always remember you as a dancer.

9

The second stage of the journey started in October the same year, at Figeac, the town where Priscilla and Hilary had ended up after my illness at Conques. As I approached the little hotel where we'd agreed to meet, I could see in the darkness through the lighted dining-room window Hilary and Priscilla sitting at a table. I dumped my pack and staff in the hall, and went through to greet them.

I kissed them both and sat down.

'You didn't think I'd be here, did you?' I asked.

'Rubbish,' Hilary answered. 'In fact, we've already ordered for you.'

She was speaking the truth. My meal arrived as I pulled up my chair.

'*El Camino es una droga*,' the Castilians say. 'The Way is a drug.'

As before, the three of us slept together.

I count the days that followed as among the happiest of my life, days of ease, well-being, contentment.

Not physically, of course. There was nothing easy in the company of my two Valkyries. They hit the road running, as the good members of 2 Para they might have been, and then they picked up speed. They stepped out, they strode with enormous vigorous steps, they bundled me along with them. We bustled, hurried, tramped and force-marched our way through the countryside.

'That's a wonderful example of vernacular architecture,' I'd plead in my most winsome voice as we passed some ancient tavern. 'Why don't we pause and take a look at it?'

'No, we must press on,' Priscilla answered, lobbing the stock-phrase back at me, '*press on*.'

We did stop occasionally, but only at ruins, churches and monasteries. Nowhere, I often reflected gloomily, which sold beer. Many was the day when I'd have bartered my soul for a demi-litre of golden frothing *pression*. With Hilary and Priscilla, my throat remained dry. Like a yearling stallion, I was kept at a hand-canter on a tight leading-rein.

In fairness to them, it wasn't so in the evening. When the day's journey was done, they could break the neck from a bottle or two of the black wine of Cahors with the roughest French peasant through those vineyards we'd tramped.

'Feel better now, dear?' Hilary would say as she extracted the cork and filled my glass.

I'd look at her, try to kick her under the table, curse her, laugh at her and, inevitably in the end, as Priscilla had promised me at the start, love her. And then we'd go on.

That first day – from Figeac to the little town of Cajarc – was one of the longest and most demanding stages on the entire Pilgrim Way, taking us over thirty-five kilometres south-west. The distance is more than enough for a fit unencumbered walker across flat countryside. To the three of us just starting out again, travelling over a steeply rising and falling landscape, and weighed down by our heavy packs, it proved a challenge we didn't appreciate when we left.

The day began well enough.

The dawn greyness gave way to sun. A fine autumnal shine and sparkle lit the morning air. The tracks were soft, late migrating birds flocked above us, the turning forest leaves glowed coppery and gold, and the tree trunks gleamed with that dew-laden dark umber I always associate with Tuscan woods at the same time of year. Beneath a stand of beeches we found a magnificent crop of *cèpes*, the penny-brown *Boletus* mushroom, and regretfully left them because we had no means of cooking them.

The *cèpes* reminded us we were hungry. We'd set out too early even to find a café open for a bowl of *café au lait*. Then at nine o'clock, we passed a little farmhouse. We had walked on for fifty yards when suddenly Hilary stopped. She flared her nostrils like a pointer, sniffed the morning breeze, turned round and headed back.

'Can't you smell it?' she demanded. 'It's wonderful.'

Hilary was right.

The farm housed a tiny family cottage industry which made *croustades*, robust but delicate filo pastry tarts filled with apples marinated in the local brandy. The family made one hundred and fifty a day, never more, and sold them only to private customers. The apples were their own, the filo made by them, the brandy distilled by the district cooperative from their own grapes too.

We were invited in. In the handsome old kitchen we watched the whole business – the mother and daughters drawing out the translucent sheets of filo, the father ladling the marinated apples into the baking tins, one brother expertly decorating the tarts with folds and whirls of pastry, a cousin supervising the baking in a modern steel oven.

'I know we're not regular customers, but could we possibly buy one?' Hilary asked.

'Of course,' came the smiling reply. 'And because, *évidemment*, you are pilgrims, you shall have it with some of our local white wine.'

We ate it round a table made out of an old mill-wheel outside in the garden. The farmer brought us a jug of his crisp chill wine, dry and clean and scented with forest grasses, to wash it down. Late roses brushed our shoulders and constellations of butterflies spiralled round us, feeding off the nectar in the still flowering lavender bushes. It was the best breakfast I have ever had.

I was infinitely glad of it by the time evening came. Lovely as the landscape was, there was nothing else on the Way except for another woman in a cabin in the woods who sold us little bags of dried *cèpes*. They wouldn't be as good as the fresh *Boletus* we'd found, but they were portable and we could eat them when we got home.

When darkness fell we'd been on the road for almost twelve hours. We were all struggling now and there were still at least two hours to go to Cajarc. For once I was struggling as much the other two. I'd slipped and wrenched my knee and, with the weight on my shoulders pulling me back, I instinctively started to favour my other leg. That transferred the strain but made things worse. The 'good' leg began to ache too. The aches drifted up to my hips and soon I was moving crab-like, quite off-balance.

Priscilla and Hilary weren't in much better shape. There was no moon, the track was rugged and rocky, we'd lost the way-marks, the forest pressed in on us with branches sweeping our faces and brambles snagging our clothes. Owls mocked us from above. Then I remembered

I had a little whisky left. It was not enough for more than a dram each, but we stopped and shared what remained.

'For this I'll forgive you anything,' Hilary said. 'Anything. It's a promise.'

I'm glad she made it. She had much to forgive me for over the many long stages ahead, and I held her to her word.

The whisky – it was the greatest of all Scotland's single malts, the Macallan – gave us just enough impetus to carry on. We saw the lights of Cajarc below us. We limped and stumbled down the sharp descent from the uplands into the town, found the wayfarers' *gîte*, raised the guardian and obtained the key, and collapsed onto the bunk beds.

'A couple of bottles of wine,' I begged Priscilla an hour later when she went out to telephone.

We drank the wine, we went out and ate, then numb and dizzy with tiredness we slept.

The morning was fine, warm and filled with early sun, and we walked on – or so we thought. At least the way-marks were clear enough, unlike those we'd lost the night before in the moonless darkness of the woods.

After an hour I stopped and frowned.

Something was troubling me. Normally I navigate broadly by eye, using the sun's position for the compass points or, in heavy cloud, by the compass sewn into my jacket, or in cloud and unfamiliar territory by a combination of compass and map. Perhaps I was still tired from the day before, perhaps I'd become careless, perhaps I was confused by the swirl of valleys and hills round Cajarc. Maybe I'd just suspended my navigational senses, put my trust in the way-marks, and settled into a day of dreaming and thinking.

Whatever it was, I knew something was wrong.

I walked slowly on. Even in the blackest of darknesses, the experienced eye registers certain patterns – contours in the ground, the presence of a group of rocks, the shape of a thicket of trees even when the individual trunks are invisible. They form a hidden map which the mind can store and recall. I knew I had walked this way before, and I knew I hadn't walked it before – unless it was the previous night.

I closed my eyes, I remembered, I went on.

I was looking for something and I found it a few minutes later behind a rock – the empty container of the Macallan. Almost invariably I carry my whisky in a battered silver flask. To save weight I'd left the flask at home, and used instead a plastic bottle. Tidy conservationist as I claim to be, I should never of course have left the bottle there. I should have tucked it into my pack, carried it with me and disposed of it in some recyclable sustainable-energy-providing bin. With my swollen knee and those thirty-five or so kilometres behind me, I'd just been too tired. I'd simply dumped it.

The bottle gleamed accusingly on the green facets of my conscience. I hurled it angrily into the bushes and called ahead to the other two. We'd been walking, I told them, in diametrically the wrong direction – not forward but retracing our steps of the night before. We'd wasted at least two hours and added eight kilometres to the day's journey. They cursed as fluently as I'd done; we all turned and set off again.

In spite of the start, it turned out to be another golden autumn day.

We roamed up and down across small gentle hills, and through little private valleys. There were late figs to be plucked from ancient trees on abandoned farmsteads. We passed great orange-yellow piles of sweet-corn, cattle food for winter, drying inside open wire-meshed storage stacks. Rows and rows of vines with a single indicator scarlet rose at each end – indicator because the roses, more sensitive than the vines, give the farmer early warning of a viral attack on his crop. If the roses blight and wilt, he knows he must take action to protect the vineyard.

Next to the vineyards were the apple orchards where the harvested but discarded fruit – a tapestry of myriad colours, bitter-green, cherry-red, damson and russet and crimson – lay in banks so high and long (some stretched for a hundred yards or more) that we couldn't easily cross the orchards, only search for gaps where the tractors had trundled across them.

The apples' rot would seep back into the earth, at least returning their nutriment to the pastures and orchards, but they were a fearsome illustration of what western Europe was doing with its riches and its land. Paying good people to grow things; paying them to harvest them; and then paying them to destroy them. In spite of all the fossil fuel waste and transport costs, it's cheaper to teach the Kenyan Masai tribes to grow alien fruit like strawberries and fly the crop to northern markets, than to pick in our own back garden. Yet politically, to buy his vote, the European farmer has to be protected from 'unfair' competition from a remote part of the world with much lower expectations of what life has to offer, and much lower costs.

The political solution is known as compensation or subsidy. It leads to the wasted drifts of the scented fruit we saw again and again that day. Like the elephant herds I had watched many times in the Kalahari, the age-old practice of good husbandry is vanishing so quickly it will soon be no more than a ghost that haunts the memory.

I brushed the bruised apple pulp from my boots and walked on.

Late in the day, towards nightfall, we reached the village of Limogne-en-Quercy. Hilary had a couple of friends, a retired British merchant banker and his wife, who owned a millhouse nearby. The husband was a keen walker and wanted to join us for the next day's stage. We waited for them to join us in Limogne's Bar Central. The bar's door was open, the evening air was chill, I was tired and cold and increasingly impatient as time passed with no sign of the pair. Eventually they arrived and I hurried the whole group off to our night's lodging.

We ate by candlelight and slept just outside the village in a *gîte d'équestre*, a farm-based summer riding centre although the stables were now closed and the horses had been turned out into their winter pasture. It was a vigorous evening. The banker was quiet and courteous, his intelligent wife far more combative and assertive. We discussed Lady Thatcher and the legacy of her conservatism. The banker's wife loathed the woman and everything she stood for. I provocatively took the other side, and we loudly and impolitely disagreed.

At eleven o'clock she swept out, heading back for her house. The banker remained; we had an early start and he'd decided to sleep in the *gîte*. The three of us, the three companions, had taken a room with four beds. Could he, he asked, take the fourth?

'I'm sorry,' I replied. 'You're not part of the group. You'll have to sleep next door.'

Which he did.

Constructive or destructive, over time a dynamic, a cohesion, develops in group relationships. A stranger has to work out his apprenticeship and pay his dues. Until he's done that, he's an intruder. He has to remain beyond the door – castle, croft, sheiling, mud rondavel, even the thorn fence. The African nations, above all the Zulus, know it well. In the north we somewhat patronizingly call the concept 'tribalism', although it applies equally to us. It doesn't deny generosity, hospitality, food or shelter, but it does say: until we know you, until we recognize your smell and are familiar with the sound of your laughter and maybe hear your song, you may not sleep with us or share our dreams.

The three of us slept safely in our own room. The banker slept next door. It was better, more appropriate, that way, and all of us rested well.

Next day we were off again at dawn. It was a quiet and gentle day along sun-filled tracks and lanes. A day for thoughts and occasional speculative talk. We unlaced our boots and ate our midday piece in a glade starred with late summer flowers and surrounded by thickets of gorse. We passed through a couple of silent hamlets without even a barking dog to harass us. We found, incongruously, a wire-netted enclosure where birds were being bred – pheasants, guinea-fowl and wild duck. It was large and evidently well cared for, but there was no one there to explain its presence.

We walked on.

Towards evening we reached the *gîte* at Mas de Vers, another little horse-riding hostel. The banker's wife joined us and was as bright and articulate as before. We ate together again, then the couple left us to go back to their lovely millhouse with its stream and wood – all of which, house, stream and wood, they were restoring and regenerating – and then back to their equally fine house in London. They had neatly organized lives. They had, I imagine, a huge pension. They had a proper sensible agenda for living.

I thought about them as I lay in bed that night after they'd left. Inevitably I thought about Francesca, too.

Francesca had no pension nor any neat agenda for her life. Only passion, interest and intellect. That and a discipline in the way she conducted her existence, a truly ruthless discipline, that might have awed the banker. If these things are up for the winning, who won? The nice banker with his pension and his spirited elegantly dressed wife? Or Fran in her frayed jeans?

I've loaded the evidence, of course, stacked the odds. I'm bound to. I'm the girl's father. But my money goes on the girl, not the banker.

The journey had reacquired its rhythm, and the days began to fold over one by one, each slotting into its place like entries by a neat hand in an old diary discovered in an attic.

The next night we reached river-bound Cahors, winding our way down into the town from the hills along lanes overhung with copper-leaved and scarlet-berried bushes that blazed like children's party sparklers in the light of the westering sun. The only rooms we could find were on the lofty wooden top floor of the rackety Hôtel Terminus. I asked Madame where the fire escape was. She looked at me blankly. I might as well have asked her to discuss some arcane dimension of advanced computer technology.

I made the sign of the cross in my mind and we checked in.

By now the canny knowledge of the ropes of pilgrimage travel was coming back to me. While the ladies sorted themselves out, I walked along the street to the bus station. Provided we delivered our packs there by 6.30 a.m., I discovered, a country bus would carry them on to our next destination and drop them off at the bar in the town's centre. I bought tickets for the packs and walked back.

The following day, Thursday, was market day in Cahors. Sensibly, as in Spain, French markets are not dawn-opening affairs – there is all that business and mischief of the previous night to be slept off before the intelligent philosophical shopper takes to the streets. Ten a.m. is considered a reasonable hour for the tape to be cut. It gave us enough time after handing in our packs at the bus station to have a leisurely breakfast and write a few letters before heading for the market square.

There are no bad markets in France: Gallic culture wouldn't tolerate them, only good, better, excellent and superb. In the last category I'd place Lyon, Aix, and the one in the little Provençal town of

Vaison-la-Romaine. There are many more and it's a matter of tossing dice to choose between them. Cahors' market probably comes between the good and the better. It's lively and entertaining. There's fresh-plucked fruit and fresh-cut vegetables; clucking chickens and scampering rabbits on the hoof; honey from the comb and honey in the comb; nuts and wine and pulses; great tables laden with hessian bags of herbs, forty or fifty different species of them; cheeses from a dozen regions and *saucissons* – black, chalk-white, ox-blood-red, bone-dry or coated with their natural fat, savoured with salt, pepper, oregano, garlic – from a dozen more.

When one looks at a provincial French market, with its satellite stalls offering meat and fish, oysters and squid, one is staring at rural France four-square in the face. The countryside French aren't much fun: enclosed, inward-looking, mean and thrifty, suspicious of outsiders, hewing only to their own – and as often as not that means just their immediate family. But when they eat – and they famously place a high value on their food – they eat like royalty. Even the Sun King, Louis XIV, was hard put to rival one of their dinners at his feasts – and the descendants of his peasants eat their dinners every day.

Caviar, oysters, truffles, salmon, venison and the finest game birds are, as is often forgotten now, the traditional diet of the European peasant farmer and fisherman. Depending on the area, they could be gathered close to home: caviar from the sturgeons all round the Black Sea (once sturgeon even swam up the Thames and their roes, with royal dispensation, fed the apprentice boys); oysters on the coast everywhere, so too salmon where the rivers ran to the sea; truffles under every copse of scrub oak; venison from the deer that still roam the forests; and game of course – pheasant, pigeon, woodcock, partridge and duck – across the entire countryside.

Where has that prodigal, prodigious and nourishing bounty gone?

It hasn't, of course, gone. It's still there, damaged, wounded and emaciated but binding up the cuts and preparing itself to feel the wind again. One cannot stop a bluebell from flowering or a falcon from flying except by destroying every last bulb and burning every last egg-laden nest. Nor can we stop the wild's harvest from returning. With the very worst will in the world, I doubt we can do that.

Optimistically, perhaps, as we made our way through the crowded scuffle of Cahors' market, I felt given half a chance and a little help the sources of the bounty would survive.

For once we set off with good provisions for our midday meal. We crossed the still mist-cloaked northern bridge, scrambled up the rock-face beyond, hauling ourselves up hand by hand, and set off into the countryside beyond. Five hours later we stopped to eat on a river's bank. As we sat there all three of us heard the co-ordinated tramp of marching footsteps. We looked round.

I stiffened. 'It's the *Herrenvolk*,' I said.

They were a group of five, three adults and two teenagers. They were all wearing *lederhosen*, and looked as if at any moment they might burst into a chorus of 'Tomorrow Belongs to Me'.

'Shut up,' Hilary hissed. 'The war's over.'

They stopped and beamed at us.

'*Guten tag*,' their leader said. 'You do not look French, no? Maybe you speak English?'

'A little,' I ventured cautiously.

'We are from Germany, from Munich. We go to Santiago. Sometimes by walking, but mostly in our Mercedes camping-waggon. Much of the way in the mountains is very hard, no?'

I remembered the snows of the Auvergne. I nodded. 'Yes,' I agreed.

'And so that part we drove altogether. Two days alone it takes us. And now for it is fine, we are walking. Tonight we sleep at a town named Montcuq. The Mercedes takes us there from the next village.'

'Have a good day,' I said.

They tramped off.

'Isn't Montcuq where we're spending the night?' I asked Hilary as they disappeared.

She consulted her notebook.

'Yes,' she replied. 'It's apparently got one small and attractive hotel with a few bedrooms.'

'Oh my God,' I said. 'It's like the sun-loungers round the swimming-pool. If we don't take action, the master race will book them all.'

I jumped up and began to run. I passed the Germans, puzzled to see me racing by, and two miles later reached a village with a telephone booth. I called the hotel and booked rooms for the three of us. As I came out of the booth still panting I saw a large and gleaming Mercedes van with Munich number plates parked up the street.

'Thank your stars I ran a marathon in the spring,' I said as the other two arrived. 'I've just saved us from a night sleeping in the gutter.'

I was right.

The hotel only had five rooms and the Germans with their back-up team would have taken them all. As it was they all had to double up with two of them sleeping on the floor. In every other way I did them an injustice. They were courteous and friendly, they bought us after-dinner liqueurs, and they offered to transport our packs onwards in their Mercedes the following day. They were undoubtedly good folk.

The problem is that racial memories, like country memories, are long. Each time I looked at their vigorous Aryan faces, their blond hair and confident blue eyes, I couldn't help visualizing the death of my father-in-law, a man I never knew. He too was fair and blue-eyed, an Old Etonian, and when he was killed at twenty-six he was Britain's most decorated pilot. A German U-boat shot down his Hercules over the North Atlantic, and the U-boat's crew machine-gunned him as he lay floating in the water.

Callously and unnecessarily, they deprived my wife of a father and my children of a grandfather. I thought too of so many of Elisabeth's relations from the strong Jewish arm of her family who were slaughtered in places with such infamous names as Belsen and Auschwitz. It's not enough to say that in war such things happen and have always happened. Not enough to argue, as the polemicists and apologists do, that comparable atrocities were committed by the Allies – I doubt they were. There's partial truth in everything, but it's still not enough.

What Nazi Germany did – and that means the German people – was to damage and scar the soul of all humanity. It's not something they alone have to live with. They harmed every one of us and the brutality is something we all have to live with. And quite possibly the parents of our pleasant companions round the fire in the Montcuq hotel that night, unfair as it was in every way to attach any blame to them, were willing cogs in the murderous and depraved machine that Germany,

79

in its greed, its vanity, its carelessness, tried to wheel across the world.

The hotel was stone-floored, rambling, warm and welcoming. I had a good hot bath, the first for days, and read the poetry of W. B. Yeats. Normally Yeats's poems for all their bleakness soothe me. Not that night. I was restless. I didn't sleep well.

We walked on – well, of course, we were constantly walking on.

It was another glorious sunlit autumn day, and the pattern of the journey had been well re-established. Sometimes we walked together and talked, often we drifted apart and strode along in silence. We formed little groups within the group. Priscilla and Hilary had many common interests based on Camberwell. They dissected friends and children, gossiped and discussed schools and local issues. I had no part of that. There I was a stranger. What Priscilla and I had in common was a family. That, apart from our love for each other, was our common ground.

So we too debated our children, examined the family structure, speculated on this or that member of the clan. None of it superficially was of any great consequence. It might have appeared trivial – just a brother and sister chattering together. I think now that like all such interchanges, it had a greater significance. We inherit or form networks of allegiances. Communication is the glue that binds them together. If we don't talk, they can fray and then dissolve. Blood is a wonderful bond, but it needs energy, constant energy, to keep the bond alive.

We spoke of Priscilla's son, my nephew Edward, an outstanding young runner studying at Sevilla university. The Spanish authorities had offered him citizenship if he'd agree to represent Spain at the Atlanta Olympics. Edward had turned them down. He wanted to take his chance on being selected for Britain at the next Olympics. We discussed our other children. And inevitably we discussed Francesca, the dying girl.

'All you can do is love her,' Priscilla said. 'There's nothing else.'

It was sensible advice. In the end there isn't anything left in the dust and cobwebs at the bottom of the cupboard except love.

It's a dangerous word. It's a raft that so often threatens to sink under a ballast it can't quite manage to support. It's so open to manipulation.

It requires and beguilingly suggests so much. It's always intriguing and occasionally noble but, my goodness, it's a wonderful vehicle for blackmail and deceit. Yet, together with hope it's all we've got and, in spite of all the shabby ways we treat it, still the best star we've got to steer by.

Priscilla was right. Give the girl love. Be patient with her fearsome impatience. Hold to that. There wasn't anything else.

We spent the night at a ramshackle little hotel with paper-thin walls in a village called Dufort-Lacapelette, where the kindly representatives of the master race had left our packs. I didn't see the hotel's name as we came in and asked the Madame behind the long spindly bar what the place was called.

'L'Aube Nouvelle,' she told me. 'We are very popular with the German tourists.'

I had to buy another drink – on the Isle of Mull it's called a 'steadier' – to stop myself falling off my stool with laughter. L'Aube Nouvelle. The New Dawn. How could our new-found German friends stay anywhere else?

IO

And then there was another lovely autumn day, another long, lovely day's walk, and suddenly this particular stage of the journey was almost over.

Although the year was winding down, the land still held its greenness and the trees their leaves. There were still late grapes, figs and apples to be picked. During the night, as for several nights before, there had been fierce rain storms. The many rivers and streams were filled and rushing and coated with peat-coloured foam. Flocks of rooks drifted away before us. The occasional solitary peasant farmer stopped to exchange greetings. I found a little laneside bar where, for once, I could buy a midday *pression*.

We tracked upwards and then downwards, speaking little.

There was no need to talk. It was a time of contentment, a time for reflection. Occasionally, high above us to the south, we could see the snow-flanked ramparts of the Pyrénées. We had nothing to eat, but the distant snows and the black and scarlet ripening berries in the hedgerows were enough to sustain us. We didn't know it then but the day, and the week that led to it, were to prove in retrospect to have been the best of the game.

We reached Moissac. We lodged in a drab family-owned hotel where we were served by a wall-eyed drooling son of the family who, in my childhood, would have been called a lunatic, but is now known as a person of severe learning disabilities. He knocked over our table and, when the glasses were replaced, dribbled into Priscilla's *citron pressé*.

'*La famille, vous comprenez*,' Madame said apologetically as he stumbled away with a glazed manic grin on his face.

Literally I understood her entirely, but hadn't the slightest idea what she meant, only that spittle was still running into Priscilla's drink. It didn't seem worth pursuing.

'Let's go out and eat,' Priscilla said, pushing away her glass.

Which we did. And in the morning, after making our way to Toulouse, we flew back to London.

On the flight home I closed my eyes and thought. We'd covered a fair measure of the pilgrim path and we'd done it in the old-fashioned way, on foot and in our own little group. Snow and rain and blizzards, we'd faced and outfaced them all in the mountains. We'd come down into the lowlands and had a joyous autumnal passage across them. There were still, in Robert Frost's words which returned to me often, miles to go before we slept, miles to Santiago with all of Spain to cross, but so far the stuff, the matter of the journey, had been lovely.

The Auvergne, with Mme Astruc's *aligot* and the storms of the Massif Central, was only a memory. Quercy and most of Gers, with its half-timbered houses and farmers – now only seen in old photographs – walking on stilts to raise them above the sodden land, was at our backs too. The Gascon lands and Aquitaine lay ahead.

Images recurred, the tales and legends we'd been told like that of the beast of Aveyron. In the eighteenth century, a creature had killed and eaten more than a hundred mountain villagers. The number may have been exaggerated in the telling and with time, but there seems little doubt the essence of the story is true. For a year or two the surrounding countryside was paralysed with fear, and the tale is still told to frighten children.

There was so much more to hold in mind. Not only stories, but landscapes and the idiosyncrasies of the people we'd met who inhabited them, so distinct all of them, so different in their cultures and domestic habits. Cascading wild flowers and glimpsed rare birds – a 'rare bird' is a phrase I've always cherished and here it was utterly appropriate – and tumbledown buildings. Hilary was even starting to convert me to consider and appreciate the broken architecture of the Way. Songs and laughter. Forests as old as Arden, rocks that belonged to ages before Eden was a garden, icy rivers frothed with yellow foam, green meadows tranquil as a well-mown English lawn.

Yet for me the connecting link in the whole mosaic, the pattern that joined it together, the inspiration for setting out and trying to make sense of the Pilgrim Way, remained as it had been from the start. Francesca. The shadow that hung over the journey was her illness.

It was, I think and hope, a rich and happy childhood, although I can only guess at the way you viewed it. Children don't tend to make judgements. Whether they grow up in the Calcutta slums or among throngs of liveried servants at Buckingham Palace, they accept what they're presented with as the norm. They don't inquire, they don't evaluate. By and large in my experience, neither a pauper nor a princess measures their lot against someone else's. Life is simply what they're given.

Yet it would certainly be true to say your childhood was an adventurous one. It was also, for four English children, highly unconventional – and that began to pose problems.

Nice children, yes. The trouble was you weren't nice English *children.*

In fact you barely used the language. You could switch effortlessly between the pure Castilian of the Madrid plateau, and the thick dialect of the Andalusian countryside, but English was becoming more and more remote to you. It wasn't surprising. Your friends were Spanish, your school was Spanish, the television and films you watched, the dances you danced, the songs you sang, the radio you listened to, all were Spanish.

It was your brother aged about thirteen who finally grasped the nettle. He confronted your mother.

'Listen, mother figure,' he said, 'someone's got to take a decision. If we stay here, we'll all go to Sevilla university, marry Spaniards, become Spanish. What's it going to be?'

We left Spain.

We packed the four of you into the VW – anarchic Honey with her gold-rimmed glasses and wandering eye, Poppy with her paint-box, Caspar, the best navigator I've ever known, with the maps, you with your books – and we headed north. Not for Britain but France.

Your mother, a superb linguist, had always been determined you would speak languages too. Not 'languages-learnt-at-school', but languages spoken with the sureness and fluency of those who regard them as integral to their culture and life. Our first language has been defined as the one in which we naturally pray, count, swear, and use when we make love. If that's so – and it seems to me a useful working definition – then goodness knows what yours is.

Your brother says he's not really aware of what language he's speaking. He turns on, as he puts it, a tap in his mind and he effortlessly reads, writes and communicates in whatever comes to mind. I suspect it's the same with you. Castilian is embedded in you, English came back to you, in France you acquired two more tongues — the Parisian of the capital and the patois of the land of the Oc.

The Languedoc takes its name from one of the two old French words for 'yes'. The other form of yes, 'ail' or 'oui', has prevailed and is the cornerstone of modern French. The country of the Oc, the mountainous landscape of the Cathars, is older, wilder, more subversive. It suited you well.

We borrowed a lonely little farmhouse belonging to Teresa, the scholarly wife of Auberon Waugh. Your mother drove the elder three of you into the local town, Castelnaudary, dumped you at dawn on the steps of the school, and told you to find your way back in the evening. Which you duly did, straggling in disconsolately one by one as the sky darkened. Your reward was a bubbling pot-au-feu and a tarte aux fraises with crème fraîche.

It cheered you all up no end. France, you decided, was a territory you could live with.

It was a harsh and icy winter.

I keep a glass of water by my bed. By morning in the Languedoc it was always frozen solid. You left for school at six o'clock, often in the snow. Your brother at thirteen was already a handsome lad and you were nothing if not a trader. On the bus back from Castelnaudary you'd barter the seat next to him to some lovelorn girl for a packet of Chiclets, of chewing-gum. No flies on you. You could have had a wonderful career dealing in rugs in the fly-blown back-streets of Istanbul or Samarkand.

Your mother painted pictures of birds and flowers in the kitchen. Honey tramped off to the local infants' school with her enamel dinner pail in her hand. When I wasn't writing I wandered the upland meadows late into the night. One evening, following a hunting owl, I found the French Foreign Legion. Castelnaudary is the Legion's main training base. What I'd encountered was a patrol carrying out a night exercise.

The Legion is led by regular French army officers from St-Cyr. I invited Philippe, the wiry and muscular young officer in command that night, back for coffee; he invited me to dinner at the mess; we became friends. Soon the farm became a Legion staging-post and other officers became visitors. There was coffee, whisky, bacon, charcuterie and eggs, and good old-fashioned men's talk, soldiers' talk of battles and the legendary Bigeard and whether or not we could bomb the hell out of Colonel Gaddafi.

One evening, picking you up from school, I stopped at the barracks for a quick drink. I left you outside in the car. When I came back a burly grey-haired man in Legion uniform was speaking to you through the window.

'Oliver Twist, I tell you, asks for more,' I heard him saying. 'More and more and more. No? Ha, I hear you saying. I read your Mr Dickens, you understand. But did he play chess, Mr Dickens, did he ask for more? Ha, I ask you.'

He was called Bradjic, Sergeant-major Bradjic. He was a Yugoslav and he'd served with the Legion all his adult life, fighting everywhere from Algeria to Vietnam. Now retired, he was still a considerable presence in the Legion's life and he ran its chess club.

Chess is much more than a hobby or interest to Legionnaires — it's the Legion's passion, its 'national game'. Taught in schools all over the former Soviet empire, it occupies a role in the Legion's consciousness close to that provided by football. One can't play football in a defensive trench on the edge of an Algerian airfield or in some isolated observation post in Vietnam, but one can always set up a board and make patterns with the queen, knights and bishops.

Sergeant-major Bradjic enrolled you and your brother in the Legion's chess club. He and his comrades taught or rather guided you into becoming outstanding players — I doubt whether chess can really be taught, it's much more like music, a matter of patterns and inventions and intuitions. And then Bradjic asked you to play for the Legion. I think the two of you were the only children who've ever done so.

Afterwards, still only fourteen, you played chess for England. And then you chucked it. You were immediately selected again, but you declined. Been there, done that, was your attitude. I think I can now understand why. You were growing, maturing, swiftly. The cygnet's shape was taking on the elegant frame of the swan that your Andalusian childhood had promised. You continued to play chess to the end, and play it superbly — you could always be inveigled into a game and invariably won — but there were other things to occupy you now. There were books to be read, words to be written, physics and biology to be studied, music to be listened to, frocks to be worn, parties to go to, boys to be entranced and seduced — poor but lucky boys, *how much they must have waded out of their depth when they encountered you.*

Damn you, Francesca.

Damn you for your wit and beauty and your magic. Damn you for the blisters on my feet. Please go away and leave me. Except, of course, you won't, will you?

Damn you, girl, for being so troublesomely unforgettable.

Letters to Francesca: 7

We came back to England.

You were offered a whole choice of schools, including London's elegant French Lycée, the one I'd have liked you to go to. Predictably you turned it down flat. You'd had enough of fancy foreign education. You wanted to see what London was really like, London in the raw, London where teenage street fashion and street credibility were all that mattered.

You picked Pimlico Comprehensive — 'this running sore on the nation's conscience', as the press was fond of describing it then. 'This educational blight where security guards have to be hired to patrol the corridors in a vain attempt to keep order.' You opted for the most dangerous of the blackboard jungles and, of course, as so often, you were right.

You were unafraid and you had steely authority and presence. Street cred seemed to have been bred in your bones. No one in the jungle ever dared cross you. In spite of your posh Kensington voice, you could deal with the gangs and coalitions of blacks and Asians, punks and 'melons' (I'm still not sure what the slang term means except I believe it's a contemptuous label for the fancily dressed middle classes). You found a few good teachers in a time when, God knows, they were as rare as star-dust. You bonded yourself to them.

And, having eyed them carefully, you chose lovely friends, all of whom have followed you loyally ever since. Yes, as I've said, you had a cat-like habit of bringing them back and dumping them on the floor. And, no, although they weren't always promising or congenial, your instinct was always right. You saw stuff and substance in awkward, ungainly, sullen teenagers to whom I wouldn't have given the time of day. Now in their thirties they are without exception among the most vital, attractive and talented people I know. Happily they've become my friends as they were yours.

You outgrew Pimlico. You'd learnt the language of the London streets, its rhythms and argot and the constantly changing culture that framed its turbulence. It was time to move on. You headed for the rather more rarefied — and considerably more expensive — cloisters and learning of *Westminster School*.

You were sometimes moody, one of your favourite words, always utterly independent, always intellectually brilliant, always a comet leaving something of a trail of havoc in your wake. 'Every boy in the school', it's been written or said to me again and again, 'was in love with her.' Which says a great deal about their good judgement, adolescent and testosterone-driven as it might have been. They were certainly wiser than your teachers.

They found you questioning, defiant, troublesome. You were what's now fashionably known as 'interesting-but-difficult'. On one occasion, famously remembered by all your contemporaries, you were punished for some misdemeanour by the headmaster by being made to run four times round the cloister. You'd just acquired the hour-glass figure you share with your sister Honey.

You set off, furious but cheerful. The boys crowded the windows to watch you. I wasn't there, of course, but it isn't difficult to visualize the scene. You with your smiling face — the idiocy of the punishment had reduced everything to a farce at which you could only smile — and several hundred young men staring down in rampant priapic rapture at your elegant legs and your jiggling, joggling breasts.

You returned that night weeping. Not in humiliation but with laughter. Someone had been made an utter fool of — and it wasn't you or your companions, the lusty red-blooded boys. No, someone else. You'd pulled authority's trousers down and shown there wasn't much there to see.

Westminster ended.

When it did, you could, as so often, have had the pick of any university you wanted. I tried to nudge you towards Cambridge, because I'd been there. I'd loved it, I thought you would too. You turned it down flat. Right, I said, then what about Bristol?

No, you answered.

Then where the hell do you want to go to? I asked in some exasperation. London, you said, for the moment I want to stay here in the smoke. You read biology. You were both the inspiration and despair of your fellow-students. As several of them plaintively wrote afterwards, it took you *a couple of hours to complete the work they needed the whole day to get through. They struggled for their doctorates. You did a short stint at your desk or in the laboratory, and left them at their labours while you headed out to go partying.*

Not that you were in any sense frivolous. You were austere, almost puritanical in the way you conducted your life. You smoked but you barely drank, a single small glass of wine — and it had to be very good, a vintage claret or champagne or, best of all, the soft aromatic Beaumes de Venise — was enough. You may have briefly experimented with marijuana — which one of us hasn't? If you did, you swiftly dropped it. Otherwise, drugs were anathema to you.

In the years before you died, the years after you were diagnosed as HIV-positive, one of your friends perceptively described you as treating yourself like an Olympic athlete. You took meticulous care of your body. You monitored what you ate, insisting everything was clean and natural and organically grown. You groomed yourself. Your hair shone, your dark eyes were bright and luminous, your skin smelt sweet.

Of course, you must have felt fear. Of course, as you wrote in your journal, you were aware of the lethal organisms raging in your body. They won in the end, but they didn't win over you. Nor did they win over your body's beauty. You kept that intact to the last. None of the now-so-familiar outward manifestations of immune breakdown appeared in you. No sores, no tumours, no lesions, no lumps.

You were born a rumpled bedraggled birdling, a sorry scrap of a thing. You grew painfully and awkwardly into a cygnet. Then you wrapped yourself in the sheen and gloss of a mantle of feathers, and became a swan. As I've written before, swans aren't easy or safe. They're beautiful, certainly, but they can also be angry and dangerous. They beat their clamorous wings, chase the hell out of the witless passengers and passers-by in their lives, and take to the skies.

Which is appropriately just what you did.

I said you read biology at university. It's true, of course, but not the whole truth. Your biology degree was coupled to another associated scientific discipline — studies in immunology.

Letters to Francesca: 8

'I'm sorry, mumsie,' you said. 'I'm afraid I'm going to throw the big one at you.'

The big one. Of course.

Being you, it was never likely to be anything other. Not something ordinary, something tidy and neat. Nothing socially acceptable like a bad case of mumps. If you were going to die, you in the fine, full and resplendent loveliness of your young womanhood, you were going to head that way with fireworks. For you it had to be the black plague of our time, God's punishment on trawling cottaging homosexuals, on needle-fuelled drug addicts, on the whole dark criminal under-culture of our society.

Yes, you picked the big one. You always did. You became infected with the HIV virus. With AIDS.

It was 1991. You were given the diagnosis on 12 January after the TB had come back. I remember the date all too clearly. The following day was your great-aunt's eightieth birthday. A large family celebration had been planned for months. Children, grandchildren, cousins, old friends, and what the Scots elegantly call 'connections' were gathering from everywhere, from all over the country and from abroad, to attend a large dinner.

Now there was clearly no question of you going to the party. The TB had made you thin, pale and weak, and the HIV diagnosis had bleakly sign-posted you were on the road to death. Two years, that was the prognosis. Twenty-four hours after hearing the verdict, it was time to stay indoors, to weep and take stock, to avoid social intercourse — most of all the pressures of an energetic turbulent family in celebration.

So like any sensible person you gracefully bowed out of the occasion with suitably vague apologies, and a kiss and some flowers passed on by messenger to your great-aunt in salutation.

Except, of course, being you, Francesca, you did no such thing.

You called your sister Poppy to your side. You cried and raged with her, your 'guardian angel' as you called her in your journal. You slept fitfully.

The following evening to my astonishment, moonlight-pale but smiling, painted like a lily into your modelling persona and looking dazzling, you arrived at our flat. We went to the party together. I never left your side, although you may not remember that. No one in the throng noticed anything. The only comments were about how lovely you looked.

Then, drained and exhausted but still with that frightening discipline of what you rightly saw as appropriate conduct and demeanour, you went home.

Years ago your mother's friend, the great biologist, Dr Miriam Rothschild, wrote one of the most illuminating books I've ever read. Called Fleas, Flukes and Cuckoos — *the title's meaning becomes clear when one reads it — it's in one sense about parasitology, but in a deeper sense it's a searching and deeply researched examination of the living mantle that covers our planet.*

Dr Rothschild sees our little spinning globe as being coated with a cloak of energy in a constant state of change and flux. We — lions, monkeys, humans, trees, diseases — invade and challenge each other, retreat or advance, succumb or survive. The ebbing and making tides of the life-charge frame and define our existence.

A great bull elephant stands level with, competes with, the tiniest microbe for breathing space. There's no difference between the two. They're both life-forms, like the flea, the cockroach and the shark, like malaria and leprosy and tuberculosis. They, elephant and microbe, just have to battle out the territory for survival.

AIDS does the same. In its own fashion, like us and the poppies and the nightingales, the virus struggles to reproduce and perpetuate itself. Maddeningly it chose your body as one of its theatres for existence. How did it first get a foothold and then invade you? You don't know, and none of the rest of us ever will.

The most likely guess is that it came from one of the tiny handful of lovers you chose so carefully in your adult years. Even that isn't sure. You tracked down the handful, insisted they were tested and, with one exception, all came out negative. The exception was fearful; he, stupid fellow, refused to be tested. You put on all the pressure you could — he was married by then and you felt he owed it to his wife — but when he rejected every argument, you gave up.

Perhaps the virus was transmitted by him. Perhaps it wasn't. The whole system of AIDS-transmission is still so little understood that you may well have acquired the virus through one of the many blood transfusions you were given as a rhesus negative child.

Does it matter now?

Not to me — except if there was someone who passed the virus on to you and took you away from me, and I found him, then I'd track him to the earth's end and despatch him. I'm sorry. You'd certainly disapprove, you'd put yourself between the young man and the gun or knife I'd be carrying. And I naturally would back off. Your generosity of spirit is so much greater than mine, and you'll have to forgive a father's rage.

Your mother likens me to an impala ram circling and coralling his herd of does, and chasing off any intruder who threatens to impregnate them. She's probably right. I've done it for years, from the moment you and your sisters brought back your first boyfriends. It wasn't very helpful even then. All I can say, asking you to forgive me, is that it's an impulse and reaction as old as the dynamic of biology — and that surely takes us back a fearfully long way.

There are only two matters about your diagnosis I can comment on.

The first is your apology to your mother when infection was confirmed. I found that extraordinarily touching and endearing. You'd been given a sentence of death and your instant response was not bitterness or self-pity, but to say sorry for the trouble and torment it was going to cause — not to you, but to others. Perhaps there are many who share your grace and compassion, and whose gift for friendship brings strength to so many others. I hope so. Certainly your words to her touched my heart.

Then there was the sheer absurdity of what happened to you. You the austere, dark-eyed, clear-eyed girl, the brilliant biologist and immunologist, the chess-player, the virtual teetotaller who scorned drugs, the intellectual and passionate reader, the fastidious thoughtful young woman who loved film and music, painting and theatre.

Why, in God's name, was the plague of our times visited on you?

I I

The taxi-driver was burly and cheerful with a southern French accent so raw and abrasive one could have honed Sabatier knives on it.

'Here to Condom?' He frowned. 'Normally sixty-five quid but seeing you're clearly a gent, sir, let's say fifty. All right?'

He spoke in French but his voice and attitude were the Languedoc's equivalent of pure Cockney. The first sound he'd heard on his birth could easily have been the bells of Bow.

'Don't spare the horses, James,' I replied.

'Trust me, squire.'

He hurled my pack and staff into the boot and we set off, skidding round the corners.

It was mid-April of the following year, and the start of the journey's third stage. Held back by commitments in London, I was catching up with my companions four days after they'd left. They'd picked up the Way at Moissac, where I'd just arrived by train. Reluctantly I had had to miss out on the small stretch between Moissac and the quaintly named little town of Condom, but I had a rendezvous with them there.

Condom lies in the heart of the French rugby-playing countryside, and one of France's greatest players of recent years had the same name as the town. He posed a fearful problem for the British television and radio commentators. Until very recently 'condom' wasn't a word to be used on air. It was rather vulgar, certainly dirty and, above all, it reeked – if words can reek – of the delightful but messy activity called sex. Prostitutes, bishops and politicians are allowed to be sexual creatures but not we, the honest citizenry. Even if we gave it a crack, 'condom' wasn't a term we used except in whispers on furtive Saturday morning visits to the local chemist.

The commentators skipped and skated round it. When the mahogany-thighed Condom advanced, carrying the ball, breaking through a tackle, or felling an opposing forward, all we'd hear was that 'the French number 7 has made a brilliant surge' or 'the Toulouse-based flanker has crashed through again'. Every other player had a name. Not Condom. He was anonymous, the original French letter not to be mentioned in polite society.

As the taxi-driver and I discussed the season's prospects and reminisced about the heroes, like Condom, of the past, I thought how potent and menacing words can be, and how strange the manner in which the unmentionable can be made acceptable. AIDS didn't just alter the vocabulary of respectability. On British television it gave back to a Languedoc farmer the birthright title of his fathers.

We reached the town in the dusk and found the hotel the ladies had booked into.

They were at dinner. There were three of them now. Priscilla and Hilary lived south of the Thames in Camberwell. A number of other elegant and interesting women lived there too. Together they formed a coterie collectively known as the 'Camberwell beauties', after the migrant butterfly that was first found there and was named after the area. The name was appropriate. Butterflies are not only beautiful but, as all biologists know and contrary to popular urban belief, bold, tenacious and tungsten-strong.

Angie, the newcomer, was another of them. Tiny and enchanting, a little shining blue-eyed shrimp of a woman, she had a keen historian's mind, much learning and a sharp wide-ranging eye. Over the days ahead she found the going difficult. Half the size of the others, lacking their sturdy frames and powerful muscles, she took a fearfully hard pounding in order to keep up. Angie was game. She didn't speak French, she looked like a child in the shadow of the Amazons, but she struggled on. She was a much-loved asset then and later on the Way.

We ate duck rillettes and the four of us slept together in a single large bedroom. It was a joyous occasion – I have a lovely photograph of three smiling ladies in their cotton nightdresses to remind me of it. Priscilla liked the hotel so much – it was tranquil and airy and scented with lemon geraniums – she decided to return there for her silver wedding anniversary.

Early in the morning we headed on. The weather for once was warm and the air sultry, and we travelled slowly, fitting into the stride of our new companion, Angie. In the afternoon we reached Montréal. Close to the village we found a farm with a little cottage annexe converted as a guest-house for tourists and walkers. We took it for the night. The weather had changed again and the sun had come out. I was standing outside in the warm and scented evening air when the farmer appeared. He was a stocky Gascon peasant with a black beret tugged down over his face. We started to talk. From my accent he took me for a Parisian. Was I perhaps, he suggested, a professor from the capital?

I shook my head.

I wasn't even French, I said mildly apologetically, I was English. I'm not, of course, English. I'm a Scots-bred Huguenot of Celtic-Breton descent, married to a Maitland Edinburgh girl with a fair river of Jewish-Palestinian blood in her veins. My true hearth isn't, as I like to claim, in Tobermory harbour or even on the holy island of Iona, although my family has been there for several hundred years and my father lives on Mull still. It's probably a Norse hamlet somewhere south of Caen. Elisabeth's is no doubt a Bedu encampment in the Bekaa valley.

In short: I'm a typical Briton, a mongrel, a cocktail of race and blood, whose children should be equally at home under the northern lights or on the heights of Masada. All of that's much too complicated to explain in quick encounters with strangers. So to speed matters up, to position and identify myself, I use shorthand. I invariably describe myself, when abroad, as English and say I live in London. I don't live in London. I live on my Ceredigion Cambrian hill farm between the hamlets of Pontrhydfendigaid, Tynygraig and Ystrad Meurig.

Consider working through that with a Gascon peasant, and it's not surprising I opt for being English and living in the capital.

'English? I'm English too.'

The farmer plucked off his beret.

He beamed at me. His hair, whitening with age, was corn-coloured, his eyes blue, his face sturdy and square. Placed on a settle by the fire in some Dorset pub with a pint in his hand, he might have been sent by Central Casting as the classic example of an English yeoman.

'Your Black Prince, he and his soldiers garrisoned the town,' he gestured up the hill at Montréal's old fortress. 'Scattered their seed. Isn't it what men do everywhere? I come from one that sprouted.'

He chuckled. Then, as he stumped away to the milking-shed, limping over his stick, I walked back to the cottage. Angie, arms crossed over the balcony rail, had been watching us in the fading light. I translated our exchange for her.

'Of course,' she said. 'The moment I saw him I knew he wasn't Gascon, he was English. All he needs is a longbow in his hands and he could have been at Agincourt.'

Later the four of us walked across the fields and up another hill on the far side of Montréal to a farm that offered dinner. The farm was a member of a network, a scheme, to promote fine, fresh and organically-produced local food. The kitchen and its young madame succeeded triumphantly. We sat at a rough heavy table. The light was dim and we had to wait. Among our companions were a rich plastic surgeon from Paris and his wife. They were cosmopolitan, *vifs*, gay, in the old sense of the word, widely travelled.

We debated, schemed, planned and plotted. We spoke of politics and books and poems. We talked of journeys behind and journeys ahead. We switched languages – there were Spaniards and Germans at the table too. When the food came it was magnificent – sturdy and honest, clean and dressed with fresh herbs. We ate it to the accompaniment of flagons of the black wine of Cahors.

We made our way back in the dark, tramping a little unsteadily along the furrows between the vines. The cottage had three bedrooms. The Amazons, the muscle, bone and sinew brigade, had naturally commandeered the largest with its panoramic views of the Eauze valley. Angie was shunted into the next.

I got the broom-cupboard somewhere down the corridor. I slept fitfully among the cans of caked shoe-polish and unwashed dusters, thinking rather wistfully that if I'd been sharing with Angie she might have put her arms around me.

The next day was grey and rain-speckled, scattered with hen's-spit as my old nanny used to call unsettled weather. In mid-afternoon, we reached the town of Eauze. We sheltered from the intermittent drizzle under a café's canopy. I left the other three over coffees round a table, and went off to find a newspaper. The sporting daily *L'Equipe* has been my favourite reading in France for years, but it took me some time to track down a copy. I returned to the café to find a stranger just leaving the table.

The ladies told me about him.

He was a tall and attractive young Belgian with fluent English and a sorry tale to tell. He too was a pilgrim. The journey to Santiago was a preparation for his entry into a monastery. Sadly, deeply sadly, he'd been robbed a week earlier. A thief had plundered his belongings in a pilgrim refuge while he was out having his simple evening meal. The burglar had taken everything – his small amount of cash, his passport, his one credit card. He'd been left destitute and stranded. Now wearily he was trying to hitch-hike his way home.

'Did he by any chance suggest he might like a little help?' I asked.

'Of course not,' Hilary replied. 'He was much too dignified for that. You could see the nobility in his face. Anyway, he didn't need to. He was a fellow-pilgrim and in trouble. We gave him fifty pounds each. It was the least we could do.'

I closed my eyes. I called for the waiter and asked for a large *pastis*.

'Immensely generous,' I said.

'What do you mean?' Hilary demanded, bristling. 'You think we were conned, don't you? You're such a terrible cynic. He was as honest as the day's long, and he had a book of signatures from others who've helped him to prove it. He's even given us his telephone number in Belgium so we can contact him.'

'I'm deeply relieved, blossom.'

A few days later we lodged in a Franciscan monastery. The Belgian claimed to have stayed there, too, and Hilary asked the Abbot if he remembered him. The Father's eyes rolled upwards in despair.

'Of course,' he said. 'The robber monk. Such a delightful young man, so plausible. He's been fleecing good pilgrims all year. He works the roads, preying off the gullible. He must have stolen thousands of francs. The police here and in Spain have been after him for months. I trust you weren't taken in by him.'

'Us? Good heavens, no,' Hilary said crisply.

She turned and glowered at me. I said nothing.

An enraged Priscilla has been unsuccessfully telephoning his number for months. Sooner or later she'll track him down. She'll probably beat him black and blue, get back the hundred pounds, and donate it to charity. By the time she's through with him the rogue will certainly have opted for a new career. After a confrontation with a cheated Priscilla, the Siberian salt mines will look appealing.

That night was spent in Manciet, a hamlet with a little bull-ring. We ate and slept, and left at dawn.

'Please, please, please,' Priscilla said the next evening, 'try for once to be polite.'

'Why?' I asked.

'Because at least they're English, not German, and they may be able to help us.'

'I'm always courteous — even to the *Herrenvolk*.'

'No, you're not. You're totally impossible.'

'Hilary loves me.'

'She doesn't. She thinks you're generally the cross a pilgrim has to bear.'

'Well, Angie loves me.'

'If she does, she's soft in the head. She should be put out to pasture.'

'Thanks very much, little sister.'

'Consider it a compliment, big brother.'

We'd arrived at the little hamlet of St-Martin-d'Armagnac where Hilary had booked us into the visitors' chalet of the single small hotel. There was one other couple there and weren't we fortunate, Madame remarked brightly, they were British. No doubt we'd all want to have dinner together. I could see the couple across the hall, grey-haired, the man in a jacket and tie, the woman in a sensible skirt and wearing sensible shoes. They were the very last people I wanted to spend the evening with, and I'd just started to mutter when Priscilla kicked me sharply.

In fact, we didn't eat with them but we did join them for a drink after dinner and, predictably, I was proved entirely wrong. The pair were learned and delightful, a doctor and his wife from the Cotswolds. We had many friends in common – among the doctor's patients was the splendid ninety-year-old artist and sportsman, Raoul Millais, a long-time acquaintance of mine – and they changed all their plans to take our packs on with them the next day.

I retired to bed suitably chastened.

The story unfortunately has a miserable ending, although not as far as we were concerned – the excellent kindly doctor and his wife did exactly what they'd promised. But that very night, we learnt afterwards, a gang of thieves drove up to their lovely Georgian Cotswold house and stripped the place bare, removing not just all the contents but even hacking out the doors and window-frames for re-sale as 'architectural salvage'. The poor couple returned to find a lifetime's lovingly assembled possessions gone, and the place an uninhabitable shell.

I tend to side with the carpenter's son. I'm not much of a one for flogging and hanging but there are occasions when I understand the appeal of the stocks and gallows for those who champion them. I would certainly like to get my hands on the thieving swine who plundered and wrecked the lives of our new-found friends.

Angie left early in the morning while it was still dark to return to London. The other two headed on. I left a couple of hours later. It was a glorious sun-filled day, the Gascon countryside was green, glowing, rich with scented grass in its summer pastures; I felt fit and buoyant. I strode out so strongly that, by early afternoon, I'd caught up with the others. However, first, I briefly lost my way. I was standing by the roadside on a small lane studying my map when a car drew up. A French couple got out.

The man was in his mid-sixties, white-haired, broad-shouldered and erect. His wife was wearing a black dress and had a cramped, scowling, angry little face. The man asked if I needed guidance. I told him where I was bound for and they both started to give me totally contradictory instructions on how to get there. Their voices rose, they started to bellow at each other, eventually the man opened the passenger door, hurled his wife inside like an unwieldy sack of beet, and clicked the electronic lock, effectively imprisoning her.

'Stupid,' he said in exasperation. 'Brain stupid. Bone and marrow stupid. Possibly the stupidest woman I've ever met. And after forty years in the army I'm an expert, I'm a world authority, on stupidity.'

'Who did you serve with?' I asked.

'The Legion first, then I transferred to the Paras for the Algerian affair. After that it was mainly staff work, desk jobs. Now I'm retired.'

'I was a soldier, too,' I said. 'Funnily enough my son and daughter played chess for the Legion.'

I explained.

'*Bon Dieu*,' he looked at me in astonishment. 'That's the strangest story I've ever heard. It calls for a celebration.'

He opened the car's boot, and produced a bottle of Armagnac and a couple of tin mugs. For almost half an hour we stood drinking brandy and discussing Dien Bien Phu and Bigeard's role in the citadel's defence and how the Coldstream Guards might have measured up if they'd been there. Behind us in the car his wife, trapped like a moth behind the window, rattled the glass and shouted insults and abuse.

It was one of the strangest, most surreal incidents on the whole journey. The man offered to take me to where I was going, but I told him the day was so lovely I wanted to walk. He inked in the route on my map and reluctantly left. As he drove away I could hear the two of them still screaming at each other.

When I look back on the journey I see it more and more as having the shape of a funnel. It started as an immense open bowl, joyous and funny, filled with optimism, adventures, laughter and delight. Everything was possible. Fran with her implacable spirit might even survive. Who knew? Certainly the candles I lit for her were lit with confidence – the human mind requires hope as the essential condition of living, and I never believed she'd tramp away. I almost convinced myself she was immortal. What was left in Pandora's box when it was opened expresses it all.

And then the funnel's neck started to narrow.

It was partly to do with the girl, with the inroads of her illness, but also with time and circumstances. I was growing older, and I felt buffeted. Strong as I was, the distances both along the Way and in the mind seemed longer. Priscilla's fortunes had been devastated by losses in the Lloyds' insurance market collapse. She had to sell her house and move to a smaller one further out in London's suburbs. Hilary's husband, badly hurt in a car crash years before, was facing yet another hip replacement operation, his fourth or fifth. Angie's husband had lost his job.

In different ways the years were gnawing at us all. Happily all three women were strong and bold and resolute. There might have been tears on occasions but no self-pity or buckling-in. Priscilla had launched a new career. Angie's husband had found a good new job, and she herself was working. Hilary was like Priscilla, confronting head-on everything life threw at her and simply surmounting the difficulties.

Each of us was still riding the waves. By the world's standards we were all still privileged, healthy and relatively well off, but things weren't as easy as they had been one year before when we'd set out. We tend not to measure ourselves by the world's standards. We take a private view. We look back at where we came from, and step forward confidently to where our childhoods have assured us we will end up – somewhere secure and tranquil, and a rung higher up the ladder, whether in learning, money or achievement, from the point at which we started.

If the Way to Santiago and the time it takes to travel it is a metaphor for human life, it teaches the pilgrim a darker and more sceptical attitude. At Cajarc we learnt what it was like to walk backwards along the track by mistake. The best one can do if that happens is mutter a curse, turn round, and head on again.

And then if one's lucky, if one does eventually reach the night's chosen refuge, all one can do is lance the blisters, light a candle of deliverance, and open a bottle of wine in celebration.

As a philosophy, it may not be so much home-spun as so old and simple it was woven on Penelope's loom. For the pilgrim, it's probably all he needs – well, that, a stout pair of boots, a few songs, gaiety, and at least a pinch of faith to savour the whole business.

12

Although it was late April, the snows were with us now.

Not close, of course: we were still in the warm valleys of Gascony, but far away there was a distant shining ice-cold presence on the horizon. We glimpsed the mountains over the hedgerows at almost every turn in the winding lanes leading us south, a constant reminder that, although we seemed to have been on the road for ever, we hadn't even completed half of the journey. The mountains had to be climbed and crossed, and then almost the full span of Spain would lie before us.

It wasn't daunting – nothing was daunting in those fresh and scented spring days – but all of us realized, I sensed, there was a fearfully long way to go with the hardest part yet to come. To sustain her, Hilary had her love of music, her learning, her fascination with architecture and history. Priscilla shared some of that but added to it a passion for birds and the wild. She also had what in the comic-books of my childhood was called 'true grit'. She would finish the journey even if she broke a leg and had to push uphill the ambulance that was meant to be carrying her.

My interests embraced or at least touched on most of theirs, but had an added dimension all of their own.

The threatened girl, the life I'd led, the life we'd led together, the candles I lit for both of us. A father and his eldest daughter, perhaps the most interesting and difficult of all human relationships. However it turned out, whatever happened between the three of us along the Way, I had to finish the journey for Francesca.

The next two days' walking, through meadows bright with wild-flowers and birch woods where the acid-green leaves on the trees were just starting to emerge, were quiet and contemplative. We lodged simply for the nights at Aire-sur-l'Adour and Miramont Sensacq. The third day dawned crisp and clear, but its bright beginnings faded into cloud and then rain. By early evening, when we reached Arthez-de-Béarn, we were walking through a deluge. Sodden and stumbling in the darkness, we found the house of the curé where, we'd been told, there was an annexe for the occasional passing pilgrim. Gruffly and grumpily the curé – hardly a model of St Francis but given we'd disturbed him at his supper, it was hard to blame him – let us in. We opened some rusting trestle beds, found a few moth-eaten and mildewed blankets, ate at a local bar, and settled down for the night.

Our only other fellow-guest was a wild-eyed Dutch youth, another pilgrim on the Way. When we got up in the morning he'd already left. Priscilla searched for her staff and let out a shout of rage.

'The bastard! He's pinched it!'

She was right. She'd bought for all three of us strong and excellent metal-tipped cattle-herding staffs from the Picos mountains in Spain. Like all good staffs they were invaluable, for leaning on across rocky country, fending off dogs, parting bushes, picking one's way through streams. And now this little thieving son of Amsterdam had stolen hers. She understandably cursed the rogue all day.

Our night's destination was Navarrenx. A lovely village. So too was the curé's large house and the curé himself – an intelligent sceptical man with a good wry smile who delighted in ferrying us round the town in his car, talked knowledgeably about pilgrimage, and refused to charge *les anglais* anything for their night's stay. We slept well in a dormitory on his upper floor. If there's something called Christian charity – something tough and cautious, generous but unsentimental – then he embodied it. He seemed to think faith should be anchored in discipline, learning and fun. I have a feeling he may be right.

The rain lasted fitfully throughout the following day, now being carried in dwindling gusting showers. The one ray of sunshine came around midday when we reached Aroue and found the Dutchman waiting for us, wan and apologetic.

'I think I make a bad mistake,' he said holding out the staff. 'I leave very early. I am sleepy. I think it is mine. I am so sorry, madame.'

Priscilla accepted his apology with good grace, but from then on she kept the staff tied with its leather thong to whatever bed she was sleeping in.

The rain had cleared completely during the afternoon, and we came to St-Palais in a clean clear dusk. We plodded through the village and found what we were looking for, the Franciscan monastery, a pilgrim haven since the Middle Ages. We ate that night with the monks in the refectory. They rightly prided themselves on their cooking and we ate simply but well – almost entirely off what they'd grown or reared in the large monastery garden.

After we'd helped stack the dishes, we sat and drank and talked with them. There were six. All of them delightful, they were grey-haired and elderly including the two who, as my old friend David Towill used to characterize those of their persuasion, were not quite as other men. A century earlier there'd have been at least fifty monks, including many young novices, and we'd have to have eaten in relays. Now there was just this relict handful with no one to follow them.

'What happens,' I asked the Abbot, searching for a suitably discreet word, 'when you all retire?'

'You mean when we hand in our dinner-pails?'

He was a Gascon. He saw through the question and was robust enough to give a deep belly-based chuckle.

'Perhaps the Church will second a few young Turks, if it's got any left, to take over from us. More likely there'll be wheeling and dealing and trickery, and the place will go to the municipality. The mayor will sit on it for a year. Then, *voyons*, *quelle surprise*, his brother-in-law will emerge as the new owner with planning permission to turn it into a hotel.'

'And you won't mind?'

'By then I'll be pushing up *marguerites*, but no,' he shook his head, 'I won't mind at all. Our Lord doesn't depend on monks, monasteries or mayors. He lives through us in faith and we through Him. Bricks even as old as these don't matter a scuttleful of coal.'

The image reminded him. He levered himself up stiffly and went off to bank the fire. I thought of Elisabeth. One of her favourite sayings – she uses it whenever another prancing bishop is caught with his trousers round his ankles – is: 'It's not the players that count, only the play.' I wished she'd been there. She and the Father Abbot would have had much in common.

In spite of the wine and the convivial talk with the brothers which lasted late into the night, I went to bed with some sadness. According to the Abbot, the monastery had been there in one form or other for at least a thousand years. Now the spiritual dynamic, the energy which had fuelled its long existence, was exhausted. It had simply run out of steam. A few weary ageing men, including a couple of elderly pederasts with dyed hair, were its last guardians. When they left, the curtain would be lowered and the show closed.

I fretted and turned and eventually slept.

Ostabat-Asme, a small village in the foothills of the Pyrénées, came next after yet another day's long and lovely walk.

We slept in a large dreary hotel on the main road. It was all we could find but it didn't seem to matter. Gascony had been, was being, so beautiful we could put up with anything. In the morning we headed on again. What none of us realized was quite how tired we were or quite how many different private pressures were tugging at us.

We came to St-Jean-Pied-de-Port at the foot of the Pyrénées, and all the concealed tensions suddenly emerged and flared.

The trigger was St-Jean itself. It's an ugly tawdry little tourist town, now relying solely for its existence on its position as the gateway to Spain. Junk from its shops and junk-food from its restaurants cascade in trays and litter-bins over its streets. One hostel we tried was a dark damp flea-pit and stank of sweat and urine. It wasn't fit to shelter goats.

We went back to the main street and had some coffee while we tried to sort ourselves out. I was planning to cross the Pyrénées later in the summer with Caspar and some of his friends, and was keen to go on and have a look at the mountains we'd be climbing. The other two, however, had to return home so we decided to stay together. We took a train to Toulouse and from there flew back to London. It was a sad and contentious end to my time in France.

13

'Ladies and gentleman, this is your captain speaking. I'm sorry for a short delay in our take-off, but three of our passengers are missing. Our staff are searching for them. I trust we'll be on our way soon.'

I sat in my window seat on the scheduled flight to Bilbao, and waited. I didn't need to ask who the missing passengers were.

Briefly, I had new companions. It was July of the same year, only a couple of months after the last stage of the journey had ended so quarrelsomely at the foot of the Pyrénées. We had made our peace since then but for various reasons Priscilla and Hilary couldn't leave London. I hadn't intended to take to the Way again without them, but when my New York-based son, Caspar, suggested that he and three of his friends should walk the pilgrim road with me for a few days through the mountains, I agreed instantly.

All of them had accompanied me on journeys and adventures in the African wildernesses, from the Kalahari to the Namib's skeleton coast. How many men are lucky enough to travel and explore, eat, drink and talk late into the night with the morans – the warriors – of the next generation? The opportunity to do it again was irresistible. Priscilla and Hilary would climb the mountain passes when they were free of domestic entanglements, we'd make a rendezvous at the point where I finished, and continue as before.

There was inevitably what's become known as a hidden agenda or sub-text to the project. For years Caspar had been going to Pamplona for the San Fermin festival, the setting for the running of the bulls which Ernest Hemingway chronicled in *The Sun Also Rises*. The plan both allowed us to walk and also to spend a few days in the town while its patron saint was gaudily celebrated.

Francesca at her brother's invitation would be there too. If I needed any other inducement to climb the mountains with his friends – I didn't – it would have been my daughter's presence when we reached Pamplona.

The three lads were difficult to overlook when they did eventually arrive. Towering James, red-haired and with the blue eyes of the Highland Celts, plays prop forward for one of Harlequins' rugby teams and must weigh seventeen stone or more. Nick, a fellow merchant banker, matches him almost inch for inch and pound for pound. Elegant Dr Charles, the third of the three, is marginally slighter but not by much.

They filled the gangway, overwhelmed it as timid air-hostesses peered anxiously from behind their shoulders, and settled themselves in seats round me.

'Sorry, Nicholas,' James said. 'We got tangled up in the traffic.'

I smiled. I'd been anxious before. Not now. I was just glad they were with me. We'd meet up with Caspar the next day when he arrived from New York.

I married when I was twenty-five and Elisabeth barely twenty-one, and shortly afterwards the whole business started.

The six Luard people arrived. The four who survived grew and flowered – with grace and elegance and loveliness in the case of the three girls, with thighs like tree trunks and rock-hard muscles in the case of their big brother – and created together a tightly knit constellation of allies and allegiances.

Constellations, the astronomers tell us, draw in other stars. The constellation they formed pulled in stars by the bucket, the bundle, the waggon-load. The mix and match, the plums plucked from the bran-tub of their lives, didn't always fit neatly together or do quite what they were meant to. The daughters put boy and girl together. Sometimes they married: sometimes it worked, sometimes it didn't. Whatever happened, they've all remained equally and lovingly members of the clan.

My companions on the flight, rollicking James, the sleepy-eyed Nick, the good Dr Charles, were part of the catch in Caspar's net. Big brother swept them up and brought them home, where their presence immeasurably enriched our lives just as the gifts of shared friendship from the offerings of the three girls did too. They were what neither

Elisabeth nor I had had any idea about all those years ago. At the time of our marriage, we had no inkling that our children would acquire such myriad companions, friends, lovers, that their gatherings of the best — only the best suited them — would become threaded into the fabric of our lives.

The four of us spent the night in Bilbao.

At dawn we left for Pamplona. We were due to meet the catalyst of our gathering, Caspar Luard, off his flight at 9.00 a.m. Tied up with business, the only way he could join us was to fly from New York to Madrid, and take the morning red-eye shuttle to Pamplona. Pamplona was the obvious place to link up, although we'd have to back-track some forty kilometres into France to begin our climb up the mountains.

Charles drove from Bilbao with the speed and skill of my old friend, the grand prix champion James Hunt. We got to Pamplona airport just as Caspar's flight landed. He strolled out, looked at us, embraced us, and took control. Caspar doesn't only speak Castilian as almost his first language, he virtually is a Castilian — or more accurately an Andalusian.

The Andalusians are hard riders, hard men and hard bargainers.

'Here,' he said in Spanish, summoning two taxis. 'Across the border, to St-Jean-Pied-de-Port at the foot of the Roncesvalles pass. The one who gets there first has twenty per cent over the clock, the other just the fare. *Me comprende?*'

The two taxi drivers eyed each other. They both knew they were dealing with a challenge from an *hombre serio*, a hard man from the south.

'*Si, señor.*'

They bundled us into their cars, heaving and pushing at us as if we'd been sheep on our way to market, and raced off.

'What on earth did Caspar say to them?' Charles asked, tumbling white-faced into my lap as we swerved dizzily round one of the bends in the pass.

There are times, I'd discovered, when it was prudent not to explain Caspar's strategy for travelling and living. It caused needless terror. He'd done just the same to me with a pair of rickshaw pedallers in

Kathmandu. Fran was with us then. She could handle her brother's style with a smile. I couldn't. It scared the wits out of me.

'I think he was just asking about the weather or the football scores or something,' I told Charles vaguely, thankful he didn't speak Spanish.

I buried my head in my arms and prayed.

'Well, that didn't take long, did it?'

Caspar beamed.

He'd given both the drivers a handsome tip and sent them on their way. We were standing where they'd left us, in a sodden meadow at the foot of the pass. The air was chill and drear. There was nothing to see except dank limp coils of mist. The day was filthy and we had thousands of feet to climb.

'Let's get it over with,' I said.

We began to trudge upwards.

The day turned out to be one of the finest, most golden days I've ever spent – a time to hold in mind, to remember and cherish in the darkest of icy mid-winters to come. We climbed through the mist, broke out of it, and suddenly we were in sunlight. Shining, glowing, luminous sunlight folded round our shoulders on a scented southern wind.

The green upland pastures reached out on every side. There were rocks, still bronze and gunmetal-bright from the rain of the night before, and the great snow-mantled ridges and peaks of the mountains. There were eagles planing on the thermals, gatherings of vultures, dartings of swifts and red-rumped swallows, a few flocks of transhumance sheep, a pair of stern-faced horsemen in thorn-scarred leather chaps watching their stock.

And otherwise nothing. Only air and cleanness and delight, the wind and the bird-calls and the silence.

There are two ways of climbing the Pyrénées through the Roncesvalles pass. By the metalled road which the vast majority of pilgrims understandably take – it's safe and secure and impossible to lose one's way on – or up this fragile, wandering, precipitous mountain path known as 'Napoleon's Way'. It was up here that the stocky little Corsican led his soldiers on the most misguided of all his adventures, his attempt to enlarge his empire by conquering Spain.

The Corsican thug, a thug of genius, could have done everything. He could easily have won Waterloo with a little more thought. Only the Coldstream Guards thwarted him there at the little farm. Moscow wasn't really a problem – he could have gone back there after the retreat and hammered sense and submission into the Slav peasantry. He could have been a much greater Alexander. He could have ruled the world.

What the pocket-sized brute couldn't do, and it was the one unforgiving mistake he made, his one great hubristic delusion, was subdue the mountain dwellers of the Iberian peninsula. He should have learnt from the blackamoors. For eight hundred years the Arabs with their scimitars, their poetry and their wisdom tried to batter the Celtic Spanish into the ground. They failed. So just as humiliatingly did he.

They went home and Napoleon did too. Now, travelling southwards in the opposite direction along his forlorn trail of defeat, we were climbing up towards the Castilian plateau.

I couldn't keep up with the lads.

They were generous enough to slow down and accompany me for parts of the climb but, strong as I was, I had to concede twenty-five years to them and they were true morans, true young warriors. On that glittering day in the mountains they wanted to test their powers, to be on their way. Towards the end they left me and strode ahead. When I crested the final ridge and walked wearily into the Roncesvalles pilgrim sanctuary, they'd been waiting for me for half an hour.

They had, bless them, each bought a beer for me. Four glasses were ranged in a row on the monastery parapet in the evening light. I thirstily drank all four. Then I heaved myself up onto the wall.

In the evening sunlight we discussed why we were all there.

14

Se llama Luz y la acompañaba hacia Compostela.

'She's named Light and I walked beside her to the Field of the Star.'

It was Francesca, of course. St Francis of Assisi used almost identical words to describe his own pilgrimage to Santiago, although his own '*Luz*', the Spanish word for 'light', was rather different – although quite how different, I'm now not so sure.

We step into difficult and, in a secular age, provocative and fiercely disputed territory here. For me the matter's quite simple: if the carpenter's son was who He claimed to be, the Son of God made man – and I believe he was – then everyone carries the light within them. The problem is that Lenin, Mao and Hitler made similar claims. I tend to prefer those who work in wood, and I like what the carpenter's boy is recorded as saying. It makes more sense than programmes of mass butchery.

I'd had the girl christened 'Luz' not because of St Francis – I had no idea then that one day I'd be following him on the Pilgrim Way – but because, as I've said, it was one of the names Republicans gave to their daughters in the Spanish Civil War, and I knew several fine women who were called it. Sometimes I found it easier to think and talk about her in Castilian – probably her favourite tongue although she delighted in speaking it with the thick raw accent of Andalucía; the deep burr of Cornish fishermen is maybe the nearest English equivalent.

All four young men knew and loved her, in her brother's case with a deep, utterly uncomplicated and utterly unsentimental passion, just as she loved him. He and his sister were immeasurably lucky in what they shared. They were wolves from the same pack, lions from the same pride. In maturity they could have split, divided, rejected each other. They didn't. They found their own space and territory, but they remained cheerfully roped together by bonds of shared experience.

They had too many secrets in common, too much remembered

mischief, too many gang wars in which they'd challenged and outfaced the adult world. And somehow they fitted together. Francesca didn't only love her brother, she liked him. She thought he was a worthwhile interesting man. She booked his flights, made telephone calls for him, sorted out and organized the untied bits and bobs in the hamper of his life.

Dear God, please give us all such sisters.

All five of us, not just Caspar and I, knew Fran was on her own swift journey towards death, and that in some way our own travels were linked with hers. Each of us put it to the back of our mind. It just wasn't appropriate to consider it. Not on that glorious day in those majestic mountains, and least of all because of the girl herself. Fran would have been enraged by thoughts of mortality.

She was already on her way to meet us in Pamplona. She had things to do, paintings to complete, people – old friends and new ones – to meet and talk and laugh with. She knew the city. It belonged to her. She had a life to live there.

The graduate immunologist, the England chess-player, the writer and artist, was eager to do what she jokingly claimed she did best in the world – to 'party'. Pamplona in the *feria* of San Fermin is the scene of the world's biggest party.

We headed on to meet her.

On the next day the temperature climbed to 54°C, the highest ever recorded in northern Spain.

I'd known heat like it before, in the Kalahari Desert in high summer, but never before in Europe and never when I was confronted with further mountains to climb. We all struggled, even the iron-man triathlete Caspar, as we forced ourselves upwards and then began the long almost more painful descent through gullies floored with jagged jarring rock.

We were each carrying two litres of water. On a normal day, it would have been more than enough to see us through. Not on this one. By early afternoon our flasks were empty, and there was nowhere to refill them. We tramped on. The sweat bubbled and evaporated on our skin. The light flared parched-white off the stones. Apparently welcoming little tents of shadow under the trees proved furnaces of trapped, suffocating and energy-sapping air. We were all dehydrated almost to the point of hallucinating.

Like the day before, the young men began to outpace me. We were travelling downhill now, but I didn't try to keep up with them. Once again, with twenty-five years in their favour, they had resources I didn't. It was a grim and in some ways a humiliating acknowledgement to make. In my mid-fifties, a marathon-runner, a Himalayan climber, an explorer and crosser of deserts, I could outlast most of my generation in the physical world – but not this lot. They were too lithe, too muscular, too highly motivated.

High up on the crests I had knelt and prayed for them by the ancient stone known as Roland's footprint. None of them knew what I'd done, they were too far ahead by then. I didn't pray for their safety; that would have been an impertinence given their confidence, their strength and their powerful sense of their own security. Instead, it was a prayer of thanks.

I was travelling with the best. I was lucky. So is the world which, I guess, they'll help mould with their money, their writing, their practice of medicine and law. The living mantle of the planet, in its strange wisdom, chose well when it sired and reared them.

'Where have you been malingering, Nicholas?'

It was Caspar, face smiling, sweat crusted in ridges of salt on his skin, energy still radiating off him. I shrugged off my pack and slumped to the ground.

'Water,' I said.

I'd made my way to a bar in the little mineral-mining town of Larrasoaña. The other three were lying on the floor beside me – I'd found them by their packs stacked outside. They were also pouring water into themselves. All five of us stayed there for an hour or more, drowsy, aching, gradually rehydrating ourselves after the savage heat-seared day.

'On your feet,' Caspar said eventually. 'We need somewhere to eat and somewhere to sleep.'

We struggled up and followed him out of the bar.

Caspar was in charge again. He examined the possibilities of accommodation for the night. In Larrasoaña, the modern pilgrims lodge in a cavernous and evil-smelling converted pelota court, a draughty great concrete-floored barn. Cas decided we could do better.

He scoured the streets. He found a small hotel, ostensibly closed but which quickly opened at his appearance. He took rooms for all of us. Clean sheets were aired over the kitchen range and beds made up. He located the only restaurant in the area that provided a decent meal, and found a taxi to take us there.

We ate superbly, beans and squid and oxtail stew with dark full-bodied bottles of Navarran wine. Then in the starlight we strolled back to our hotel.

'How's the senile old buffoon holding up?' Caspar asked me as we walked.

It's his invariable description of me. I think it's meant to be an affectionate joke, but I'm never quite sure.

'If you don't make it in international banking,' I said, 'I'll give you one hell of a recommendation as a tour leader on the Pilgrim Way.'

Caspar grinned. 'Get some sleep tonight,' he said. 'Tomorrow it's Pamplona.'

15

The walk from Larrasoaña into Pamplona was dreary and hot, a sultry sweaty tramp along the rocky lanes that scar the scalp of northern Spain as it tilts down in all its baldness from the mountains onto the central plateau, becoming dirtier and dustier with every stride.

Because we had a spare day before the start of San Fermin and Francesca's arrival, we did not stop in Pamplona when we reached the fortress town but found a taxi to take us out to the nearby town of Puente la Reina where we spent the night. The next day we walked back to Pamplona, reversing the Pilgrim Way.

When we arrived in the late afternoon Francesca was waiting for us in her favourite café. The café was just up the street from a lofty, creaking, tumbledown house with lopsided porthole windows that gave dazzling glimpses of the city in which Caspar had rented an apartment to house us all.

Fran was wearing Pamplona party-wear, a crisp white shirt tied at the waist with a scarlet cotton sash. She looked thin, but serene and happy. Her black eyes shone with pleasure at our arrival, and my heart dipped and turned over at her beauty. The girl was more than three years into her illness, and only four months away from her death. My journey was halfway through, hers was approaching its end. None of us, whatever we knew rationally about the inevitability of what was coming, could have sensed it that day.

She embraced her brother, kissed the lads, then turned and confronted me. She tossed back the hair cascading over her face and inspected me.

'Dog's dinner,' she said smiling at what I was wearing. 'I'll have to sort you out.'

An hour later, stripped of my mountain clothes, I'd been redecorated. Wearing the same white shirt and scarlet sash as Francesca, I set out with her onto the streets. We traced the route the bulls would follow the next day.

'Good morning, Michael,' the young man said to me amiably if a little vaguely next morning.

It was 8.30 am. Fran and I were on our way downstairs, he was on his way up. I looked at him startled.

'Good morning,' I replied.

I frowned at Fran as he disappeared.

'Am I going potty,' I asked, 'or was that my son and your brother?'

'It was.'

'Then surely after thirty years he must know I'm called Nicholas, not Michael?'

'Forget about it, dad. It's San Fermin. Let's have breakfast.'

We went out into the already warm morning sunlight of Pamplona's calle San Sebastian, and headed towards Fran's favourite bar for coffee and coils of salty *churros* for her and a sugary *anis* for me.

Pamplona was in *feria*, Pamplona in celebration of its patron saint, Fermin. Rickety, rackety, old Pamplona was host to one of the biggest, gaudiest, most exuberant, exhausting and — if one chooses to run with the bulls — most hazardous street parties in the world.

Only in Pamplona, in my experience, can a son be so dazed by a night on the tiles that returning home at dawn he can't remember his father's name.

Mainly owing to Hemingway's writings, many people assume that bull-running is peculiar to Pamplona. In fact, it happens at festivals in towns, villages and even hamlets all over Spain, a single calf sometimes being all the municipal purse can run to. Although it gave birth to the bullfight, the running of the bulls originally had nothing to do with the *corrida*.

To the Scots, the wide open hill is home. Unlike them, the Spaniards are natural *pueblo* dwellers, urban people. They like to congregate close together in compact settlements, classically in the white lime-washed villages which polka-dot the plains or cling like swallows' nests to the lofty mountain ridges, and venture out from there to tend their fields and rear their herds, returning at nightfall to the safety and companionship of their clustered houses. When they need meat, they drive the animals from the *campo*, the open countryside, into their villages to be slaughtered, sold and distributed for food.

For thousands of years the staple meat of Iberia was beef, and it remains prized to this day. And so are the traditional ways in which it reached the table.

The so-called 'bullfight' is not a fight, not a contest, nor least of all a sport. It is a moment of theatre, of challenge and confrontation between man and animal, on the bull's inexorable journey towards death. The *corrida* has much to do with drama, ballet and sculpture, far more with even more elusive concepts – grace and courage and intuition in both the animal and the man.

In the end, though, the bullfight is about food. Its spiritual and physical home is in the kitchen. The abattoir which delivers it there is open to the public.

The Masai demand their young warriors kill a lion to prove their worth. All cultures have created similar challenges, whether in the shape of lions or dragons, and their own morans who must overcome them, young men with charges of sexual and energy hormones flooding their bodies, out to prove themselves. The Spanish morans run with the bulls. They are noble and brutal adversaries, Iberia's more-than-equivalent of the lion. They are a worthy test of an apprentice warrior.

As they swept in a raging pack down some village's cobbled streets, how could you fail to leap out, run with them, dance with them, lean in to touch the bony hump between the lacerating horns, skip away and laugh as one of their slashing blades cut by you, and then run again amongst the panting, snorting and enraged bellowing, the spraying scatter of sweat, the pounding beat of hoofs on stone, the staring red-veined eyes, the jostle and press of massive animals, coralled by the walls and racing in blind fear and fury?

It was the start of the bullfight.

As far as anything is known about the modern *corrida*, it began with a couple of brothers, the Romeros, sons of a middle-class family of cobblers from southern Andalucía. They took the ancient practice of bull-running, explored, extended and codified the movements of the 'dance' that had evolved to accompany the animals on their way to slaughter, formalized the lures the young morans used to provoke the beasts – the sweeping crimson and yellow cape, the scarlet scrap of the *muleta* – and so created the rituals of today's bullfight.

The Romeros or their predecessors or their followers – the *corrida*'s history is largely oral, its development impossible to chart step by step – probably drew on the horses and lances of the gentry. A bull cannot be 'run' and killed by a man on foot until its head is lowered. Unless that happens it is virtually unconquerable.

Using lances, as the armour-suited picadors – the rustic hard men of the *corrida* – do from their horses, the bull's great mass of neck and shoulder muscle could be partly broken down, forcing the animal to lower its head and horns. Then it could be 'passed' at close quarters by a man on foot using only a square of red cloth in the last and most important phase of the ritual, the *faena*. Finally, it could be killed, ideally with a single sword thrust.

The spectacle is grim – grim, savage, barbaric and dangerous.

At its rare best, on those sunlit afternoons when both the *toreros* and the bulls are equally brave and sure of themselves and create together a flowing fleeting series of sculptures in black and gold, scarlet and blood, it can be ennobling and inspiring. A man, on our behalf, presents himself effectively naked before one of the most lethal creatures on earth.

The creature embodies death. With skill and grace and courage, the man tries to control and dominate it – *mandar* and *templar* are the words the Spanish use. If he succeeds, he has bought us all a brief respite against mortality, a brief defiance of death. We go away calm, exhilarated, purged of fears – the matador has taken them from us. That is if the *corrida* works. Mostly it doesn't. Mostly what happens in the arena is an inept, timid and bungled act of butchery inflicted by frightened men on bewildered animals.

Is there any way the *corrida* can be defended, let alone justified?

Years ago Ernest Hemingway decided it couldn't, but that it didn't matter, and he went on celebrating and writing about it anyway. Years ago I might have agreed with Hemingway's view about its indefensibility. No longer. We live in a world whose moral landscape

of political correctness and witless frozen attitudes was chillingly anticipated by the poet, W. B. Yeats:

> *We've fed the heart on fantasies,*
> *The heart's grown brutal with the fare.*

Brutality means coarseness, the inability to think, to discriminate
and make choices, to dream and hope. We have lost the ability to
wonder and learn. We tell the 'Eskimos' to stop hunting whales when
most of us wouldn't recognize an Inuit if we woke up to find one of
them in our bed. We tell the fragile remaining clans of Kalahari Bushmen
– they refer to themselves as the San peoples – to halt their pursuit of
gemsbok and eland antelope with poisoned arrows. Within living
memory we shot the animals as 'vermin'.

How many of us have ever encountered a member of the San race?

Yet we pout and posture, our faces flush with indignation, we know
we occupy the moral heights. We've lost our faith but we've learnt
how to chatter and by God, our forgotten God, we feel it a duty to
tell the lesser foreign breeds what to do – the Eskimos, the Bushmen
and notably the Spanish with their addiction to the barbarous practice
of bull-running. We cannot tolerate a brave man confronting a brave
animal, yet we continue to eat beef. We accept unquestioningly animal
factory-farming – the shelves of every major store dip and creak under
the load of the products from our abattoirs. Almost all of us wear
leather shoes, stripping and plundering the hides of creatures for the
raw material.

And yet we condemn the Spanish for what we complacently accept
in a far more coarse, cruel and corrupt manner every day.

Interestingly, the abolition of the bullfight would have only two
certain consequences: the disappearance of the fighting bull as a species,
and the devastation of vast areas of Spain's remaining truly wild land.
Whilst a source of excellent beef, to a farmer the fighting bull is not a
cost-efficient animal. Almost any Charollais-cross produces animals
with much higher meat yields.

Next, the pastures on which fighting bulls range are notoriously
under-utilized by modern intensive farming criteria. The bulls thrive
on wilderness, on the margins, on saline flats, rugged rolling pastures,

great untamed sweeping tracts of landscape which they share with communities of birds, flowers and animals. Where bulls roam and breed, trees grow, orchids flower, red-rumped swallows and golden orioles nest, butterflies cloud the earth, mongoose and genet cats hunt, eagles fly.

Take the land from the bulls and it will be cleared, zoned, put under mechanical ploughs, fertilized with chemicals and made, as agricultural lawyers say, 'to wash its face'. The yield will be piled up as another grain, cereal or beef mountain to rot somewhere to the west of Brussels.

I think of Antonio Ordonez, perhaps the greatest *torero* who has ever lived, placing himself before a bull in the ring at the little harbour-town of Tarifa, the southernmost point of the European landscape. Ordonez looks at the bull and a strange fascinated smile comes over his face.

Francesca, a child, sits beside me.

'Watch this, Fran,' I say to her. 'We may be about to see something odd.'

She puts her chin in her hands and looks down.

The bull is small but extraordinarily brave, one of the bravest animals, Antonio says to me afterwards, he has ever faced. He dismisses the lances of the picadors, the darts, even the scarlet *muletas*. Nothing has touched the creature. In his short grey jacket and his tilted sombrero – it is a charity *corrida* and he has dressed not in a suit of lights, but in the countryside-riding uniform of the Andalusian *caballero*, a gentleman farmer – he runs the bull with his hands.

He provokes it. The animal hurls itself at him. He guides it away with his outstretched palm. He spins on his feet, faces it again, challenges it, leads its tossing horns into his body and then away from him again. The dance, the man and animal weaving, threading, blending together, seems to go on for ever. One, the animal, is black fury. The other, the man, is speculative, delicate, smiling.

Antonio decides it's enough.

He and the bull have done the *faena*, the job, to their satisfaction. Antonio moves forward. He leans out and incites the animal for the last time, bringing it towards him, steadying it, holding it in place, balancing it carefully so that it is calm and composed with its forefeet together. Then he swoops over it with a thrust of his arm. The gesture would have been deadly if he'd been holding a sword, but his open hand taps the animals on its shoulder and glances off. The bull snorts. It sweeps up its horns, inspects him, and lowers its head again.

Antonio pats the animal on the cheek. Then, as the fisherfolk of Tarifa rise to their feet and applaud, several of them weeping, he uses his hand again as a lure to guide the bull out of the arena. Unharmed, untouched, it will be taken away as a stud animal to breed and hand on its genes to generations of bulls to come.

Ordonez returns to the centre of the ring. He stands there laughing and exhilarated but his eyes are remote. He isn't thinking of any of us, of the still cascading applause, of the dry Tarifa wind, of the tumbling gulls overhead. He is pondering the movements of the rare creature, and his own interaction with its charges.

He scuffs the sand and walks away. That evening he and his friend and protégé, another great *torero*, Miguel Mateo 'Miguelin', dine with us in the rambling white house in the forest. Fran and her sisters dance *sevillanas* for them – the elaborate formal dances foreigners think of as *flamenco*.

The following day Fran does her first childish drawing of the bullfight. Years later, still drawing, she sits with me in Pamplona and gives one of her sketches to the rich lady who leans over her shoulder. And two years later still, by then taking her rest in a Sussex graveyard, her *corrida* paintings hang in a London gallery.

The gun-toting chess-playing *képis blancs* of the Foreign Legion and two of Spain's legendary bullfighters aren't the most usual companions of an English girl's childhood. To Fran they were quite normal. She took them all in her stride and learnt from them.

They were all witnesses to her life.

Letters to Francesca: 9

By the time of our visit to Pamplona you'd been harbouring the virus for three and a half years.

I remember the first evening after we joined you there, walking back from the restaurant where we'd eaten with your brother and his friends – like you I had sweet white pochas, beans stewed with plump mountain partridges – brushing off the pickpockets as we pushed our way through the crowded streets, laughing and talking and singing. Then for some reason I thought of the day the diagnosis was confirmed.

Frail and sick with the effects of the second attack of TB, you behaved at your great-aunt's birthday dinner, as I've written before, with the exemplary courage you showed to the end.

I felt inept and helpless, but somehow for me it was comforting to be by your side. I don't think it mattered a tuppenny damn to you. You wanted the sometimes quarrelsome but always powerful presence, comfort and support of your sisters. In my view, they aren't your sisters in the normal sense. Until your late teenage years the three of you had barely spent a night apart.

I see you more as triplets. Utterly distinct in personality, in attitude, talent and presentation, but beans from the same tight pod – blood of blood, bone of bone, companions, rivals, fellow-conspirators from the start as you formed strategies to frustrate adults as you squatted round the earliest of the family's hearth-fires.

You were all wonderful wool-pullers, at least over my eyes, convincing me you were innocent little cherubs, ignorant of anything to do with sex, never casting a glance at boys, dismissive of the vanity of fashionable clothes, disdaining nicotine and all other bad habits. And I, God help me, almost believed you. I almost convinced myself I was the first father in history with three daughters destined for sanctity.

Your mother had no such illusions. She saw all of you for what you were – subversive, funny, mischievous, reckless, creatures of blood and passion, tears and temptation, hitching up your skirts and tucking them into your knickers, a fag in your mouths and a winsome beckoning glance to some likely lad in your eyes, to behave well or badly as the fancy took you.

I know little about the relationship between the three of you. What I do know is the bonds, the love, are profound and unshakeable, unbreakable. Lucky old you, all three of you — and, of course, big brother who provides the fourth strong oaken leg to the four-pillared milking-stool. The four of you together — not forgetting the guiding abiding presence of the family's lode-star, your mother — saw the matter through over the hazardous time that followed.

You were well embarked on what might have been an interesting and successful career in journalism. You had just come back from a survey of Cuba, one of the few British writers to take a look at ageing Castro's corrupt and creaking island society. Journalism wasn't fulfilling enough, certainly not now. You threw it up. You needed time to think and reflect. You did what you always did both at moments of trouble and distress and when you wanted rest — you headed back for your beloved Spain and its sun.

For six months you lived alone in a little white-walled pueblo *in the sierras. You walked a little, warmed yourself in the clear Andalusian light, read the local newspapers over coffee in the bars, embarked on your journal. Once again you had come home.*

I wrote you postcards and sent you a subscription to The Spectator. *To my anguish the first issue that reached you contained the first article of what was to become a bitter and continuing tirade against AIDS by the polemicist, Paul Johnson. For me it was made worse by the fact that I knew Johnson casually. I wrote to you and apologized. You sent me back one of your lovely postcards. You said, laughingly, that I should save my pity for Mr Johnson. He needed it, not you. You added you were enjoying the chess column, and reading about the adventures of my friends, the flamboyant Greek boy, Taki, and your brother's rogue godfather, Jeff Bernard.*

You must have had — well, I know you did, I have mentioned it before — periods of intense fear and doubt and anger. But that buoyant generous response was far more typical of you.

You came back to Britain, bouncing across Europe in your little scarlet Citroën 2CV with your mother as navigator and co-driver. And you started to paint. Again it was your mother who encouraged you. All the family paints. As a very young man I studied with Cézanne's and Renoir's friend, Survage, in Paris. Elisabeth is a professional painter. Both your sisters paint. Poppy's now an art director, Honey an art historian. Even Caspar can wield a mean brush when he sets his mind to it.

Painting, it would be fair to say, is a central part of the family culture. For some reason you hadn't previously embraced it. Not any longer. You began tentatively and then hurled yourself into it. Your first works were a series of self-portraits. They're somewhat awkward, stiff, exploratory. They're also among the strangest and strongest studies I know — bleak and penetrating and dangerous.

For the portraits, you dressed yourself in a wonderful array of clothes and hats, Breton berets, a straw boater, my Andalusian riding sombrero. You looked in the mirror and painted what you saw. The images, and the constant refrain of your night-black eyes which link them together, are chilling and unforgettable.

That was the start. You were hooked. In paint you'd found a passion and a cause. You gathered together some paintings you'd done in Wales and trudged off to the Byam Shaw School of Art. You didn't exactly ask to be admitted as a student; in the words of the principal later, you demanded it. Sensibly the Byam Shaw agreed. Such was your emerging, surging talent — and, I'd guess, the force of your personality — that the school awarded you a major scholarship.

Throughout your time there no one knew that you were even ill, let alone dying. When you didn't arrive for that final term — and I find this characteristic and engaging — it was assumed you'd run off with a boyfriend. Of course. That's what beautiful girls do. Except not you. You simply didn't want to load anyone with the burden you were carrying.

My goodness, you were strange, Francesca. Strange and brave beyond the telling.

It would be absurd to make extravagant claims for you as an artist, any more than for you as a dancer. You were still a student when you died, with a brief two years of painting behind you. You were learning, exploring, studying every day. Hunger and passion for art suddenly fused in you. Like an athlete — and the term crops up often in your life — you were running against the clock. Yet it wasn't just the urgency. You had found something true for you. You'd have held to it, continued with it, enlarged it, made it flower and blossom.

And it would be equally silly to fail to acknowledge not just that you'd shown huge promise, but real achievement. Your oil-crayon studies of the bullfight, so fast in their execution, so bright and brilliant and sure, are memorable. They remind one, as several critics commented, of the young Picasso. They have his energy, his conviction, his falcon-gaze and economy of line. A number of them line the wall above my desk as I write. To me they are doubly haunting. They are both you, expressions of your own painter's vision, and emblems of my own friends in the dangerous craft (should we call it art?) of the corrida – the running of the bulls.

You date and label your sketches carefully and I can see their names now.

Antonio Ordonez, the man who took bullfighting back to its classical roots, redefined it, and then in the constant presence of death set standards of courage and excellence it was impossible for anyone else to approach. I remember your mother dancing with Ordonez at a party at some ranch in the sierras. He wore the short grey caballero's jacket, she was wearing a long flounced sevillana dress, black and white spotted.

They spun and laughed and stamped their heels and your mother gestured with her graceful hands just as you did. You met him often as a child, and he'd always lift you and give you a kiss, holding you tight to his scarred chest. Like you, he had his wounds, great clusters of them.

The difference was that in Ordonez's case, they weren't lethal.

But perhaps that's where it started. In your sketches you caught Antonio, and Miguel Mateo too. 'Miguelin', the finest natural athlete I've ever seen, was often a guest at the house – do you remember the Christmas dinner when he warily examined the silver sixpences in the plum pudding and made you wash them for him? There was a host of others, and I took you to watch them everywhere from Arles to Pamplona.

I'm far from sure you really engaged with the corrida. You read the books of course, Hemingway and The Wounds of Hunger and the critical treatises, and you scanned the journals your brother collected. But to you, I think, it was much more a matter of theatre, a dangerous display which provided you with a kaleidoscope of images for your art. You took from it what you wanted.

On our last visit to Pamplona you were sitting beside me sketching in the oil-crayons you loved to use, with the same controlled intensity and focus you brought to your chess-playing — and the same tranquillity too — when, as I've said, a rich Basque matron in a Givenchy suit and laden with gold jewellery made her way down through the tiered seats. She'd seen what you were doing. She was captivated and entranced. She offered to buy everything you'd done that day.

You gave her your cautious gentle smile, and shook your head.

No, you wanted to keep your work and study it. But because you appreciated her interest, you'd give her one of your sketches. You plucked one of the best from your pad. The woman tried to pay you for it. You refused to accept anything. Puzzled but delighted, the Basque lady went back to her seat with her prize. I wonder where the sketch hangs now. I wonder, too, what you might have done as a painter given time.

Letters to Francesca: 10

'Just leave me alone,' you said angrily. 'It's a bruise on my breast, that's all, a bruise I got playing football. Don't even ignore it.'

It was a lie, of course, one of your valiant defiant lies.

It wasn't a bruise. It was the first physical expression of that rare cancer, T-cell melanoma, which eventually killed you, although none of us was to learn about that final fatal affliction until the last few weeks of your life. But I believed you and backed away — I always backed away in our confrontations.

We were on the Hebridean island of Mull, in my homeland and heartland. Pamplona was a couple of months behind us. The day was sun-filled, the seas silvery, the bay below the house thronged with seals and the occasional passage of an otter with its trail of spring-bred cubs. The Treshnish Isles and their puffins rested calm and clear on the ocean to the north. Further north still we could glimpse Rhum and the dark ramparts of the Cuillins on Skye.

Foraging red deer had come down from the tops during the night and their droppings were steaming in the warmth. A golden eagle planed the thermals above us. Your sister Poppy, working on a film at Fort William, had taken the ferry over to join us for lunch. Your friend Peter — what a funny combative relationship the two of you had — was picking through and mending his fishing tackle.

There was a fine picnic lunch — lobsters from Croig, wild-gathered mushrooms, Chrissie's homebaked bread, superb wine Peter had brought from the south, Tuscan olive oil and island herbs to sauce everything — and all was well with the world. All was sweet and scented. It was a day of loveliness, of perfection.

Except now for my rage and regret that you were dying; you were launched on the river that was going to carry you away. The rage is against myself for my sheer stupidity. The regret is much the same, that I didn't realize the cause of your weariness, that I quarrelled with you and blamed you for not enjoying the glory of the day, that I even accepted the explanation about the bruise on your breast.

Peter went off to fish.

The two of us made a rough form of peace. I watched as you dozed fitfully in the sun, huddled under a coarse plaid rug with a scarf woven in the family's tartan — that pattern of scarlet, oatmeal, rowan-red and skeins of harebell violet you loved — round your throat. Your ancestors wore the tartan on the field of Culloden. Your dark eyelashes were so long. Your hands, fingers knitted together, lay over your breast. There was no trouble or disturbance in you, only weariness as you travelled, I guess, through your dreams.

I longed to touch you. I didn't. Partly for fear of waking you but much more for the fear of stirring a sleeping leopard — not a leopardess, alert and keen feminist as you were, you hated politically correct gender distinctions. You were a leopard. Supple and taloned and dangerous like your mother and sisters.

I retired to the little garden hut to write.

I find the generosity of children towards their parents extraordinary. You were exhausted, in pain, and dying. I with ox-like obtuseness registered none of that. I was simply irritated at your silence, your sleepiness, your lack of interest in the glory of the Hebridean day. Afterwards in the short time left you bore no resentment. You treated me as you'd always done; with impatience — your flashing eel-quick mind was as fast as my own — with that razor-sharp blade of your judgement, with an occasional smile, and invariably with something for which the only proper and grown-up word is love.

Against all odds — I was a man, older, a figure of authority, and I'd stacked the odds — you dealt love out to the last. 'Beware of the old,' your mother sometimes quotes Dr Rothschild as saying, 'we care only for ourselves.' Dr Rothschild is right. The old can become profoundly selfish. I wasn't old — or not as I judge it — but compared to you I was ageing. I had lost your tolerance, your compassion.

I was becoming in my worst moments sour and intractable. You, for all your tempestuousness, remained sweet and flexible. Together we probably made up a classic paradigm of the interaction of generations, of the relationship between father and daughter, across history.

We quarrelled furiously all our lives. We debated, argued, pondered and plotted. We raged over films and music, paintings and politics. We fell out again and again. You cursed me with venom and I cursed you back. And yet somehow you invariably found it in you to forgive me. You handed love back.

You decided I was your father.

You encouraged me, urged me on when I was wavering, instructed me in your street phrase to 'go for it, main man'. You frightened the daylights out of me as no woman has ever done. But you made me do things that without you I'd never have done. You encouraged me to stand for Parliament, you urged on my work in conservation, you taught me patiently at the chess table, you tried to persuade me to paint again. And in spite of all your curses, the terrible ghetto swear words you used in your battles, I think perhaps, just perhaps, you took a little pride in me.

Proud, fastidious, clean and as strong-shelled as a cobnut, dangerous as a leopard — the image is used by so many of your friends that it comes back again and again — you continue to prowl round the camp-fires I've lit against the darkness in my mind. You wrote in your last journal: 'I am unremarkable except for the fact that I believe myself to be truly remarkable.'

You're right. You were truly remarkable, Francesca. No wonder I light candles for you. No wonder I weep.

Letters to Francesca: 11

And then for ten days at the end of October Elisabeth went away, leaving you in the care of your sister, Poppy, and me.

Elisabeth was exhausted, having looked after you throughout the summer and autumn. She had a long-standing engagement to address an international conference in Morocco, and make a television programme there. Like all of us, she had no idea quite how ill you were. Perhaps you did, but it was impossible for the rest of us to know. Yet I sense there was intuitively more behind Elisabeth's decision to go than all the known or unknown considerations.

I think she wanted you to be with me for a while, for me to look after you in peril. If I'm right it was the wisest, most far-seeing decision she has ever made. I had you, my daughter, to myself. For a proud and frequently careless man, convinced of the invulnerability of his issue, to cherish a daughter in illness and danger – and I hadn't cherished you anything like well enough over the past twenty-nine years – is, I discovered then, perhaps the richest, most rewarding and humbling experience available.

We had a turbulent and eventful time, you and I, during those ten days. We roamed the desolate corridors of St Thomas's Hospital as the doctors tried to work out the reasons for the sudden and accelerating deterioration in your health. Sometimes you were instructed to stay for the night. Sometimes you were released to sleep in your own flat. I slept wherever I could, scouring London for bedspace from my friends and relations.

'Nicholas, get round here now and fast.'

It was your voice on the telephone on the Wednesday after your mother had left. You'd stayed in the hospital for the night; I'd found a bed with a friend; we'd arranged to meet at midday.

But now I drove straight to the hospital. You were waiting for me dressed in jeans and a T-shirt by the lift on the twelfth floor. I suddenly noticed how extraordinarily thin you looked, starving-sparrow-thin.

'What is it?' I asked.

You didn't answer directly. 'Down,' was all you said.

We took the lift to the ground floor. Outside it was a warm October day. You gazed at me in the car park, your dark eyes fierce and steady and concentrated as always.

'T-cell melanoma,' you explained then. 'A rare form of cancer. They've only had two cases here in the past ten years. But that's it.'

I remember frowning and rubbing my face. 'What do you want to do?' I asked.

'Chinese lunch.'

Chinese lunches were an integral part of the family's past. They had been instituted by your mother. Hating the contempt and disapproval with which northern nations view small children in public places, she had always searched for little culinary havens in cultures and races with a different attitude to the nuclear family — to its noise and laughter and ladders of relationships from grandparents to babies. In London she found it in Soho's Chinatown and its mushrooming extension into the West End.

We drove to Trafalgar Square.

In your company things somehow always worked. The huge car park was full and the illuminated sign on the door said 'Closed'. 'Go in,' you instructed me. I did. Unaccountably one space among hundreds had been overlooked by the attendants and was empty.

It was the same at the restaurant. The place was packed and there was not a table to be had. 'Follow me,' you said. I did. A couple were just getting up from what was probably the best-placed table there. We sat down, ordered a selection of your favourite dim sums, and talked.

Understandably, you were pale, tense and wary. At the age of twenty-nine, a great beauty, coming into your full powers, finding yourself as a painter and writer, longing to have children, you had just been given, as we both knew, a sentence of death. As we talked, random inconsequential talk, you relaxed a little. By the end of the meal we both managed to laugh at some of those jokes that get woven into the private culture of all closely knit families.

Then we went back to the hospital.

While you returned to your bed, I spoke to your kind and helpful doctor — and not all of those who treated you were as courteous as he. Diffidently and awkwardly, trying to avoid giving a name to finality, he confirmed what was obvious. There was no way out of this one.

Afterwards the river began to run towards the sea.

We had some fearful wearisome ordeals to go through first, or rather you did while I, as your trolley-wheeler and minder, could only share them in some small part at second-hand. We went back down into the hidden vaults of St Thomas's. Because chemotherapy might be at least a temporary palliative, there were CAT and PET scans of your body.

The scans involved drinking strange liquids and lying in booming chambers, reminding me of old-fashioned iron lungs, while sonic waves toured your bones and arteries. Sometimes you, the fiery quick-tempered girl, got fed up with the drinks you were told to pour into yourself. Equally, devoted to the young nurses who attended you and not wishing to be thought a difficult patient, you didn't want to leave the glasses of the potions untouched.

Always a pragmatist, you came up with a simple solution. You made me drink the contents of the glasses. Goodness knows what radioactive computer-recognizable washes coursed through my own bloodstream. Perhaps they still do.

As I look back on that time, I have to accept that I wasn't much good. I was impatient, my fuse of tolerance as short as yours. I paced restlessly during your interminable examinations, longing for both of us to be somewhere else. We continued to quarrel, and the fault was invariably mine. No, I did not redeem myself.

Yet something came out of it which I shall treasure always. Raw and barbed as our relationship was, between the storms and collisions we often sat in companionable silence, we held hands, we talked and joked and laughed together. It was a gift of grace. You handed it to me. It will mark me like a benign brand for the rest of my days.

Elisabeth came back from Morocco. She and Poppy took you, fading but still fierce and fearsome, into their guardianship. Your mother and younger sister united to escort you to where you were bound. The river became a cataract sweeping with terrible swiftness over rapids.

We spent three weeks at the house in Wales. You were tired and listless. Your temperature soared up and down, you were feverish, you couldn't eat.

Occasionally your mother persuaded you to take a short walk on the Tregaron marsh to watch the red kites overhead. All too soon it was clear you were so ill that it was time to return to London and try the doctors again.

Elisabeth has chronicled the last week of your life, the week the three of you shared, in her book Family Life. *I find what she wrote almost unbearably distressing but also extraordinarily inspiriting. As you died, you all found peace and reconciliation. Not between the three of you. That was never an issue. Given the immeasurable love you shared, the richness of your common past and experience, your bonds, allegiances and attachments, mother to daughter and sister to sister, that was never going to be called in question.*

No, what you did together — and the three of you took equal shares in the task — was to confront and stare down the last great spectre of our frightened secular age, death. We've reluctantly learnt to tolerate the notion of sex, and we're starting to acknowledge that even money may not be the unmentionable vulgarity we were taught. Yet for most people mortality remains the ghost at the feast, the final subject that cannot be spoken of in polite conversation. Not to you. You all faced up to it, you defeated it, and you went on your separate ways.

The women of the family, as so often in the past, had ruined ruin. Elisabeth and Poppy took you across the river. And then having delivered you safely, because you loved candles they lit them for you. As I do.

Candlelight always became you.

16

St Thomas's Hospital is set on the south bank of the Thames immediately opposite the Houses of Parliament, and beside the bridge which links the two sides of the river.

'Napoleon called us a nation of shopkeepers,' the former prime minister, Sir Alec Douglas-Home, once remarked about some Anglo-French dispute. 'We have built a memorial to him at the heart of London. It's a railway station named Waterloo.'

Trains thunder in and out of the station which lies alongside the hospital. Traffic roars over the bridge. Barges and ferries nudge their way up and down the river. The bustling noise continues until late in the evening. Then abruptly it dwindles and stops. During those last evenings, I would walk out from St Thomas's and stand looking across the river.

I could see the lights of the taxis drawing in to take the Members of Parliament, among them many friends of mine, back to their houses. I could almost hear the patrolling policemen calling out, almost jokingly as they do today, the ancient cry 'Who goes home?'

It was late November, but still warm.

I would listen to the water flowing towards the English Channel. I would inhale the night air. Then I would go back into the unshapely inelegant building and take one of what must be the slowest lifts in the world up to the twelfth floor. I would usually be surrounded by neat crisp young nurses, eagerly chattering young doctors, mostly Bengali or Pakistani, the crippled, the lame, the halt, the drunk.

My fellow-passengers would trickle out and, almost always by the time I reached the twelfth floor, I would be alone. There is a filthy space disdainfully and contemptuously put aside for smokers, and I often sat down on a bench there. I hadn't smoked for years but it was the only place to sit, and a sad reflection of the grim and growing influence of the health police. T. S. Eliot wisely observed humanity could only tolerate so much reality. Cigars and cigarettes have always seemed to me to be entirely acceptable palliatives in dealing with the troubles of life. The new health bully-boys don't agree; claiming 'health-care tax-waste' from behind their expensive desks, they promote guilt, worry and misery as they goad and accuse.

Somewhere in a room along the passage would be three of the four most important women in my life.

I had little role in the dark event they were handling. It was work for the women of the family. I was the gofer, the chauffeur, the fetcher and buyer and carrier of the odds and ends they needed as the journey towards the end swiftened until it was swept along on a raging cataract.

I used to sit there and stare into the night. Sometimes, an awkward stranger, an uninvited guest, almost a gate-crasher, at a party no one else wanted to attend, I visited her.

I lean over the girl.

There's precious little time left. She has difficulty in hearing and speaking. I put my mouth close to her ear. I tell her of a meeting I have attended earlier in the day, a meeting of the management committee organizing the British joint services' mountaineering expedition to tackle one of the world's highest and most dangerous peaks, Gasherbrum in the Pakistan range of the Karakorams.

The committee included a general, an admiral, an air marshal and a cluster of brigadiers and colonels. I'm the expedition's special adviser. Whispering, I tell Fran what we've been up to.

We've been discussing CAS-EVAC, casualty evacuation, the rescue of accident victims or, in the worst case, the case of fatalities, what to do with the bodies. We've got two choices: do we bring them back in body-bags or leave them in a glacier near where they'd died. What does she think?

Francesca ponders the question.

She is dying, and we're measuring time now not in weeks or even days but in hours. To anyone else what I ask her would be intrusive and macabre. Not to Fran. Even at the last she can deal with accidents on mountains, with deaths and body-bags. For heaven's sake, she's climbed with me and her brother high into the Himalaya. She knows the risks. She has always tackled matters head on. She enjoys the hazards. To try to molly-coddle, to shield her now, would be an insult. She'd be enraged and, besides, her judgement remains as sound as the great bells of St Paul's.

'Ask the climbers' families,' she says. 'Go with what they want. I think they'll opt for the mountain.'

Of course. It is thoroughly sensible advice. (Later we did exactly what she suggested. We wrote to the families – it was a difficult letter to write, posing a sad hypothesis – and they all responded. Without exception, just as Francesca thought, they wanted the bodies left on the mountain.)

'What else?' she asks.

The words are so faint it is difficult to hear them. I bend even closer to her.

No time for silliness or sentimentality now, not that there had ever been with Fran. Only for toughness, objectivity and matters of substance. I am finishing a book and I tell her about it. The process is damnably hard, like breaking stones. She smiles. She knows all about the fearsomely difficult business of writing.

I remind her of the pilgrimage we had done to Rocio when she had been eight or nine, and I speak to her about the John Muir Trust, the wilderness conservation body I helped found. It is a cause as dear to her heart as to mine, and she's been a staunch supporter from its beginnings. I tell her about the Trustees' latest deliberations, the disputes, the fierce arguments, the areas of agreement.

We'd just bought the Strathaird estate on Skye. I tell Fran about my visit to Lord Rothschild, chairman of the Heritage Memorial Fund, with my begging-bowl in my hand for help in buying the land. Turner had painted Strathaird's great mountain, Blaven, and the Loch of Coruisk below. It is one of Turner's masterpieces and I asked the noble lord how much he thought the painting was worth.

If one can't ask a Rothschild how much something is worth, who the hell, I thought, can one ask?

Jacob Rothschild looked at me warily. 'About twenty million – if it ever came on the market which, of course, it won't.'

'Give me one-twentieth of that, just half a million, and I'll buy you the original,' I said. 'It'll last longer than Mr Turner's canvas, too.'

Jacob went on staring at me. Then, bleak and brilliant banker as he may be, he burst into laughter. Later, after consulting his co-trustees, he wrote out the cheque.

Fran manages a glimpse of a smile at the story. I know it has pleased her.

'Keep our clan together,' she breathes rather than speaks. 'Keep them questing.'

Poppy is near me, Elisabeth is near me. I put my fingers to my mouth, give them the shadow of a butterfly's kiss, and place it on the girl's forehead. I leave the room.

Across the road from the hospital was a pub called the Florence Nightingale. It was large and expensively decorated, 'themed', I think the word is, in the style of a St James's Street men's club, all leather and brass and polished mahogany. I went there often, but as far as I could tell I was the only person who did. In lonely splendour I had the place to myself.

I always carried a newspaper with me, a security blanket to occupy my attention and somehow disguise me as if I'd been a spy. With the paper in front of me I looked confident and respectable, not the father of a girl wasting to death in a room above me across the way. In the morning it was *The Times* which I reckoned had become bland and banal; in the afternoon or evening it was the much more robust and entertaining *Standard*.

It was Wednesday. I couldn't read anything. I glanced at my watch. It was 4.00 p.m. London time, 10.00 a.m. in New York. I walked back to the car and dialled Caspar at his bank on Wall Street.

'Listen, old fellow,' I said, 'the girl's not well. Please come back now.'

It was the most unnecessary request I'd made in my life. Caspar's finger was tapping out the digits on his other line to call up his travel agent even before we'd finished speaking. He flew through the night. I met him at Heathrow and we drove to the hospital. It was 10.00 a.m. when we got there.

Over the next couple of hours a number of things happened that will haunt, disturb, and in a way sustain me for the rest of my life. Cas and I went into the girl's room. If there's a conflict called sibling rivalry, there must be its opposite – sibling compatibility. The brother and sister, big bro and first lady as they were known in the family, had lived together and loved each other all their lives, given of course the necessary turbulence, the surging tides of quarrels and peace-making in any deep relationship.

I looked at them as they greeted each other. I felt humbled and numbed. I felt confused. I was in the presence of passion, and I was no part of it.

Caspar lowered his head and brushed his hair across the girl's face. He reached for her hand and found it, a tiny riven claw now, somewhere under the sheet. He grinned at her. The waif, the sparrow, the fragile spinning frame in the foam of the cataract, grinned back at him. They were together, safe and companionable.

No sentimentality here. No frivolity or nonsense. Not an eye's-blink of sadness on either side at the imminent separation. Just the raw power of shared experience, of lineage, of common blood and bone and sinew – and feasts and festivals, births and deaths. They'd shared far too many hot dinners, too many secrets, too many furious disputations and their resolution, for uncertainty now. The pulsing quivering bird and the man built like iron stood shoulder to shoulder.

And something else too. Something that Caspar and his sister, and the two other girls who make up the heart of the clan share equally, something to which we give the name love.

I backed away.

The morning of 29 November 1994 was grey and sullen but mild. I stood looking out of a hospital window at the clock-face on Big Ben on the other side of the Thames. As the hour-hand approached half past eleven, I heard a disturbance behind me. I turned. Poppy had come out of the room. She hadn't actually 'come' from the room in the word's usual meaning: she'd thrown the door aside, sprung through the opening, and hurled herself into the passage in a tidal wave of anger.

The consultant was standing in front of her, surrounded by his acolyte support group of doctors, students, nurses and assistants. They were probably fifteen in number. Poppy confronted them, challenged them, outfaced them all.

'Go away,' she shouted. 'Away with you all! I want drugs left for me to give my sister in case she has pain and needs them. Otherwise, be off, all of you!'

I had never witnessed anything like it.

She isn't tall but, like her sister and although in an entirely different way, she has great beauty – blue-eyed with a fine-boned face, cascades of wheat-coloured hair, and a slender supple willowy figure. Her gaze is thoughtful, penetrating, and she has the presence men dream of.

Not that day. That day she was the stuff of nightmares.

She chased the hapless medical team away like the money-changers from the temple. They looked at her, quailed, broke ranks, and ran. Poppy looked at what was left. A handful of teenage nurses.

'Come here,' she beckoned to them. 'I want the painkillers left outside the door. I want hypodermics. If I need your help, I'll call for you. Just be there. Understand?'

'Yes,' they chorused.

The authority in Poppy's voice was so powerful she might have belonged to sixteenth-century royalty. The little black nurses waited. I waited.

I and the black girls were waiting for Fran to die.

Which she did as Big Ben chimed midday. They came past me running, racing, like windswept seagulls, Elisabeth and Poppy, pale as moonlight, harrowed, shadow-eyed, sunken-cheeked, tormented, bursting from the room and flying on furious bitter wingbeats down the passage. I tried to catch them as they passed. Poppy hurled me away. Elisabeth simply ignored me.

They vanished. I knew the girl had gone.

'Listen to me, Nicholas, listen carefully –'

It can only have been minutes later. I was sitting dizzily in a room close to where Fran had died. Caspar was kneeling at my feet with his arms folded round my knees.

I stared at him.

'Remember what we had together. Remember the lovely times. They're her. Remember Rhoshan and the ridges and the stars –?'

I nodded.

Rhoshan was the head sherpa who'd led our expedition into the Himalaya. The knife-like ridges and the falling dreaming spiralling stars were what the three of us remembered best about the journey. That and the ice and snow.

'And the snow?' I said.

It came back to me.

Cas was probably the strongest young man I'd met. When we encountered deep snowdrifts close to the Tibetan border and our porters tumbled into them, Cas would wade in, pick the porters up, and carry them out on his shoulders. Fran and I would watch, shaking with laughter. The porters were paid to carry our possessions. Cas was toting not just our baggage, but the porters too.

'The snow, too,' Caspar chuckled. 'But that's only part of it. There's so much more. She loved you, Nicholas, loved you for the best.'

A retinue, a flock, a clamorous crowd of doctors and nurses and administrators erupted into the room like a laval flow. They were kind and sympathetic and sensitive, with all manner of questions to ask and neatly ruled pads to note down the answers in the appropriate boxes.

I glanced at them and then back at Cas.

'She was safe, wasn't she?' I asked.

'My sister had Ma and Pops with her,' he replied. 'She was always safe, she's always been safe.'

17

That first night tumbled restlessly through darkness into day.

I woke at dawn. Leaving Elisabeth asleep, dark-eyed, white-faced, and drugged with tiredness, I got up and wandered the streets. I walked up to Fran's flat in Kensington Park Road, and stood gazing at her door. The geraniums I'd bought her were still in flower in the window-box. The milkman brushed by me as he delivered her morning pint and a carton of yoghurt.

The postman appeared.

He had a recorded delivery letter for Fran to sign – she was overdue on her Visa account – and a bulky package from British Airways with special offers for their 'Frequent Fliers' clients. I said I'd deal with them both.

'Thanks, chief,' the postman said.

He wheeled his trolley up the street. A moment later he trundled it back.

'Forgot about these,' and he handed me a bundle of magazines. 'She doesn't half like to read, your daughter, that is. Something new every day, but here's a real collection.'

I looked at the labels under the cellophane wrappings. *Vogue*, *Vanity Fair*, the *New Yorker*, the *Literary Review*, *The Spectator*.

'She's a classy chick,' I said, repeating the slightly sardonic phrase she liked to use to describe herself. 'She's got to keep up to date.'

'Good luck to her, squire,' he grinned. 'I can't even spell my own bloody name.'

He wheeled the trolley away again.

I picked one of the geraniums, a small scarlet one, and stuck it through her letter-box. Then I went back to our borrowed flat.

Months earlier I'd agreed to introduce Sir Laurens van der Post at the inaugural meeting of one of the several conservation bodies I chair, the Wilderness Trust, at the Royal Geographical Society. The meeting was to take place that evening. Given Sir Laurens's stature and the magnetic effect of his addresses, the event was expected to attract a capacity audience of one thousand people.

Twenty-four hours earlier Fran had died and my heart had been broken. The stuffing had been knocked out of me in a manner I am only now beginning to consider, let alone absorb and accept. Grief and decorum should have dictated that I gracefully bow out of the engagement — with tactful understanding sympathy from everyone involved — and let someone else do the job.

The trouble was Fran. And the trouble was that Fran would have kicked me sharply in the butt. Unfortunately, grief and decorum weren't listed in her vocabulary.

'Get a life, Nicholas,' was one of the last instructions she gave me. 'You love that old man. So speak for him and make it good.'

She had been on the cataract's edge with bandages over her eyes, but her spirit had still been intractable, irrepressible. She had had private business left to tidy up with her mother and sister, but still just enough energy to deal with me too.

Damn you, Francesca.

Damn you, beautiful sparrow, beautiful lady, damn you for still haunting my life, for dominating what I think and feel. You thread my hair, you shine in my eyes. You colour my being. I can't wipe or rinse you away. You run in my blood, your calcium cells have become the building blocks of my bones — and I always thought it was meant to be the other way round. You're the presence which inhabits and wanders, at your own elegant ease, through the mansion of my mind.

Go away and let me be, girl. Except you won't, will you? Any more than you did on the day after you died.

I didn't want to address that audience, but I promised you I would and so I did. I went down to the RGS. There were indeed a thousand people there, and happily among them your brother. Sir Laurens arrived in a wheelchair, delivered by an ambulance. I brought him and Caspar together. Caspar knelt down by the chair. I waved the attendants aside, backed away, and left the two of them to speak quietly to each other, the old lion and the young lion in a private communion that belonged to the two of them and no one else.

The lights dimmed, Sir Laurens's chair was wheeled up onto the dais, and I stood up to speak. I made a fair beginning. Then I faltered.

Then through the wandering dust-strewn spirals of the lamp-light in the dazzling darkness in front of me I saw Caspar. His face was smiling, energetic, powerful, urging me on. His eyes had the same intense glow as his sister's. They were a bonny pair, the boy and his sister, so were the other two girls who made up the four. They were all salt and rock. Turbulent, truculent, combative, difficult, but wonderful.

I grinned back at him and went on. Then I sat down and let Sir Laurens take over. He spoke as always with his characteristic passion, eloquence and grace. When he finished the entire audience rose and applauded him in affection and respect.

I wheeled his chair out.

For a moment the two of us were alone in the half-darkness of the corridor. Laurens knew what had happened. A few weeks earlier his friend and comrade, the doughty South African conservationist, Dr Ian Player, had stayed with us in Wales and held Fran's hand as he said grace in the tongue of his adopted people, the Zulu nation, over our midday meal.

It was a strange and extraordinarily appropriate and conciliatory gesture. Food of course should always be blessed, but there was far more to his grace than that. Kwa-Zulu had triumphed at the battle of the hill of Isalwandana, breaking the spirit of the world's mightiest empire, only to have its own spirit broken twenty-four hours later at a little farm named Rorke's Drift on the bank of a Natal river.

Now, a century later, a white South African, a descendant of a Voortrekker who'd fought with the British soldiers, was blessing food in Zulu in the Welsh-speaking heartland of Ceredigion from where many of the Rorke Drift's garrison had come.

Laurens took my hand.

'Ian tells me your daughter was a warrior,' he said. 'I have spoken with Caspar. He is one too. They are the same. Dream of them, Nicholas, dream of them together.'

Caspar was forthright and uncompromising.

'My sister is beautiful,' he said. 'I'm not having her buried in the urban squalor of London. She'll lie in a place as lovely as she is.'

The chalk-bedded orchid-starred whale-backed Sussex Downs, cropped tight by sheep and armoured by bronze copses of beech, must be one of the most beautiful landscapes on earth. The skies above them are immense. They're lit by light reflected from the Channel seas. In winter often under snow – the frosted upland pastures are steely-hard – they glow with spears and blades of rose and gold; in spring and summer they ripple with scented green.

The little village of Ripe – the name is wonderfully appropriate – lies close to the Downs' feet. The settlement is very old. It's recorded in the Domesday Book but clearly existed for centuries before the bastard Duke William sent out his surveyors and map-makers. Today it consists of a cluster of handsome ancient houses, a pub and a church.

My mother lived in the village for years. Her second husband, my stepfather, a kind and gentle man, is buried there. So too is the writer Malcolm Lowry. Lowry, author of that strange, savage and wonderful book *Under the Volcano*, completed his alcoholically driven suicide-journey in a wooden cottage up the lane.

'Ripe,' Cas said, 'I'll deal with it.'

I smiled.

I said nothing. One doesn't argue with six feet of bone and muscle deciding with passion and an intellectual vigour to match his sister's where the girl is going to rest. I kept my peace. I enjoyed the idea of the two, Lowry and Fran, lying side by side.

Lowry poured himself into his grave, awash with any liquor – from bourbon to scrumpy – he could grab. Fran occasionally sipped a glass of champagne, and then only if it was *brut* and preferably from a fine vintage year. I didn't envy Lowry his bed in the Sussex soil. He was about to get a fearfully strict companion in the bed next door.

Horses.

Grey horses in the early December air, cantering and roaming and shaking their manes. Late roses still spilling over garden hedges. Mist and flinty walls and pigeons thronging the yew trees, and those immense silvery-mackerel-flanked Sussex skies lit by the light reflected off the stormy waters of the Channel which is where her brother, Boychild, rests beneath the waves.

And there in Sussex soil close to the Boychild was where we left the girl with a pottery emblem of the *blanca paloma*, the white dove of Rocio, on her coffin.

The grave-digger crossed his arms and leant on his spade under the yew.

He surveyed us all – the family and Fran's hundred or so friends who'd gathered to see her on her way – and spat on his hands. He knew my folk and had dug graves for them before. He didn't belong to the twentieth century. He came from Shakespeare's time and he spoke with the rhythm and accent of centuries before.

I went and stood with him. There was a touch of frost on the ground. We watched the wheeling tumbling crows. He pocketed without comment the traditional note I gave him for a drink at the tavern.

'Dug it deep,' he said. 'Dug it clean. Put the flints as came out up there by the gate. She'll sleep well, your girl will.'

On the way out I picked up one of the stones, chalky, gleaming and steel-grey on its cutting edges, hard and defiant as the girl's spirit, and took it home with me. It sits now with her boots on my desk.

And then that part of it was almost over. I embraced and kissed the inhabitants of Fran's world whom she'd made members of our own clan: the gaunt-faced Peter, grieving ashen Amy, weeping Dr Day with her enchanting little daughter, stern and thoughtful drummer Joe, so many, many more. They were the boldest and the best, companions of Fran's heart and now of mine.

Damn you, strange and darling Fran, damn you for walking out on all of us.

That particular part of the tempestuous event should have been over. It wasn't.

The girl had died, we had laid her to rest, we were trying to assemble our hearts and wits to handle what was left. The trouble was that Honey Abigail, her youngest sister, didn't know what had happened. Honey was untraceable somewhere diving in the South China seas. She came back a few days after the funeral. Elisabeth and I went to meet her at the airport.

It was 6.00 a.m. – and it was one of the most heartbreaking moments of my life. She was welded into the same litter, she had been reared in the same straw as her brother and sisters. The four were indivisible. They were each other's support systems, the porters of each other's troubles, the counsellors and resolvers of each other's problems – from broken hearts to withdrawn credit cards. They discussed and argued the issues of the intellect from art and literature, politics and finance to films and music.

The flight landed, Honey appeared behind the barrier, she saw us and ran forward throwing out her arms. She was tanned, golden-skinned, a lissom and elegant beauty in her tattered salt-faded jeans just as her sister had so often been on her return from her travels, and with the same hour-glass silhouette.

Honey checked.

She'd seen something in our faces. The laughter went from her. The impulsive rush slowed and became hesitant. Her mother pushed away the barrier. She caught her and held her and told her. She had no need to. Honey already knew.

To her immense and eternal credit, Honey showed extraordinary fortitude. There were no tears – those came later – only smiling confident instructions to me to find the car and drive us back into London. Which I did. We returned to the flat, the curious base we'd used as a camp-site during the days of peril, and thankfully found Poppy there.

The three of them, the mother and two daughters, folded each other in their arms. They sat laced and threaded together, occasionally murmuring, occasionally laughing, occasionally weeping. I felt the warmth of their touch as they stroked each other. Woven into each other so delicately, so tenderly, with such suppleness and grace, the three women could have been a model for a carving by Michelangelo.

Big bro, exhausted, was asleep in the bedroom. I went and lay down beside him.

The months passed.

The winter on my little estate in Wales had been chill and drear. My tenant farmer on the land, Will, came up daily to feed the sheep and see all was well in the house. A stocky grey-haired Welsh-speaking peasant, Will is among the finest and kindest men I've ever known, a person of laughter, loyalty and limitless generosity of spirit, a true son of the Cambrian mountain people.

He had cared for the whole family – Francesca above all, he loved the girl and used to take her clay-pigeon shooting – from the moment we arrived in Wales. Fran's death had come as a fearful blow to him and his own family.

'*Dhu, dhu, dhu,*' he kept saying after he heard the news, shaking his head grimly and sadly.

Dhu is one of the relatively few words common to both Gaelic and Welsh. In both languages it means dark. *Dhu* bread, black bread, is what you eat yourselves. White bread is for feasts and guests.

Dhu is rough, hard, bleak, signifying both sorrow and reality. *Dhu* is the nature of things. *Dhu* is what we all had to live with.

His wife, the grey-haired grandmother Jane who looks after the house, cried for days. They put an announcement in the little local Welsh-language magazine which spoke with eloquence of the community's sadness at the girl's death. From all around the farmers sent cards of sympathy, lovely cards embossed with silver crosses or wreaths of roses and printed with touching little scraps of doggerel verse.

Will and I used to go out, look at the snow-laden sky over the mountains, examine the fields under their crackling mantle of frost, talk about the flock and the prospects for lambing. They were all sturdy living matters and Will did his best to lift my spirits with them, but nothing worked. The girl had gone. What was left seemed paltry and insignificant. The salt, the taste in things, had been stolen. A thief had broken into my larder and stolen off with the best of my stores.

It was the same for all of us. There is a common belief that death brings people together. It is a fallacy. In a closely knit family it's much more likely to create ruptures and divisions, to separate and sunder the clan.

'When someone so extraordinary dies,' our friend Venetia perceptively remarked, 'everyone wants to be part of the event, to have their own share in the grief.'

She was right. From the centre of the family to comparative strangers, everyone wanted Fran. Within the family I'd assumed she meant the same to all of us; that powerful as she was she was the same person to each and every one of us. I now realized that was a fallacy, a delusion. The intensity of the grief was the same, but we were all trying to come to terms with the loss of a different person.

And because there were five of us, we were dealing with five different Frans. Multiply that by the loss felt by her multitude of friends, all again with different perspectives and relationships, and the numbers added up to hundreds of Frans.

'Don't tap too hard on the cracks,' Elisabeth said.

I tried to follow the instruction while she held the group – the family and the friends – together through a perilous time. But, grief and desolation aside, I often felt angry that others didn't see her in exactly the same way I saw her. I couldn't understand why people didn't unquestioningly accept everything I knew her for, and everything I was determined to do on her behalf.

For Christ's sake, I was her father, she was my oldest daughter, we'd had a fierce and combative relationship but apart from her mother, I'd known her for longer than anyone on earth. Holding her in my arms on that icy night of her birth, I'd helped save her life. I must be right.

My goodness, what folly, what arrogance!

Yes, Fran belonged to me. In equal and sometimes far greater measure she belonged to her mother, her brother, her sisters and her friends. Many of their claims on her were infinitely stronger than mine, although in the end she belonged to us all. That was her gift as she died.

I wasn't aware of it during that first winter.

All I knew was the cold and frost and cheerful Will's companionable talk about the flock, and the ravens wheeling overhead and a terrible sense of bereftness. Where the hell was Fran? Each time the telephone rang I leapt for it, certain it would be her. At night I'd go out and shout at the stars: 'Please, mister, can we have our girl back? Just throw her over the garden fence. That'll do fine.'

Silence. Complete silence apart from the occasional hooting owl. Silence and the icy air and solitude.

Elisabeth and I went to New Zealand in the early spring. We fished for rainbow trout and swam with dolphins which Fran had so longed to do, and drank the fine red wine from the new vineyards. We returned and left again for Africa. We camped out in the Okavango delta, we watched the elephant herds coming to drink at dawn and evening, we listened to fish eagles screaming and watched malachite kingfishers plunging into the lagoons, we filled ourselves with Kalahari sun. We went to Canada, to Quebec, walked in the forests, and studied beaver dams.

We returned and nothing had changed. Nothing had made the slightest scrap of difference. Inside me was a cone of ice. She was my daughter and she had walked away from me and I felt bitterly cold.

PART II

PART II

18

'Meet us in Pamplona,' Priscilla said as June approached.

It wasn't a good start. Pamplona was where Fran and I had spent our last funny and happy time together, but I took the flight.

As a former special forces soldier and seasoned traveller, I'm usually well prepared and well equipped. I arrive at the departure point fit and well briefed and ready to tackle anything. Not this time. I was desolate, confused and drifting. Instead of taking my sturdy and comfortable walking boots, I simply threw a pair of lightweight deck-shoes into my pack which I filled up with odds and ends at random, and set off for the airport.

The taxi-driver who drove me into Pamplona was a Navarran and deeply proud of it.

'Navarre first, Basque second, and Spanish maybe, maybe, a long way third,' he said.

I sat beside him brooding and silent.

'If I may ask, are there *cosas*, matters on your mind, *señor*?' he went on.

'Yes,' I answered abruptly.

'Come back in *feria*, in San Fermin. You will forget everything then.'

Not Francesca, I wouldn't. I didn't say that at San Fermin a year ago I'd been here with her. I was due to meet the others at a restaurant off the main square, but I asked him to drop me in the square itself. I started to walk.

I knew I was going to be late for the rendezvous, but it didn't matter.

I stopped in front of the Basque club where her brother had taken us for lunch, shouldering his way through the Spanish secret police who were checking everyone who went in. I went to the bar where Fran liked to drink her breakfast coffee, and I used to have an *anis* to set me up for the day. I walked up the street where the bulls ran and stood looking up at the apartment Cas had rented for us. Behind the iron bars of the *rejas*, the window sills were laden with geraniums. The pink and scarlet petals shone in reflection on the glass.

I turned and headed for the bullring.

On the way I passed the high wooden stockade onto which I'd heaved her up so she could perch, feet dangling, laughing, while the lads with their frosted bottles of beer gathered below. There was a light evening wind swirling round the ring and the old bullfight posters were flapping and rustling. I read some of the names. They were achingly familiar: Chamaco, Domecq, Litri. I'd watched all of them or their fathers, and known several of them well for my entire adult life.

So had Fran. I saw her again a year earlier, sitting beside me inside the ring and furiously sketching the strange drama of the *corrida* taking place beneath us. I remembered the drawing she'd given the rich Basque lady, and then Francesca quickly returning to her work. There were the great Miura bulls to be caught in the spinning coloured webs of her lines, and that was far more important – particularly when time was so short.

Oh, beloved Fran, why the hell did you leave us, first lady?

I swung away from the ring, trudged back into the centre of Pamplona, and found the others.

This time we were a group of five. Priscilla and Hilary were there, of course. So was buoyant little Angie, another of the Camberwell beauties who'd walked with us on the previous stage through Gascony. The newcomer was a woman called Liz, quiet, sensitive and reflective. She was confronting a tragedy close to mine. Her eldest daughter had been killed in a road accident which happened barely a month after Fran died.

I was probably unhinged, close to lunacy and madness and all the points of a spinning compass between. Gentle Liz had remained sane.

Why, Fran, did it take you the four agonizing years we had to live through?

What a foolish, reckless question to ask. You were the clan's leopard, prowling and dangerous. You challenged all of us. You never did anything by halves – neither in life nor in death. When you left it was bound to be in trouble and turbulence and accompanied, given your matching gentleness, by trumpets and peace too.

Damn you, Francesca Luz. You baffled me in life. You baffle me now.

We ate in Pamplona that evening.

For me the town was too full of ghosts, of memories. I was uneasy. I wanted to get to where we were sleeping that night. We finished our meal and took taxis out to the pilgrim hostel at Cizur Menor. The main dormitory was almost full, but the overflow adjoining barn was empty. I pulled two truckle beds in the barn together and asked Angie if she'd sleep with me there.

Angie put her arms round me and tried to make me sleep. Like Will and with the same great generosity she did her best, but again it didn't work. I dozed fitfully, never for more than twenty minutes at a time, and I kept getting up to roam the garden outside. When daylight came I was red-eyed and exhausted.

We set off south-west across the Navarran plain. The day's walk was the one I'd done with Caspar and his friends in the opposite direction the year before. Then it had been lovely, a day of splendour, a fresh golden day of sunlight and birds and keen grape-scented air, with a satisfying weariness and Francesca waiting at its end.

This time it was different.

The day was hot but overcast and a troublesome east wind was blowing. There was a dull, harsh cast to the countryside. The vines were dust-covered and the flanks of the surrounding hills seemed to glower at us rather than shine. I trudged on. By midday I was struggling.

It wasn't just that I was unfit and exhausted, physically and mentally drained. It was the shoes I'd so carelessly and thoughtlessly tossed into the pack. They'd done me well enough in New Zealand and Africa, but there I'd been walking on pine needles or sand. Here the track underfoot was uneven and littered with sharp broken stones. I began to stumble, my ankles kept twisting, the jagged pebbles dug through the thin rubber soles and bruised my feet.

I reached our overnight halt, the little town of Puente la Reina, well after the others and stripped down in the pilgrim refuge. Peeling off my socks I saw my feet were swollen and corrugated with blisters. The Camberwell beauties made token murmurs of sympathy, but there was nothing they could do and I knew what they were thinking.

How on earth has this tough and experienced soldier got himself into this ridiculous and unnecessary pickle? For goodness sake, doesn't he know you wear boots and not shoes on a long hard hike? Where has he been all his life?

If I silently cursed them, I cursed myself much more savagely. The next day, I knew, was going to be worse. So it proved – and it got even worse as the week wore on.

The nature of the journey was changing, and not just because of my own disaffection, my weariness and raw feet.

The two landscapes, the one inside the mind and the physical one without, were different. We'd started with gaiety on an adventure. The three of us had travelled alone, roaming and wandering through some of the loveliest countryside in Europe. We'd taken our time and slept where we wanted. We'd met almost no one – in the first five hundred miles we'd encountered fellow-pilgrims on less than a dozen occasions.

There'd been hard and demanding passages, of course – the snows and rain of the Auvergne, my sickness at Conques, limping treks in the dark when all of us were so tired we could barely speak, the occasional angry quarrel, invariably sparked by me. But my overriding memory of France will always be one of sun and delight. Wild orchids and narcissus, immense skies, circling kites and eagles, fine food and the sturdy black wine of Cahors, talk and quiet companionship and affection.

Spain was different. Spain, as I knew well, was the land of the *leyenda negra*, the black past. The best of the game, I sensed, was behind us.

Wherever one goes in Spain the land has the texture of a bull's hide. All of France's gentleness and softness vanishes as soon as you cross the Pyrénées. The earth bristles aggressively with thorn. The light is bleak and bold and clear, the midday sky challenging you to stare it down and invariably forcing you to lower your eyes. The stones hurt. There are still wolves in the mountains and the eagles are real eagles, not distant elegant silhouettes but creatures who dive with razored talons and kill mercilessly in front of you.

Horsemen ride by.

They wear spurs and worn leather chaps and flat grey caps tilted down over their narrowed eyes. They seldom smile. They are not mounted for fun, they are at work and on business and the prancing, cantering horses, superbly as they ride them, are simply tools. The food is either trawled from the sea or hammered out of blood, meat and lights, and packed for storage into the translucent entrails of the prey animal's gut.

The bread – the Romans rightly thought it was the best bread in the world – is grey, rock-hard, and salted from the deposits on the Cadiz flats. When I lived in Andalucía the local baker would make me huge circular loaves which he baked in his wood-fired oven and stamped with a cross and his initials. They were known as charcoal-burners' loaves because they were taken into the forest where the charcoal was made. You needed a machete to cut them, and they lasted not just for days or weeks but for months.

Franco used to say: 'Europe ends at the Pyrénées. The *pueblo* is African.' In Spanish the word *pueblo* embraces everything from a hamlet to a city to a nation, a people. I have known and loved both Spain and Africa for most of my life. I know just what the little 'most general' meant.

Spain is separate and apart. Spain is different.

The pilgrimage approach roads come together close to the French border at the foot of the mountains. Afterwards they funnel into a single path. The first and most noticeable consequence for anyone travelling the Way is that one is suddenly accompanied by people all moving in the same direction. On the first day's walk westwards from Pamplona we met more fellow-pilgrims than on our entire journey across France.

So we had companions now. We were numbers of a much larger group, occasionally it almost seemed a crowd. Once that week we found ourselves walking with seventy-eight – I counted them – teenage Japanese girls in day-glo cerise, avocado and lavender anoraks. They were chewing gum, they flash-photographed each other endlessly, they hopped and skipped and their squealing giggles made the hedgerows ring.

I wished Caspar was with me to find out why they were there. Among his many languages he speaks limited but adequate Japanese. I have hardly a word. The appearance on the Way to St James of a bunch of adolescent Shinto Buddhists – they can't have been anything else – will remain one of the pilgrimage's mysteries. As they whirled and shrilled like migrating swallows, we hurried on past them.

Happily their itinerary didn't include lodging for the night at the next pilgrim's hostel, a *refugio* as it's known in Spain. In France we'd been able to pick and choose. Hilary and Priscilla are experienced travellers. They'd done their homework, studied maps, consulted pilgrims who'd walked the Way before us, reached for their telephones, and – where they could – made bookings in advance. We'd slept in farms, monasteries, *gîtes*, priest's houses, little hotels.

The standards of accommodation varied wildly but the manner of our sleeping was always safe, secure and generally warm. The nightly stops were planned and organized. Not in Spain. Beyond the Pyrénées we were forced to take pot-luck.

For most of the week we lodged in the pilgrim *refugios*. While I haven't yet been incarcerated in prison or slept out on the street slums of Calcutta or Rangoon, the pilgrimage journey taught me what it's like to live in a Third-World shanty town. It's a nightmare.

There are exceptions, but most of the *refugios* are sheds. Stacked inside them are cramped tiers of iron beds. The passages between them are roughly 18 inches in width; even someone as slim as I am had to turn and shuffle sideways to negotiate them. The beds are full of pot-bellied German and Belgian penitents. They all have filthy underwear, haliotosis and digestive problems. They rinse their intimate clothes and hang them out sodden and steaming to dry. Then they toss and turn all night, creaking the rusty bedsprings as they triumphantly expel their stomach gases with explosions like artillery fire.

The next night at Estella I slept with brown-streaked underpants flapping across my face, foul-smelling steam condensing on my skin, and Teutonic farts in my nostrils. At three o'clock my neighbour in the bunk above climbed down for a widdle. He was a bald nineteen-stone Bavarian, a massively muscled former prison guard and member of Germany's Olympic water-polo team who'd decided in mid-life to become a monk. On his way back to bed he misjudged where he was. He placed his heel on my groin and levered himself up. Well over two hundred and fifty pounds of Black Forest bulk and bone ground down on one of my most sensitive personal areas. I thrashed like an eel and screamed like a banshee.

'*Bitte, mein freund*,' he said. 'There are people here who wish to sleep.'

He gave a final crushing and reproachful heave on my testicles and crashed down like a beached whale above me.

We tramped on. My crutch felt as if a Sherman tank had been parked on it throughout the hours of darkness, and my feet had started to bleed. It was another long day. I lagged behind the others and only caught up with them when they stopped in the rare little village for a coffee. In the late afternoon I hobbled into Los Arcos, our destination for the night.

All I wanted was a deep hot bath, a good dinner and a comfortable bed – preferably with a down pillow and lavender-scented sheets.

'I fear it doesn't look very promising,' Priscilla said grimly.

19

Priscilla had already been there with the others for an hour.

'The refuge is closed,' she went on, 'the only *pensión* has gone out of business, and there's not much in the way of food. However, we've found Eduardo and he's heard of an old biddy who may give us lodging.'

The tall and handsome Eduardo, a fellow-pilgrim travelling with a friend who'd tacked himself on to us, was already negotiating with the old biddy.

She was tiny, white-haired, filthy, and what the Spanish call *bruta* – coarse and suspicious with a sophisticated calculating machine of a brain over anything to do with money. She owned a hovel with three tiny rooms for rent. The washing facilities were a chipped enamel bowl filled from a dripping cold water tap, and a stinking broken lavatory without a seat.

We took the rooms. There was nowhere else. She grinned wickedly and pocketed our money. One pair of Camberwell beauties slept together in two tiny beds. Priscilla and Hilary shared their room with the old harridan and her husband who farted all night. I was left with Eduardo and his friend, Diego, in a space smaller than a Victorian broom-cupboard. There was a single straw-filled mattress on the scrap of floor, and two *vaquero*'s hammocks, tarred jute bags used in the field by cattle-herders and slung above each other from a worm-eaten beam.

I took the mattress.

'For what she's charging us for this,' Eduardo remarked as he heaved himself into one of the hammocks, 'she's a real *hija de puta* – a whore's sprog.'

Diego, his friend, was already lying down and reading his Bible.

'Wash your mouth out, Eduardo!' he shouted. 'We are on pilgrimage. You cannot use such vile language. I must go and pray in expiation.'

Diego managed to tip himself out of the jute bag – the tar on the cord was melting in the afternoon heat – somehow clamber over me, and head downstairs for the church.

Eduardo shrugged.

He crossed his arms behind his head and began to doze. I looked at my feet. I hadn't been able to take my shoes off, I wouldn't be able to until the swelling went down when the air cooled, but I could see blood seeping out from the welts. I lifted my head and smelt the stench from below. A mangy goat with diarrhoea was roaming the courtyard and its discharges had blocked the drains.

I decided the only sensible course of action for a mature responsible adult was to go out and get drunk.

I succeeded triumphantly.

With at least two bottles of wine under my belt, I went back to the old biddy's hovel as if I were elegantly tap-dancing, walking like Fred Astaire on air. I was unaware of my feet, I gave the goat a friendly pat, I didn't notice the stench, not even when I tripped over one of the slurry-choked drains. I climbed smiling up to my bed, toppled onto the straw mattress, and slept.

In the grey early morning light the world looked rather different. Choosing alcohol as an anaesthetic fell into that category of decisions – quite a good idea, but not a very good idea. At one end of my body my feet were just as painful. At the other I had a pounding hangover. I struggled up and set off with Eduardo.

Eduardo and I walked all morning together.

It wasn't the worst day of the journey – that came later in the week – but it was a bleak and painful one. My feet were raw and patterned with blisters and sores. I was moving slowly and I often had to stop to remove stones or thorns which had crept into my unsuitable shoes. Whenever I did Eduardo waited beside me.

'Good heavens, Don Nicholas,' he said, gazing anxiously at my blood-sodden socks, a dripping mass of red, 'those are the true signs of Calvary. You will gain much merit from this.'

'Shut up, Eduardo,' I snapped. 'It's my own damn fault for not wearing my boots. And don't address me as Don Nicholas. Nicholas, or Nick as my sister and the others call me, will do fine.'

'Yes, Don Nicholas,' he'd reply, kneeling to tie my laces.

I limped beside him as we went on.

Eduardo was an athletic, dark-haired and dark-eyed young man, well over six feet tall, who came from north-eastern Spain. His father was an affluent butcher, a member of Spain's emerging middle classes, who had great hopes for his son. Eduardo had gone to university to study law and spoke fluent unaccented Castilian, but he'd never quite fulfilled his family's expectations. He found the Spanish legal system trivial, and the lawyers who taught him meretricious and corrupt.

He'd returned home to work in the family business. A potential QC, at least when we encountered him, and perhaps finally a judge was hacking away at bones and stuffing animal intestines to make *chorizo* sausages on a marble counter. What Eduardo wanted, he decided when he met me, was to be me.

'I wish to write books, maybe poems, travel the world, speak languages, influence events,' he said. ' I would like to be like you, Don Nicholas.'

They were almost exactly the same sentiments, although expressed in a different language, that little bow-legged Jean-Paul, the French pilgrim with his house on his back, had voiced. What is it, I wondered, that makes so many yearn to be writers? Why not opt for a glittering – and financially much more rewarding – career as a bank manager, estate agent, or even a publishing excecutive? So much safer, so much more social, so much more pensionable.

I thought of telling Eduardo of the hazards, problems and demands, but decided not to. At twenty-six, as he was, everyone is entitled to their dreams. Only the heaviest of hands – and sadly there are many – bring down the clenched fist to try to crush them.

'Just call me Nicholas,' I repeated wearily instead.

'*Si, señor.*'

We tramped on.

There was a lovely youthful gaiety about him, a natural courtesy which showed itself in his concern about my blood-sodden feet and an intellectual curiosity in his constant uninhibited questions – about life and the nature of human sexuality, about history, books, ideas and international relations. There was too immense patience which, together with gentleness, may be of all human gifts the greatest.

That day I was stumbling and struggling. Eduardo was buoyant, ready to leap and run as I had been on that now distant time in the mountains of the Auvergne. He held himself back, he waited for me, he made himself available, a companion to the bruises on my spirit and the blood in my shoes. It was an act of instinct, of generosity and kindness. It came across the generations from one stranger to another.

It belonged to pilgrimage.

So even more vividly was what happened later. Eduardo and I caught up with the rest of the team, the group. The old Pilgrim Way lay along the metalled highway. The detour, recommended for walkers by the Spanish Tourist Board, ran close to it just to the west. Nursing my feet I chose the highway. Apart from being the original route, the level road was gentler on my blisters than the rugged track through the hills and woods which the others opted for. We all eventually met up at our destination, the little fortress town of Viana.

Walking along the road I was normally recognized as a pilgrim by the approaching cars and trucks. They saw my staff and pack, they knew it was the Way to Santiago, they moved out to overtake me and would salute me with a tap on their horn or a blink of their lights. The occasional vehicle took not the slightest notice of me. They gave me no space and I had to leap for safety into the hedgerow.

To them I was riff-raff, a wandering tramp.

By the time I arrived at Viana I'd decided I was lacking something. I knew what it was. I wasn't wearing the scallop shell of the true pilgrim. If I'd had one round my neck and the cars had still driven at me, I'd have been faced with heathens, barbarians, but I was fairly sure the most committed atheist fuelled with road-rage would have swerved rather than confront that potent talisman.

The *cuadrilla*, the ladies and Eduardo, were resting on the ground in the tree-shadow of the monastery courtyard at Viana when I limped up to them. I gave them my offerings: I'd bought some cherries, figs and wind-dried mountain ham on the way. Then I heaved off my pack and slumped down.

'How did it go?' Priscilla asked.

I told her. I said that if I walked a highway again I had to have a shell hanging on my chest. Eduardo spoke a little English, but not enough to understand. He asked me what had happened and I explained in Spanish.

As the rest of us ate the fruit and *jamón*, Eduardo retired to the shade of another tree. An afternoon wind had risen and he stood there, pensive and frowning, as the branches tossed round him. Then he came back to us.

'Don Nicholas —'

'Nicholas,' I cut him off. I was exhausted and the blood in my boots was beginning to cake and abrade the skin on my feet whenever I moved. 'Just Nicholas.'

'*Si, señor,*' he smiled. 'You are a true pilgrim. I wish to give you this.'

Hanging from his neck on a cord of woven jute was a large shell. Ivory-white and rimmed with the flaring orange stripes of the scallop, it was the first thing I'd noticed about him when we met. It was simple and beautiful, heavy and real — the true mark of Santiago, the dwelling and shelter of Christ's disciple on his sea-wanderings. It was just a shell.

'I carried it with me on my first pilgrimage,' Eduardo went on. 'Now it belongs to you.'

He took it from his neck and held it out to me.

I stood up stiffly. I protested. I refused to accept it. I said it was his and he had earned it. I cursed him for even trying to make me a present of it. I swung away from him angrily and hobbled off into another cone of tree-shadow. I waited for an instant. It was a ritual but an essential one, demanded by the graceful formality of Castilian social intercourse. Then I returned, put my arms round him, kissed him and we both wept.

'For you and for your daughter,' he said.

Eduardo's gift was rare and extraordinary, the most valuable thing he had to give. It wasn't something one could accept easily and lightly. Its very importance meant it had to be denied and rejected. I wasn't being presented with a bauble: I, a stranger, was being given part of a man's heart.

As the poet W. B. Yeats pointed out, hearts are not had as gifts, hearts are earned.

Eduardo placed the shell round my neck.

'Travel safely, Don Nicholas,' he said.

We finished the meal. Eduardo lifted his pack and set off ahead of us in the afternoon sunlight. We lifted our hands in farewell as he left.

'I think you've changed that young man's life,' Hilary said.

'Bugger that,' I replied. 'He's much more likely to have changed mine.'

I slept that night with the shell under my pillow.

20

My sister Priscilla's husband Mark is an entrepreneurial businessman. Educated at Madrid University and a lifelong fluent Spanish speaker, one of the main areas for his activities is inevitably the Iberian peninsula. Among his many Spanish friends is Primitivo, 'Primi', Gurpegui, the managing director of a large family-owned Navarran winery. Priscilla telephoned Primi after Eduardo left us.

We were in Viana, she said, we'd love to see him.

'No problem,' Primi replied. 'You are less than an hour away. I pick you up at the *refugio*, and we dine at the *bodega*. Be there at the gates seven o'clock sharp, please.'

We were.

Primi arrived late. It was no matter. Timing in Spain is measured on a different scale. Foreigners scoff and sneer at what they call the '*mañana*' mentality. They believe every appointment is of equal importance. It doesn't matter what the issue is, only that the hour is met. Not the Spanish. If the matter is of consequence, if it involves a sick child, the Spanish drop everything and are with you long before the emergency services of the advanced industrialized societies could hope to be there – even if it means fording rivers at night on horseback.

A leaking tap is different. That can indeed wait until tomorrow. One of the sadnesses of modern emerging Spain is that the national *pueblo*, the sons and daughters of Franco's Africa-beyond-the-Pyrénées, so desperately wants to be like the *países formados*, the old structured countries of the north, while those same northern nations have everything to gain by trying to be more like Spain.

Spanish priorities are different.

Mañana is a considered concept, a considered choice. It places the stricken child leagues and distances and limitless vastnesses of effort before the leaking tap. One is vital, it merits moving heaven and earth for; the other can be put on hold. Very flat, Norfolk, as Noël Coward said. Very wise, the Spanish *pueblo*.

Primi arrived in his handsome Mercedes. The five of us climbed in and set off for the family winery. We made a couple of detours on the way to pick up supplies for dinner. An hour later we reached the *bodega*. Primi, an immensely energetic and attractive Navarrese in his mid-forties who spoke fluent idiomatic English, took us on a tour of the cellars before leading us to the boardroom dining-room.

For one of Navarra's oldest and most successful wineries, the huge size of the chill vaulted tunnels of oaken barrels and the stacks of ageing bottles wasn't surprising. What was surprising was what lay between them. Some cocooned in plastic dust-sheets, some open to the air — they were being serviced or polished — was an extraordinary collection of vintage cars. There were Bentleys, MGs, Ferraris, early T-Model Fords, ancient Rolls-Royces, a magnificent hearse, a pair of pre-World War II taxis.

Waxed and gleaming, their steely bonnets and wings glistened like a school of sharks under the barrel vaults in the light from Primi's hand-held candelabra. The collection was the hobby of his father. Primi liked the cars, he said. He would keep them and look after them, but he didn't have his father's consuming passion for them.

'Except sometimes historically,' he said. 'Look at this.'

He lowered the candelabra to illuminate the interior of a powerful, bulbously designed, late thirties sedan, a Bugatti, perhaps, or an Alfa-Romeo. The dashboard was oak and the upholstery on all the seats was velvet, coloured in imperial purple.

'Franco gave one to every bishop in Spain once the Civil War was over,' he went on. 'Just a friendly personal present, but to remind them where their allegiance lay and where they owed their dues.'

Chuckling, he led us through to the dining-room.

Primi was both a gourmand and a gourmet. A sturdy hungry trencherman, he was also a passionate connoisseur of good food. To him that meant the cleanest, simplest, finest of local ingredients served with care, in their season, and at their best. As a defiant gesture of protest against the fast food restaurant conglomerates, he'd founded a maverick eating club called El Caracol, the snail. At Primi's table one ate very slowly – and very well.

He laid out the dishes, he handed us the knives to slice the various regional *salchichón* and *chorizo*, he put on an apron, and he asked us to get to work to help him.

We ate that evening as well as I've ever eaten in my life.

There was nothing fancy or elaborate or sauced. There were the simple honest meats and vegetables, the sweet fruits and tangy cheeses, of the Navarran countryside. The wild asparagus and the strange local artichokes in a light benison of cloudy emerald-green olive oil were a matter for dreams. It was a feast, given to us out of courtesy but almost with a carelessness – as if Primi were saying, how can anyone ever want to eat except like this?

And of course we drank.

We started with the year's vintage, oaken-red and warm and substantial. Then we ranged back. Primi opened bottle after bottle, selecting them from our birth dates or from his own favourite vintages. Our heads sang and our brains reeled. Primi vanished and reappeared in the crimson gown and feathered hat of a medieval troubadour. We drank again. Finally, reluctantly, Primi agreed to drive us home.

The Mercedes careered through the night along the bright and winding moonlit road. A *Guardia Civil* patrol car tried to follow us. Roaring with laughter Primi accelerated and left the police far behind. We reached Viana, tumbled out, embraced our host gratefully, and headed for the late-night bar near the pilgrim hostel.

Our key had been left with the 'dwarf' who washed the dishes. He was indeed a dwarf, tiny, red-headed, strutting like a little game-cock, and delighted to see us – escorting us to the *hostal* relieved him of at least fifteen minutes' plate-scrubbing.

We stumbled upstairs and collapsed on our bunks.

Priscilla had set her alarm clock for 5.00 a.m., less than three hours after we went to bed.

Within twenty minutes we were on our way. All of us were nursing hangovers from Primi's munificent hospitality, and we barely spoke. We set off across the flat industry-zoned plain towards Logroño. The thin pre-dawn light was grey and grainy with dust, the few trucks on the road still had their headlamps on, and the air was heavy with the night's dew.

It was the ugliest stage of the journey so far.

We tramped past brick and cement factories, round shallow lakes filled with brackish water and patrolled by a few weary herons, along narrow detour-lanes surfaced with powder-like sand and jagged stones. We circled diesel filling stations and graveyards for rusting automobiles. As the morning advanced, the hum of traffic increased until it drowned out the songs of the resilient local birds.

At midday we crossed the old stone bridge over the Ebro and entered Logroño. Logroño fits the model of what over the years I've come to recognize as characteristic of Spain's ancient cities — overlapping rings of dirt, squalor and tawdry urban sprawl enclosing a jewel at their centres. It holds good for the great towns of Andalucía: Sevilla, Granada and Córdoba. Set in a circular frame of grime and flaking concrete lies a small gay heart of glory and magnificence.

Logroño doesn't have an Alhambra or a Mezquita, the latter the shadowy bull's-blood-and-white-stone pillared Moorish temple which must be, even more than the fairy-cake pavilion of the Alhambra, one of the world's supreme man-made achievements. What Logroño has is a sturdy scatter of lovely fountains, mansions and fortified churches dating back to the Dark Ages. The streets and squares of the old town are paved in worn stone and are tranquil. They all belong to pilgrimage and they resonate with peace.

An old Logroño citizen, eighty or more, half-blind and leaning on a white stick, found us. He insisted on escorting us round his *pueblo*, that complicated word again but here meaning his home and hearth. He told us a good deal of truth and even more of what, I either guessed or knew, was pure nonsense. The Spanish, like any race of natural story-tellers, have never let fact or the established historical record come between them and a good tale.

'There he is,' the old man pointed up at a carving of St James on the tower of Logroño's main church, 'a true disciple of Jesu Cristo. The kindest, gentlest man who ever lived. A man of peace. And because of that, naturally a saint.'

Which Santiago no doubt was. The trouble was the carving showed him in his *matamoros*, his blackamoor-killing, mode with his sword drawn, an Arab's severed head impaled on the blade, and his rearing horse clearly eager to trample underfoot any other troublesome little Palestinian mercenary who got in his master's way.

'How serene, how gentle he looks,' Priscilla murmured politely.

The old man beamed. 'Ah, *señorita*, you have true sensitivity.'

I gave him five hundred pesetas for a couple of restorative brandies at the nearby bar. He hobbled away happily, and we headed out into the countryside to the south of the city.

Something had got into the two Amazons, Priscilla and Hilary, some charge of adrenalin-fed vigour.

They surged away in front of the other three of us, and within half an hour of leaving Logroño they were out of sight. My feet were not just suffering now, they were a constant lacerating source of pain, spilling blood through the welts of my shoes and making me wince each time a stone on the track impacted against the few remaining unburst blisters. Liz was in much the same condition. We hobbled along together. Angie kept us company.

As we walked through the arid heat of the afternoon, Liz and I tentatively spoke about our daughters. The deaths of children are tragic.

It was therefore a quiet speculative exchange, an interaction between two people who barely knew each other but who had a shared experience of what I'll now firmly call tragedy. The great Dr F. R. Leavis, my tutor at Cambridge and the intellectual guide to so many generations of undergraduates, used to insist the word 'tragedy' had to meet several conditions before it could be properly used: hubris, high birth, reckless-ness, talent and beauty, a challenge to the gods, were among them. They invited retribution. They invited the vengeful sword of fate.

Francesca met his criteria. She was flamboyant, well born, defiant and dangerous. She had extraordinary gifts, in words and paint. She was more beautiful, when she chose, than any woman has a right to be. She soared and she was cut down.

Yes, she met Leavis's conditions.

21

In the immediate aftermath of the massacre of the Dunblane children, I listened to an old woman being interviewed on the radio.

She too, a young war widow at the time, had lost her child, her only child, years before. Quietly, temperately and unintrusively, she'd devoted much of her life since to helping other parents facing the same experience. She was evidently much too wise to fall into the category that contemporary jargon labels 'counsellor'. She was just a mature and thoughtful old lady, one of those vanishing sea-anchors which stabilized the traditional support systems of European families.

Bleakly but compassionately, she made some telling points.

'There is no death like a child's,' she said. 'When a child dies the world ends. What's happened is contrary to nature. You can start again tomorrow, you have to start again, but you're embarking on a new and different life. Don't expect understanding or sympathy. No one except another parent who has shared the same grief will have any inkling of what you feel.'

The experience Liz and I shared allowed us to talk about matters that I, certainly, felt awkward and inhibited in discussing with other people. We both wanted our girls back. We wanted the untidiness, the scattered clothes and tights, the books and magazines left open – Fran, I can understand your reading *The Spectator* but what on earth is that gloomy intellectual shroud, the *Guardian*, doing by your bed?

We talked too about the respective services and I remembered Fran's putting to rest in that flinty little Sussex church. The hymns had been bellowed out with far more gusto, passion and blind choking grief than tuneful elegance. There'd been a certain pagan barbarity to the committal – rage and tears rather than soothing musical cadences. For a moment I felt in retrospect a certain embarrassment at the rawness of what we'd done.

*

Petunias.

They've never been one of my favourite flowers, but as we walked wearily into the conical village of Navarrete – it's heaped on a granite and clay pillar like a tiny dormant volcano – I stopped, startled. The cobbled streets and white-washed houses were silent and deserted. Outside every door in ranks of great earthenware bowls, spilling from window-boxes, cascading from pots, was the finest most exuberant display of petunias I'd ever seen.

Blazing scarlet, Schiaparelli pink, ice-veined white, coppery fire-yellow and translucent aquamarine blue, the flowers poured like spray from fountains on every side. A breeze-tossed rainbow of colour, a festival of blossom, enveloped us in the evening air. I'd never seen anything like it before. Spanish *pueblos* are traditionally decorated with geraniums. This was something strange and distinct.

Had an energetic silver-tongued travelling salesman in seeds passed that way, seduced the village's *señoras* with his descriptions of the delights in his packets, and unloaded his entire stock on them – to vanish with his empty van into the night? There was no one to ask.

We walked through the tumbling blooms and found the little hotel we'd booked into for the night.

The day had been dry and dust-filled, the air arid, the heat of the Logroño plain fierce, the stones on the tracks as sharp and jagged as ever. I limped upstairs and unlaced my shoes. Slowly and cautiously I unpeeled my socks from my feet. They were matted, saturated, with blood and sweat. I hobbled down the corridor, leaving a sorry set of oozing prints behind me, and cleaned myself up as best I could in the bathroom.

I made my way back to the room Hilary was sharing with Priscilla, and slumped down the floor.

Hilary looked at my soles horrified. Where blood wasn't seeping out, they were swollen with corrugated lumps of black and grey blisters. She didn't need to say anything, nor did I. We both knew that for me this stage of the journey was over.

'I'll find a cab in the morning,' I said. 'I'll take your packs with me and join you for lunch. Then I'll head back.'

Hilary nodded.

It wasn't a major change in our plans. I was due to return to Britain before the others anyway – I had long-standing Trust meetings to attend. All I was going to miss were two days of our long journey. It was still a frustrating and humiliating interruption.

Liz came into the room then. She settled herself stiffly on one of the beds. Her feet had been causing her pain, and her face was pale with tiredness and coated with the day's dust. She has great tranquillity of spirit and, although not one of life's natural travellers and explorers, immense physical and intellectual fortitude.

'How was the day?' Hilary asked.

'We talked about our daughters,' Liz replied.

Hilary glanced at me. 'I know you have faith, and you know I don't. Has your faith helped you?'

It was an intriguing question, not trivially posed – Hilary only asks questions to which she wants serious and considered replies. I thought about it.

'No,' I answered. 'Not one whittle or tittle, scrap or jot. Not the merest whisper on the wind or the faintest reflection from the stars. No comfort, no warmth, no consolation. The only God I know is an abiding, distant, immanent presence – funny and loving but utterly outwith our experience. He, or more likely She, framed the universe and keeps a benign abstracted eye on it. I accept that as a gesture of faith. Trying to understand and rationalize Him or Her is like trying to play golf with a corkscrew. Golf courses weren't designed to be played with corkscrews –'

I took a deep breath.

I glanced at the floor. Blood from my feet was staining the pine boards. In terms of a consideration of God, it was most appropriate. His Son's blood had been spilled everywhere. We were even asked to drink it each Sunday at communion.

'I like the little Palestinian,' I went on. 'I like carpenters. I like what they make with wood. I like Jews and a few, not many, Arabs. I think the Christ bedded down with the lovely Mary Magdalene – He'd have been a damn fool if He didn't. I like His fondness for wheat and grapes. I like the way He liked to go fishing. I like everything about Him, most of all His sanity, His generosity and gentleness, and his way with words –'

I stopped again.

'He'll find Fran very difficult. But they'll discuss the lovely kitchen table Ramón Sosa made for us in Spain – no nails or screws, all wooden dowels, as befits a true shipwright's work, and inset with Sevillan tiles – and they'll reach an accommodation, my daughter and the Son of God.'

'Is that a statement of faith?' Hilary asked.

'It's a statement of bruised and battered feet on the Pilgrim Way,' I answered.

I slept in late the next morning. It was almost 7.00 a.m. before I rose, and the others were long since on their way.

I took the village taxi out to meet them in the little town of Nájera for lunch. The driver, Joselito, a truculent bald Navarran with a scarred face, looked scornfully at the heavy packs as we heaved them into the back.

'What are your companions doing, *señor*?' he asked. 'Are they on pilgrimage or are they moving house?'

'They're women, José,' I answered.

'Women!' he snorted. 'No wonder! A proper woman's place is in the home, not out on the *Camino*.'

'Don't tell them that when we find them,' I said. 'You'll end up tarred and feathered, and probably knee-capped. Believe me, José, they're *muy seria*, these ladies. Also, what about St Teresa?'

'That's different. She was a bride of Christ.'

'This bunch are collectively Christ's mothers-in-law. Want to argue with them?'

He thought for a moment, chuckled and shook his head.

On the way José insisted on making a detour and showing me a derelict abandoned graveyard a mile or so from the village. Until we got there I couldn't understand why he was so keen I should see it. We walked in under a ruined arch and I realized.

Set into the eighteenth-century walls on either side of the gate, almost plastered against them like ancient postage stamps, were a number of carved sandstone panels. They'd been found, Joselito told me, in the retreating waters of the local river after a devastating flood a century ago had washed away the remains of a long-abandoned monastery.

The carvings were the boldest and most vivid I'd ever seen. They showed cantering horses, devils and satyrs, rampant sheaves of wheat and brimming bowls of fruit, naked human couples energetically coupling, baying wolves and hunting owls, and a huge man with a thick erect whatnot, as broad as a tree's span and reaching to his ribs, surveying them all with a grim grin.

It was a joyous, dangerous, subversive panorama of the delights of the flesh and the terrors of the spirit, Dionysian in its riotousness and somehow sweet and subtle in its rendering, although the acid rain of modern Castilla was starting to break down its clean outlines.

I whistled and shook my head in wonder at the sheer surprise of finding the frieze there.

'Santiago's sword!' Joselito tapped the giant's massive organ and laughed. 'Good seed from that. Fertilized most of Spain.'

We went on.

We found the Camberwell beauties in a little restaurant beside the river that threaded Nájera. I'd forgotten it was Sunday and the Christian feast of Whitsun. The streets were carpeted with rose petals and lacy grey-green branches of thyme that gave off a heady oily fragrance as one trod on them. We watched dancing children in maiden-white dresses embroidered with yellow flowers, and listened to the town's brass-and-wind bands as they paraded the cobbles.

We ate outside under an awning against the hot sun. We had simple country *tapas – albóndigas, calamares,* fried *pimientos,* a *tortilla de patatas,* all the counter-served dishes Spanish wayfarers know so well – and drank pitchers of the rough local wine. The river's waters were covered with rafts of tiny white lilies with coronets of golden stamens, just like the children's skirts.

I watched a school of trout nudging their way lazily through the reeds, and once a heron flapped by. Everything was quiet and gentle and contented. Everything apart from my feet. They burned and throbbed like a martyr's wounds.

The bus that was going to take me back to Logroño arrived. Accompanied by the others, I limped across the bridge to board it.

Their destination for this stage was Burgos, which they were to reach after overnight stops at Santo Domingo de la Calzada, Belorado and San Juan de Ortega. From Logroño I took a train to Bilbao. There was no flight to London until the following morning. I hailed a cab and asked the driver to take me to a simple but comfortable hotel where I could spend the night.

He took me to the hotel on the river where I'd stayed with my son Caspar's friends a year earlier before we joined him in Pamplona to climb the Pyrénées. I booked in. The hotel had some four hundred rooms. By some strange coincidence I was given the same room, 307, I'd shared with Charles the last time I'd been there.

I sat down and glanced at the telephone. It had only rung for me once on the previous occasion. The call had come from Francesca, somewhere in France on her way to Pamplona. She rang to check — she was always methodical in confirming arrangements — our arrival time the next day.

'Nicholas, Cas is coming in on the flight from Madrid arriving at nine.' I could hear her voice as clearly and vividly as if she were speaking now. 'It'll take you three hours from Bilbao. Please don't let the lads lead you astray and get you drunk. I want you there in one piece. I suggest Charlie drives.'

'Yes, Fran,' I said obediently.

One year later. Same city, same star-dappled river, same hotel, same room, same telephone. Only now the girl wasn't out there in Pamplona to call me. It was, I decided, a maudlin and unworthy reflection. I put it from my mind and went out to eat. The trouble was the only good restaurant I could find was the one Francesca had told me to eat in a year ago.

I looked at the menu and swore.

As I ate I thought of the only pilgrimage I'd made before, one that we'd done together. That too had been at Whitsun.

Letters to Francesca: 12

Do you remember the Rocío, Fran?

Of course, you do. How could any of us ever forget it? It was the first pilgrimage we made together, the only pilgrimage where you accompanied me in the living flesh and bone of a nine-year-old child rather than on this one, the Camino *to Santiago, as the unseen adult companion of my heart and mind.*

Rocío is a village lost in the marshes of the Guadalquivir river to the south-west of Sevilla. Sevilla was once capital not just of Spain but of the Spanish empire, the entire continent of South America. Up the Guadalquivir from the new world flowed a matching river of galleon-borne treasure, of gold and silver, emerald, amethyst and rubies, that made Spain briefly the richest nation on earth, and then as the wealth was recklessly squandered, it bankrupted the country.

The hamlet of Rocío barely noticed.

Rocío had its virgin, the blanca paloma, *the white dove of the marshes. The grim and stony-faced little lady was worth more than all the riches Columbus found — and the Genovese Italian-Jewish sea-captain was wise enough to delay his first epic voyage so his sailors could visit her shrine and pray to her for their safety before they set sail on the voyage over the edge of the world.*

The edge was Cape Finisterre, in sea miles just around the corner of the Iberian peninsula to the north-west. St James's body had been beached on one of Finisterre's coves. The two hamlets, the one in the marshy estuary, the other bordering the Field of the Star, had much in common.

The legend of the Rocío virgin, the white dove, is known to every Spanish child. In the early thirteenth century, a peasant farmer hunting the wild boar of the marshes stumbled on a wooden carving of the virgin in a thicket of gorse. The carving had clearly been hidden hundreds of years earlier to prevent its capture and destruction by the advancing tide of Arab invaders. The farmer tugged the effigy out of the thicket, heaved it on his shoulders, carried it for a time, and then, exhausted by the morning sun, dumped it on the ground and lay down to rest.

When he awoke, the virgin had vanished. The farmer tracked back and found her once again embedded in the thicket. The next day he returned with a group of his fellow-villagers. It happened again when they too tried to remove her and paused to rest in the summer heat. The virgin returned to what the Spanish call her *querencia*, the singular small space where, like a fighting bull on the open sand of the arena, she felt safe.

A shrine was built to her in the tangled reeds and scrub of the Guadalquivir basin. Over the centuries, again like the Field of the Star, the white dove began to attract visitors.

The pilgrimage to Rocío never rivalled the one to Santiago, but to her passionate adherents, and particularly to the fiercely proud Andalusians, the white dove of the marshes is just as potent a talisman as the carpenter's disciple. For all but five days of the year Rocío slumbers, a dusty and almost deserted huddle of lime-washed cottages and tethering posts wavering in the heat-hazed light's reflection under the southern Spanish sky in the loneliness of the delta.

And then Whitsun comes and for the five days and nights Rocío fills and erupts, strains and throbs and becomes delirious with music, dance and the dry white wine of Jerez in celebration of its virgin.

Like Pamplona in San Fermin, like Rio in carnival, it is one of the greatest parties in the world. From every compass-point the dove's admirers travel to honour her. They come in hermandads, *brotherhoods*, each with its own banner at the head of the column. Because they are Andalusians, and by definition the finest riders in the world, they travel on horseback escorting the ox-drawn waggons that carry their supplies. The men wear the leather chaps, short grey jacket and tilted sombrero of the southern working caballero, *the women perched behind them in the brilliantly coloured, polka-dotted skirts of the formal attire of Sevillan ladies. We proudly rode with them, members of the brotherhood of Sanlúcar de Barremeda.*

We headed off into the sinuously rolling dunes and pine forests of the river's delta. We had a scarlet cart with a canvas awning pulled by a tough and recalcitrant mule. Round us streamed a calvacade of riders on shining grey and chestnut horses. The horsemen would gallop towards us, check and *rear above the little platform seat where you were sitting. They'd scoop you up, whirl you round in their strong arms, place you on the saddle behind them, and gallop away again with you clinging to their backs. Later, sometimes hours later, they'd return you to the cart. Both you and the horseman would be laughing and panting.*

We slept beside fires in the warm and watery reaches of the delta. Owls called all night and bursts of fireworks lit the sky, and in the morning herds of deer and wild boar scattered before us. Throughout, day and night, there was dancing, the elegant formal patterns of the Sevilla arabesques that you and your sisters performed so well.

'Ai, que gracia!' the Sevilla ladies called as they clapped their hands in rhythm while you turned and shaped your wrists into swans' necks and snapped your fingers to the guitars and castanets.

And then, moving through the great tunnels of dust thrown up by the horses' feet, we came to Rocío in the tumult of its yearly festival. There was not even a chance of sleep now, only surging crowds and galloping riders, trumpets and more fireworks from dusk to dawn. We watched as the burly sons of the peasant farmers of Almonte paraded the white dove through the sand-floored streets. We went to one of the endless masses in the virgin's church.

We pinned on the dove's favours, a silver-gilt medallion hanging from a blue and white ribbon. We drank a last copa. We set off for home. Somewhere along the way, I can't remember where, we'd acquired a sturdy unsmiling lad, a native of the Sevillan slum of Triana, as our all-purpose deck-hand and mule-driver.

'Anda la mula!' he shouted as he cracked the whip over the sullen animal. 'Get on with it!'

Tangled in a heap with your brother and sisters on the cart's floor, neither you nor they heard the owls cry that night or the deer bark next morning. Cubs in the pack, you all slept exhausted until we reached the river.

It was the emblem of the white dove who'd led us that I placed on your coffin.

The past is another country.

I wonder.

I incline more to William Faulkner's view: 'The past is all we've got,' *he said. What of your past, Fran, what, for instance as we're considering pilgrimage, did you make of the Rocío that year? What do you remember best about the Rocío, I remember asking you as you lay in your hospital bed? The riders who swept you up? The fires and the fireworks? The dust and the dancing? The parades and the trumpets?*

You frown and think.

'That tortilla *Ana made to take with us,' you answer. 'And the* chorizo *we bought in Sanlúcar to eat with it.'*

I close my eyes in anguish. Then I open them and laugh and hug you.

Your priorities of course and, as always, you are right. You travelled the Pilgrim Way to Rocío, you danced to guitars and castanets and saw the cascading rainbows of fireworks and slept by fires, you rode pillion on galloping Andalusian stallions and attended the Virgin's mass to the sound of Almonte's trumpet-led band. And what do you remember best?

A cold potato omelette and a fiery wind-cured sausage.

The Palestinian carpenter suggested that bread be broken and wine drunk to celebrate what He stood for — wheat and vines, love and life. You agreed. You barely drank wine but you could make meals with the best.

The difficulty for me now is that I'm recalling the past, and I've no real time for that. I have to, in our constantly used phrase and at your urging, press on, press on. *A pilgrimage isn't done until it's done. Nor is the full story I promised you told.*

22

Priscilla and I flew to Madrid, and took the train to Burgos.

It was April again, the spring of the following year, and the start of the last stage of the journey which had begun three years before. By coincidence, the next day when we'd begin walking was 23 April, St George's Day, the anniversary of our departure. Hilary had travelled separately, in order to listen to the medieval plainsong sung by the monks in a monastery near Burgos. We were due to meet her at somewhere called Itero de la Vega, a name that didn't feature on any of my maps.

The train trundled north across the barren expanse of the Meseta, the great plain at the heart of Spain. At the end of our carriage was a video screen. A smartly uniformed young *señorita* came by with a trolley of drinks and complimentary earphones. I bought a chilled bottle of beer and plugged in. The film being shown was John Ford's *Mogambo* with Clark Gable and Grace Kelly. It's a magnificent movie, one I'd seen often before but I was delighted to see it again.

As I watched Gable boldly shooting his leopards and sardonically corralling his women, I pondered briefly on the incongruity of it all. Here was I, ostensibly travelling the ancient Pilgrim Way on foot and yet in reality drinking beer in a comfortable seat while I was carried at sixty miles an hour across the plain with twentieth-century technology providing me with entertainment.

And then, I thought, it wasn't so incongruous at all. Any sensible medieval pilgrim would always hitch a lift on a passing waggon. The beer was the same, well, probably stronger then. And as for the entertainment, there might not have been video screens and a muscular Clark Gable, but there were jugglers, *jongleurs*, and story-tellers – and they certainly didn't flicker or fall silent when the current wobbled as it did frequently on the train.

Styles and modes of passage change, but the core of things remains the same. It was, I thought, an acute insight and I leant over to communicate it to Priscilla. She was sleepy and grumpy and disinclined to listen. I went back to watching Gable embracing Grace Kelly against the background of my beloved Africa.

From Burgos we took a taxi. No one, not our driver nor any of the colleagues he consulted, had ever heard of Itero de la Vega, but the driver was game to try and find it. He set off confidently in the right general direction. As soon as we left the highway his confidence evaporated. Understandably. We'd entered a maze of rambling and unsignposted country lanes. Most of them were axle-deep in water.

Overhead the few scraps of open sky were blue, the shining luminous blue, the blackbird's-egg blue, of the skies when we left Le Puy. Framing the blue were great banks of dark cumulus cloud. They coiled and rolled and tumbled, threatening more of the rain with which they'd already deluged the Meseta by the barrel and bucket. And it wasn't soft or gentle rain, either.

'Nine months of winter, three months of hell,' as the Castilians wearily describe their landscape and home.

We had caught the backend of the Meseta's winter. In the days ahead as we climbed into the mountains the rain was to turn to hail, then sleet, then snow. For the moment it was just wet. The land was saturated. It exhaled and smelt of water. So did the dank damp air. It reeked of wetness from the brimming ditches, the sodden meadows, the puddled lanes.

As we made our way along them, our driver was seized by something close to panic. With the spray rising round us, he clenched the wheel, muttering and cursing as if he doubted he'd ever see Burgos again. Finally, to his immense relief, we found Itero. He dropped us off outside the church and roared away, his face set grimly, almost before I'd closed the door.

It wasn't surprising I hadn't been able to find Itero on the maps.

It wasn't a village, hardly even a hamlet, just a tiny cluster of dilapidated cottages lost in the damp and misty water meadows. A stocky grey-haired man with a hearing-aid was waiting outside the one little bar. This was Paco, a fellow-pilgrim Hilary had picked up and posted on the rutted street to watch out for our arrival.

Hilary herself was waiting inside the bar. The three of us embraced each other with laughter, companions brought together for the final time, persuaded the reluctant bar-owner's wife to make us a *tortilla española*, and sat down to discuss what lay ahead.

We'd given ourselves some twenty days to cover the last 500 kilometres. On paper it didn't look too challenging. As so often, what's written down in the comfortable warmth of a London drawing-room, even by seasoned travellers, can prove very different on the ground. The weather apart, we had to cross the mountains of León. Galicia beyond would be slightly warmer, but scoured by rain. We were carrying heavy packs. 'Rest' days – it would have been folly, for example, not to stop and see the glories of León – would eat into the schedule.

It was a daunting and demanding plan, although quite how demanding none of us realized as we crossed the street to our night's lodging at the *refugio*. Itero's pilgrim refuge was little more than a shed with a few stacks of the now-familiar iron bunks. Paco was asleep and snoring. His friend, an energetic little Majorcan named Jorge, was reading by torchlight.

I slid onto the evil-smelling straw-filled mattress on my bunk. Outside, the air hadn't only been dank but suddenly icily cold. Shivering all night, I slept little.

We left Itero in the chill grey light of dawn.

Within an hour a sharp easterly wind had risen and rain was falling, the keen piercing rain of a Meseta winter. The Pilgrim Way follows the course of a branch of the Pisuerga river. There was water everywhere. Above the turbulent fast-flowing thrust of the river, stippled and clamorous with the deluge, wet grey mist coiled and spun upwards into the clouds. Ankle-deep puddles, grainy with the clay undersoil, sucked at our boots. The branches of the trees were bowed under the water's weight, and the burgeoning grasses in the neighbouring meadows flattened.

We trudged on seeing no one.

There were a few farmhouses on either side of what was quickly becoming a torrent, but the good folk who lived in them had prudently decided to stay inside. At midday we reached Fromista, and slumped down, drenched and shaking, in the first bar we encountered. Hilary was pale and uncharacteristically quiet. I felt bone-chilled and wretched. Only Priscilla seemed buoyant. Her buoyancy, it turned out, was fleeting.

Under the rain, Fromista is a dull and tawdry little town, but close to its centre is one of the loveliest buildings I've ever seen. Its scale is small but in my mind it belongs with the greatest of all the world's religious monuments. Scarcely larger than a chapel, it ranks with Chartres, Winchester, Salisbury and St Paul's. Pale and clean, it has a nobility, a serenity, a scale, a balance and proportion, inside and out, that take one's breath away. The carvings that adorn its pillars are magnificent, both lusty and elegant.

From that moment on I stopped being sardonic about the cold, empty and crumbling buildings we passed. I paused and glanced at them all. Unfortunately, jewels like Fromista's are, well, jewels, few and rare and far between. There were no more than a handful until we reached Santiago.

We set off again.

Hilary's face was not so much pale now as grey. The cold and wet of her journey from Burgos to Itero had entered her bones as the chill of the water meadows had entered mine. She walked more and more slowly, and then began to stumble. When we reached the next village she decided she couldn't go on.

Our destination for the night was the small town of Carrión de las Condes. Priscilla suggested Hilary should hitch a ride there and that I should accompany her, while she walked on. I agreed gratefully. The first car we hailed swung in and stopped. The driver was a photographer, his companion a young priest from the monastic foundation based on La Valle de los Caídos, the burial place and memorial to the late 'most general', Francisco Franco.

Hilary was feeling giddy and ready to vomit. What mattered was getting her to Carrión de las Condes, and into bed. As soon as we reached the town, we tucked her into a familiar iron bunk in the pilgrim *refugio*. The kindly priest in charge of Carrión's church, alongside which the refuge nestled, fetched her extra blankets and she fell asleep.

Several hours later in the early dusk Priscilla arrived. She'd completed the day's journey on foot, but she was to pay a harsh penalty for it.

The rain of the Meseta's tail-end winter had set in hard. A chill easterly wind with a knife-edge cut to its gusts was scouring the plain. Priscilla was wearing shorts. When she walked into the refuge her sturdy legs were tinged blue and corrugated with goose pimples, and her muscles were seizing up with cramp. The cold of the Castilian plateau had got to the marrow of her. We were all suffering.

We all slept fitfully.

It was a sorry, tattered and weary trio that set out next morning. The wind was waspish, tugging and plucking, teasing and irritable, bitterly cold one moment, almost benign the next. And then the sun rose and the temperature soared and we walked. We walked and walked through an arid sun-glazed and toasted and oven-baked landscape as flat as a billiard table, except there was no nice green nap to it, only jarring pebbles underfoot and whining hornets and the occasional sentinel tree — so rare they were marked on the map.

'Nine months of winter, three months of hell.'

The saying came back again. The Castilians have my sympathy. I thought of my home, certainly my heart's home, in the green and silver sea-ringed isles of the Hebrides. We could do without the Meseta's winter months there but the months of hell, of baking sun, we could certainly make use of them.

Terradillos de los Templarios really shouldn't be there at all. It's a nothing, a fragment of habitation, a tiny forlorn cluster of ochre-coloured adobe-built birds' nests somewhere on the Pilgrim Way. The winter rains should have swept the village away long ago. They haven't. Against all odds and all probabilities, Terradillos survives — although not by much. The pilgrim refuge, rather more sturdily built than the mud-walled dwellings on the muddy lanes round it, sits at the entrance to the hamlet.

Once again we were caught up in a little caravan of fellow-pilgrims whose journey rhythm coincided with ours. They arrived one by one or in pairs. There was the stocky, ebullient, pot-bellied Jorge, a restaurant owner from Palma in Majorca, and his grey-headed friend, the carpenter Paco. They spoke together in Majorcan, took long open-air siestas after their magnificent lunches whatever the weather – neither snow, gales nor sun disturbed them – quarrelled ferociously, laughed uproariously, and were fine companions.

There was Luc, a middle-aged homosexual Belgian who'd dyed his hair orange and hadn't the slightest idea where he was, how he'd got there, or what he was doing. Helmut, a shy German body-builder in his early twenties who washed his clothes whenever he could – three times a day, he said, was his ideal. Strength through Joy, and cleanliness, lives on in Bavaria, as it did with our now-absent friends in their *lederhosen* from two years before. And there was the French-Alsatian couple, Christiane and Serge.

Serge, the quiet patient husband, was Christiane's minder. Christiane was a handful or rather several hands'-ful, and certainly filled poor Serge's hands until they overflowed in desperation. She was a dietitian, a biologist, a civil servant who'd lost her job through 'devilish intrigue' and, most important of all, a 'Christique'. I hadn't encountered the Christique cult before. I asked her to explain it.

'We are Christ,' she said. 'We identify totally with Him. He becomes us, we become Him. His sufferings are ours, ours are His. He and we are inseparable. I am His presence on earth, He is mine in what lies beyond. We cannot be divided.'

Pain and suffering lay at the core of Christiane's belief.

She had problems with her feet and legs, sores and blisters and inflamed tendons. The worse the problems were, the happier she became. Each agonizing stab, each eruption of blood, each torn muscle, brought her closer to the carpenter's son. She would, I realized, have welcomed crucifixion with the same enthusiasm as other pilgrims on the Way would have greeted a hot dinner.

Happily Christiane was also French and by upbringing a country-woman. On the way to Terradillos she'd gathered a basket of St George's mushrooms. She asked the refuge-owner to cook them as part of our supper. He recoiled and refused point-blank. To most Spaniards all mushrooms are toxic and the fruits of the devil. Anyone who eats fungi is sure to die – and where would his business be then?

Christiane shouted and raged. The owner backed away, grudgingly allowing her – entirely at her own responsibility – to cook them herself.

If anyone else ate them they were, in his unspoken judgement, suicidal fools. Christiane tossed and fried them with olive oil and presented them in a light little omelette. They were superb.

Dear passionate Christiane, with her obsession about the wounds inflicted on the Son of God, and her long-suffering husband who tended to her needs and carried the bags behind her. I hope she gives him a gold watch after twenty-five years' patient service, as British Railway porters used to be given. Yet I have a feeling she would be happier as a biologist and cook – the smile on her face when she served up the mushrooms was as radiant as the refuge owner's scowl was dark and suspicious – than as a self-mutilated Christique.

'Good woman, that,' Jorge the restaurateur said as we finished our wine after supper. 'But needs a sharp slap on the *culo*.'

23

We went on.

It was winter cold when we rose and set off, and then suddenly the sun lifted over the Meseta and for the midday hours our clothes were sodden with sweat. We passed through the drab little town of Sahagún, its streets cramped, its people furtive and mean-looking, its bars reluctant to offer us anything except slabs of coarse potato *tortilla*.

All that redeemed the place were gleaming brass replicas of the *concha*, the pilgrim shell, set in the pavements and sidewalks. They confirmed the direction of our journey, they pointed us on our way. We headed out into the countryside. The plain was bare and barren. We turned off the truck-laden, diesel-stenched highway onto a newly created pilgrim path.

The path must have been the idea of an imaginative young planner in some office of the city fathers. He clearly wasn't a walker himself. Underfoot the surface was covered with lumpy pebbles. It was one of the most taxing, uncomfortable, ankle-jarring surfaces I'd ever travelled across. The path was lined with newly planted trees, alders and limes. They'd been put there to provide shade. One day those that survived probably would do just that, although many of them were dead or dying. For now they were nothing more than random vertical scraps of hesitant vegetation.

Every mile or so there was a municipal picnic area. A cluster of elephant-grey concrete benches surrounding a dowdy concrete table. They looked almost unbearably forlorn, designed not even by a committee but by its progeny, an unhappy and dyslexic camel. No one clearly had ever used them. Only the wild flowers found any purpose in them as they coiled round and up their pathetic pillars.

Yet the path and its themed areas were the way of the future, the Way of St James to come. Families with their portable CD-players, their ice creams – Häagen-Dazs was available even in dowdy Sahagún

– their photo-friendly journals – *Hullo!* magazine was of course born in Spain as *¡Hola!* – would come and invade and colonize the path. It's trivial and patronizing – not to say profoundly politically incorrect – to complain.

Yet as I tramped along – my feet were bleeding and painful again – I thought of all the pilgrims who'd trodden the Way before me. The saintly and the bandits, the holy and the scoundrels, the passionate and the cynical. Häagen-Dazs and concrete benches didn't square with any of them. They didn't square with me.

Hilary was somewhere ahead, Priscilla a long way behind. I plodded on, hot and fretful in the afternoon sun. Towards evening I came to the scrappy little village of El Burgo Ranero, a tiny dusty handkerchief of cottages tossed down on the plain. The pilgrim refuge looked imposing. Even if its walls were adobe, stained the colour of ripe old peaches, at least it was tidy and modern and clean.

The reality was somewhat different.

The showers spat and muttered. The walls turned out to have been made of damp cardboard. The wind from the plain penetrated every crack and crevice. By the time the sun dropped, I knew we were in for a chilling night. I found the refuge's *guarda*, a handsome and sympathetic grandmother. In Spain I learnt long ago one can only be bold. Weasel-words, cautious excuses, delicate explanations, cut little ice and touch none of the Castilian or Andalusian rock that informs the spirit of the Iberian Celtic people.

Timorous complaints are taken for what they are – ignominious whimpers of a feeble spirit. Extravagance, fantasy, cascading tears of distress, are something completely different. Entirely alien to modern Anglo-Saxon urban life, they remain for the Mediterranean peoples the stuff of existence, the poetry and condition of living. They are real.

I told her I'd been a poorly struggling child from birth. I said I had a clan of dependants, including an infirm near-blind wife. The survival of all of them depended on me – and I wasn't sure I was going to make it through the night. I urgently needed protection and covers against the cold. As a writer I was, of course, a skilled and experienced liar, a wonderful deceiver and teller of fibs. But this time I was telling the truth.

The north wind had risen. The Meseta night was going to be icy. In the cardboard and adobe dwelling my blood was going to curdle with the chill.

The *guarda* was a true Castilian, who understood the plain's weather, and, bless her, was sympathetic to my plight. She went away and returned with a collection of carpets and rugs she'd unearthed in her attic. They were the dustiest, filthiest, most flea-ridden scraps of odds and ends of cloth I'd ever seen. Not even the most impoverished passing tinker would have thought of trying to unload them at a car-boot sale.

But they were warm. I piled them under and over my slatted bed. I coated myself in them. Ancient faded tapestry, stinking of urine, was my bed linen. I scratched and itched for days afterwards, but at least I slept.

From El Burgo we headed to León.

It was still the Meseta, flat and bleak and barren. The three of us started to drift and separate. I was briefly buoyant that day, striding easily and confidently ahead. Hilary lagged behind me; Priscilla, stubborn and defiant as always, trailed limping in our wake.

We gathered at Mansilla de las Mulas, a strangely claustrophobic and oppressive little town. León, only ten miles away, was our destination for the night. After a short but acerbic argument, Priscilla and I decided to take the bus into the city – the approaches were urban and ugly. At first Hilary opted to walk but at the last moment she changed her mind and came with us on the bus. In León we found a small hotel near the cathedral, and we had a time of delight.

León's cathedral is not Chartres. It doesn't have Chartres' bleak and fragile methods of addressing God and the sky, the shifting watery underpinnings – Chartres floats on water like Salisbury, it's more of a ship than a cathedral – and the trout-swimming presence of the streams that flow by it. It lacks Winchester's towering fortress-like magnificence and Rufus the Red's blood on the stones. It doesn't waver and hover like Ely, a dreaming mist-cloaked cloud of stone above the Fens. Paris's Notre Dame resounds far more with history, silent trumpets echo the names of those who've used it as a platform, a launching-pad for their careers, or, more simply, just as a place for sanctuary and prayer.

Vienna's Stefansdom, my favourite of all, is Europe's still-burning candle of faith. St Peter's in Rome, that massive acknowledgement to *pierre, pedro*, the rock on which Christianity was built, is fine in its way. It's still not Chartres, the crowning pinnacle of all the wonderfully strange architectural achievements of the Middle Ages – how on earth did the masons and carvers, the planners and glaziers, come up with that magical palace?

León doesn't rank with the cathedrals I've known all my life. Yet it's still fine, it's bold and haunting and beautiful. The three of us gathered there as the sun was setting. We stood shoulder to shoulder in the nave. The sun dipped over the city. It flooded, it irradiated, the great west rose window. There was light everywhere, dazzling light, rose and crimson, lemon and gentian-blue, honey and barley and emerald. I couldn't handle the sheer incandescence of what was being hurled at me.

I walked away.

I emptied the candle box – the verger had to come and fill it behind me – and lit every one. Then I knelt and prayed. Take the girl, I said in my mind: you, the carpenter's son, are welcome to her. Welcome to her dark eyes, her tempestuous rages, her boldness and her brilliance. Take the woman off my mind and out of my hair. What do I need a daughter like that for? Far too fierce, far too dangerous. She's yours. Enjoy, enjoy, as our cousins, the Americans, say. But please just take her away. I want no more business with her.

And then as so often I cried.

We had a splendid evening.

Hilary treated us to several bottles of vintage white Navarran wine in the glorious Monastery of St Mark, built by Isabella and Ferdinand as a pilgrim hospital and now one of the world's great hotels. We prowled the stately corridors and cloisters, but were soon chased away by important flunkeys in uniforms.

Were we part of the group? We were our own somewhat raggedy group of three. Had we been invited to that evening's important function? No, not exactly. In which case, out – or back to the public bar where at least we can relieve you of some of your cash. And, yes, we do take credit cards if you're short of folding money.

We finished our wine. We went out and stood in the dusk among the roses gazing up at one of the most majestic Renaissance façades in Europe, all balance and elegance and dark heather-honey-coloured stone with the impetuous flourishes of the architect thrown in, little colonnades and peeping windows, shields of rock and mischievous adornments. So much of Spain's history is carved in stone for all to read.

We ate fish that evening.

It was a sweet, fresh, white-fleshed bass, trawled up somewhere off the Galician coast. The Spanish, even those of the dusty inland Meseta, love their fish. One of the most abiding memories of anyone who, like myself, has driven thousands of miles along Spain's highways, must be the grinding trucks leaking water behind them as they make their daily deliveries of the sea's gathering to the cities.

A few years ago I was sitting on the tiny pier at Ulva Ferry on Mull in the Hebrides when I heard the sound of an approaching truck. I looked round. It was a Spanish fish truck and it carried an SE – Sevilla – number plate. I talked to the Andalusian driver. He told me he came up to the Hebrides every two weeks throughout the summer to collect the crustaceans the islanders wouldn't eat. He transported them back to southern Spain, and delivered them to bars and restaurants along the coast. Before there were trucks, the fish was carried by mule.

He'd been doing it for years. One of his drop-off points on his return was the Bar Marinero in Tarifa, the southernmost point of Europe. During the many years we lived in Andalucía, little Tarifa with its lighthouse and crumbling Moorish-built walls facing Africa had been our home town. The Bar Marinero was our local 'pub', the place we went to on Saturday nights for *tapas*, shellfish and *copas* of *vino de Jerez*, of sherry.

The *tapas* and the *copas* might have come from Spain, but the shellfish I discovered had always been mine. They came from Mull.

In the morning I bought a thick woollen jersey and a sleeping-bag.

We were heading for the mountains, there was snow ahead, and the cold was going to become even sharper. We gathered for lunch in the bar of the grandly named Hôtel de Paris. No pre-arrangement or rendezvous had been made but one by one the members of our latest band of pilgrim-companions drifted in: the Christique Christiane with her silent husband, the ebullient little Majorcan restaurateur Jorge, his grey-haired carpenter friend Paco – and a couple of Germans, new acquaintances and still warily regarded like the unknown family of one of one's children's spouses.

Somehow the fellow-travellers of the *Camino*, like spies, like members of the resistance in an occupied country, instinctively know where to find each other. We huddled together and studied maps. We discussed plans and possible safe-houses ahead. Then we parted and set off again.

24

We left León in the late afternoon.

We walked to the station, found we'd just missed the last train which would take us out through the suburbs to where we planned to continue on foot, and hired a taxi instead. Hiring taxis to carry us even for a few kilometres always made Hilary bristle and protest. She was like a good old-fashioned gardener. The earth had to be dug deep by fork or it wasn't properly done. In our case that meant the path had to be covered with boots on the ground.

The very few occasions when we did use transport I christened Hilary's little tragedies.

'This one's so tiny you don't even have to ignore it,' I said. 'It fell off the edge of the table without you noticing. Pile in.'

She sniffed the diesel-laden air, looked at the concrete and convoys of container trucks churning out their fumes in front of us, and reluctantly agreed.

The driver dropped us off on the far side of León, and we walked for a few hours as the sun fell. Unfortunately there was no choice except to keep to the main road. Apart from the roar and whine of the traffic it was a lovely evening stroll. The soft western light shone in our faces, a gentle wind from the distant Atlantic cooled us, the verges were starting to blossom with wild flowers.

Towards evening we came to Villadangos de Páramo, an ugly straggling village on the highway but with a fine new pilgrims' *hostal* in charge of a delightful woman named Rosalie.

'How good to have British *peregrinos* here, but how sad so few of you come this way,' she said as she searched through the register to see when the last Briton had been by.

She couldn't find one for months. 'Tell me about your country. Tell me about your wonderful Senora T'atcher. Now there's a woman all the world admires.'

I swallowed and did my best.

Apart from Ramón we had the *hostal* to ourselves. Ramón was a fat, swarthy and evil-smelling young man, the stench of sweat and garlic lifting like steam from every pore. He came from Granada and claimed to be a student. He was shifty and penniless, and he had a sackful of improbable stories to tell. If he did come from Granada – and he certainly had an Andalusian accent – his home was almost certainly somewhere in the gypsy dwellings on Sacro Monte, one of the red hills that surrounds the Alhambra.

Priscilla's warning antennae, like those of a moth at the approach of a hunting owl, flared. When we went out for supper, she insisted we locked our packs and took all of our saleable goods – our cameras and binoculars, passports and credit cards – with us. She checked all of our possessions as soon as we got back. Everything appeared to be still there.

Ramón was asleep. The smell coming out from his cubicle was something between the stench of an abattoir and the raw fungoid aroma of a rugby league team's changing-room before the cleaning ladies had come in and sluiced down the tiles.

We opened every window in the place.

The next day across the Meseta was hot and long and dusty. Hilary and I strode ahead; Priscilla, still struggling, was a long way behind us. We crossed the magnificent rippling and cobbled Roman bridge at the little town of Hospital de Orbigo, arch after arch spanning the now shallow river – its waters have been divided, sluiced and plundered to irrigate the surrounding farmlands – and waited for her to catch up with us.

While we waited, Hilary went off and bought an immense sweet loaf coated in glazed sugar from the village's baker. It served us for both breakfast and lunch. Priscilla limped in. We ate the loaf accompanied, in my case, by several glasses of the light Spanish draught beer which has, at its best, a foam at the glass's top and a clean golden sparkle to the liquid inside. Then we headed on.

Towards evening under dark gathering clouds and spats of rain we came to Astorga. Astorga is strange and interesting. One of the great way-stations on the pilgrim road, it lies at the foot of the León mountains with their often snow-covered peaks rearing above it. It thrives, or now more probably survives, as it's done for centuries on wool and its carpet- and rug-making enterprises. The farmers from the surrounding countryside bring in the fleeces from their flocks. The Astorga merchants deal in them and the town's manufacturers turn them into goods.

It's somewhat like Wilton in Wiltshire, the eighteenth-century centre of Britain's carpet industry. Unlike Wilton, it has a cathedral, a massive but grim and sombre building; a bishop's palace designed by the catherine-wheel and roman-candle Barcelonan architect, Gaudí, in one of his more restrained planning moods – maybe the bishop's bursars tugged the purse-strings tight when they saw the plans; and a cluster of bars, pavement cafés and restaurants – a couple of them devoted to Maragato food.

I had never heard of the Maragatos before. They are a curious and interesting folk, quite distinct from the Castilians and probably descendants of some ancient branch of the Romany people. For centuries they had a reputation as bandits and cut-throats, preying on pilgrims and the locals alike. Today, still distinct from the Spanish but quickly diminishing in numbers, they have become something of a cultural oddity.

By chance a family of three, father, mother and child, all dressed in traditional Maragato costume – the man in pantaloons, the woman and daughter in embroidered skirts – were in the pharmacy when Priscilla went in to buy something. I tried to talk to them but their Spanish was stilted and awkward, and they were shy and evasive. They got into an old pick-up van and vanished. The clock on the town hall wall struck the hour and there, in a sense, they were again – carved figures dressed exactly as these ones had been, beating out the hour at the top of the tower.

We joined up for dinner that night with two new companions on the Way, two young Swiss women named Caroline and Christine or 'Kinou' as the latter preferred to call herself, using her childhood nickname. They were about thirty, university-educated with business school diplomas, smart, chic, equally fluent in English and French, and earning large salaries as executives with the European Commission in Brussels. In spite of all their talents and achievements and money, something was missing from their lives.

Guardedly they told us of love affairs that had soured, of difficulties with their parents, of careers which for all the rewards they offered didn't really satisfy them. They had heard of the *Camino* and decided to test it. Both had been drained but entranced by the experience, Kinou in particular.

'I'm seriously considering giving up everything,' she told me as we walked back to the *hostal* in the dark. 'I've never known anything like this. It's so rich, so fulfilling. I may become a pilgrim for the rest of my life.'

It was a delightful child-like declaration, naïve yet full of goodwill and hope. I didn't confront her, point out she'd never carry through her ambition, or add she'd be a pilgrim for the rest of her life anyway. Instead I asked her mischievously if she had any frocks by Givenchy.

'Of course.'

'Then when you do set out on the road for ever,' I replied, 'parcel them up and send them to me. You won't need them on the Way, but my daughters are the same size as you. They'll wear them happily in memory of your previous incarnation.'

She laughed. 'It's a promise.'

The mountains were ahead.

Priscilla brought us a *pain au chocolat* at a bakery open conveniently early, and we tramped on. Rain was in the air but the start of the morning was warm and sun-filled, and as soon as we left Astorga the scents in the air were sweet. We made a detour to visit a village named Castrillo de Polvazares which had been a post on the Pilgrim Way. Virtually abandoned for several centuries, it was being restored and renovated as an arts and crafts colony.

The little houses were delightful, golden-walled, their doors and window-frames freshly painted, and with the medieval stone flags and cobbles of the streets clean and weed-free. Yet the place was silent and melancholy enveloped it. Our voices and the clatter of the rare horse's hoofs echoed mournfully. The village needed to be filled with people and bars and children and laughter, with the whole dynamic of a human community. Maybe one day it will be, but I was glad to move on.

We began to climb.

We could see the late snows above us. The vegetation became darker, more cramped and coiled into itself as we moved upwards. A northerly wind blew over us. On the plain it would have been welcome and refreshing; here it carried a chill edge to it. In the mid-afternoon at the height of some 3,500 feet we reached our destination, the village of Rabanal del Camino.

I like to think I'm not a chauvinist. I've travelled much of the world, I brought up my children to speak several languages and educated them in several countries, I'm an honorary Zulu and an honorary Nepalese sherpa. The trouble is experience has taught me that when the British decide to do something, they do it better than any other nation on earth.

The pilgrim *hostal* in Rabanal was adopted by the London-based Confraternity of St James. It was a ruin when they took it over. The Confraternity cleared the grounds, raised the walls again, restored the *hostal* to its former state – simple but elegant and comfortable – and now run it with the dictatorial efficiency of the Empire. The bunk-beds are clean and comfortable. The showers are hot. A comforting log fire burns in the communal living-room on chill evenings. There's an excellent small library to be consulted, a resident warden – when we were there the helpful and knowledgeable Alison – breakfast from dawn onwards, nowhere else were we offered that.

Being British there are rules, of course. No smoking, the puffers had to go out and light up behind the bushes. No sex, naturally: an exuberant young Swedish couple had to share their embraces in the same bushes wreathed in Spanish smoke. And many more prohibitions – no this, that or the other, particularly if it involved fun or love or laughter. But the place works. It has discipline, confidence and energy in honouring its vision of the Pilgrim Way.

The Empire is alive and well and living in a tiny village in the León mountains – and all three of us, like those of our companions from the lesser breeds without the law, felt grateful and privileged that someone was still shouldering the white man's or woman's burden.

The splendid Rabanal did us fine. In my prayers that night I mentioned Cecil Rhodes, Rudyard Kipling and Enoch Powell. My goodness, those fellows knew how to create a worthwhile legacy.

25

It rained throughout the night and although the downpour slackened in the early hours, it was still drizzling when we left Rabanal.

We climbed through mist and cloud to where an iron cross marks the head of the pass. A huge cairn surrounds the cross. Traditionally every pilgrim adds a stone to the cairn. A lifelong opponent of cairns for the way they impose on and disfigure the natural contours of wild landscapes, I declined to make a contribution. Priscilla and Hilary were too damp and tired even to think about it.

On the way up to the pass we went by a little stone cottage. A man in a brown cloak ran out ringing a goat's bell. Hilary and I waved but walked on. Priscilla, still straggling behind us, stopped and went into the cottage. It housed, she told us later, a little hippy commune, a forlorn relict of the flower children of the sixties. They survived by selling coffee, scrolls and odds and ends of artefacts they'd made to passing pilgrims. Sitting by the fire was the plump young Ramón, the foul-smelling gypsy from Granada we'd met several days earlier. Somehow he'd found his way there and installed himself among them.

He jumped up beaming when Priscilla walked in and held something out to her.

'Your brother must have left this by mistake in Villadangos,' he said. 'I found it in the dustbin. Please return it to him.'

It was the useless little sack in which the manufacturers had somehow managed to cram the sleeping-bag I'd bought in León – useless unless one had three Turkish wrestlers to heave, kneel, strain and pack it away again. I'd dumped it in the hotel bedroom's waste-basket. Hilary with her magpie eye had spotted it and pulled it out.

'You can't throw this away, for heaven's sake,' she said. 'It may come in useful some day.'

I didn't argue. You don't argue with Hilary. I took it from her and then, when I knew she wasn't looking, I put it in the bin once more. And now this wretched gypsy had retrieved it *again*. I sighed. I took it from Priscilla. It was clearly the albatross round my neck. I put it in my pack. I still have the damn thing.

We began our descent from the pass.

The wind was cold, and became colder and colder. All round us were gulfs and valleys, mountains and snowfields. For a moment the sun came out. On a high upland farm, at the furthest extent of the transhumance pastures, I glimpsed a small white galloping horse, cows the colour of Hebridean peat smoke, faded velvety acorn-brown, and calves with chiming brass bells round their necks.

The clouds returned and the descent became steeper. I was tired and my knees were aching and I started to shiver. We reached the village of El Acebo two-thirds of the way down the mountain, and went into the bar. At the bar's centre was a wood-fired metal stove. The local farmers and labourers came in with their midday stew-meals in pans. They heated the pans on the stove, bought a bottle of wine, and ate. It was obviously a workable form of trade for both sides – the bar-owner and his customers.

Hanging on the bar's walls were a number of crudely printed posters and pamphlets. I studied them while the bar-owner, his wife and his daughter watched me anxiously.

I've never been exactly sure what pornography is. Even my old friend Ken Tynan, a lifelong student of the matter, was stumped until he decided there was no such thing. The law with good intentions but all the dexterity of two babies trying to pass a rattle between them describes it as material with 'a tendency to deprave and corrupt'. I wonder. But if pornography does exist, then this was hard-core stuff. This was real filth. I certainly wouldn't have allowed my wife or servants to read it – not that I can stop Elisabeth doing anything, nor do I have any servants.

The famous flood-gates burst open within months of Franco's death. For half a century, with the connivance of the Roman Church, sex wasn't merely unmentionable in Spain – it didn't happen at all. All births in the growing population were tacitly attributed to immaculate conception. And then suddenly when the little man with the moustache was carried up to the great censor's office in the sky, flies were unzipped, blouses unbuttoned, and knickers dropped like confetti.

People began to make love. If they didn't, they could at least read about physical coupling. Sex can be difficult and challenging, wonderful but messy and perhaps leading to all sorts of other complications, children and lifelong entanglements for example. What does one do confronted by difficulties and challenges? Humanity's good fairy left laughter as a present in our cradle. We use it to make jokes about sex.

I turned from the walls. The anxious gaze of the three was still on me. Had I been reading filth? Or were the pamphlets nothing more than robust and riotous jokes that Chaucer's Wife of Bath, no sluggard herself in the ways and means, the stratagems along the way to the final panting delights of sexual congress, would have enjoyed and shared with her companions?

I laughed. 'Give me a *caña* on the house, and I won't tell the *guardia*.'

I got my free glass of beer but the bar-owner smiled as he handed it to me.

'You don't need to tell the *guardia*,' he said. 'Everything you've read came from them.'

We went on, Priscilla and Hilary ahead now.

For a few hundred yards I hitched a lift on an ox-drawn cart. The oxen had dark patient eyes and scything horns the colour of Cornish cream. The owner, an old peasant farmer, took me into the stable below his house and showed me how to remove and replace the animals' yoke. The house at the far end of the village was like all the others there. A tiny balconied top floor rested above the animals' quarters. The cattle gave heat that rose upwards to warm the family in winter, dung to fertilize the fields, milk for the dairy, muscle to draw the carts, and fine if sinewy meat when their life-span was over. It was a thoroughly satisfactory arrangement, place and people and animals fitting well together.

I took to the road again.

It spiralled down from the high ridge above. There were cuckoos calling and larks singing, banks of white wild cistus rose and drifts of ivory broom. The clouds rolled away, the sun appeared, the air was sweet-scented and warm. It was a magnificent afternoon to walk the

Camino. The trouble was my knees ached and throbbed, and my feet were leaden. We'd already gone too far, too fast, and the most demanding days of the journey still lay ahead.

I lay down and slept for a while. Then I heaved my pack onto my shoulders and, stumbling, headed on. I just made it to Molinaseca, 'the village of the dry mill', which was to be our night's sleeping quarters, but when I crossed the stone bridge over the river and discovered the pilgrim *hostal* was a mile further on still, I thought the hell with it.

I went into the bar at the end of the bridge, threw the pack to the ground, and asked not just for a *caña* but a whole jugful, a whole *jarra* of beer. The pitcher came and I slumped myself across the table staring at it.

What on earth was I doing?

The steam was seeping out of the journey as it might have done from an old rusting railroad engine whose plates were cracking. Worse, the steam was seeping out of me. I went outside and did some limbering exercises to try to loosen my joints, my knees and elbows and hips. I raised the pack again and set off for the *hostal* once more. I arrived reeling like a drunk.

The *hostal* was in what had once been a church. Priscilla and Hilary had already made camp on the upper floor. The air was beginning to chill and Hilary, using all her formidable armoury of charm, wiles and guiles, persuaded the guardian to light a fire.

I drifted into sleep with the firelight flickering below.

The morning was damp and grey with the constant threat of rain.

We walked through a soft undulating countryside of farms and vineyards, uninhabited, it seemed, apart from colonies of storks. On the way was Ponferrada, another great staging-post on the pilgrim path with a ruined Templars' castle, a fine clock-tower, and a cluster of ancient buildings. The city fathers, in a lavish brochure, proudly claim Ponferrada is one of the great undiscovered glories of Spain.

They may well be right. It is certainly still prosperous and energetic. But fruitlessly searching its streets in a dank mist for a café that would give us a breakfast roll and coffee, I felt I would sooner be in Granada, Sevilla, Córdoba or Ronda. The Andalusian cities may not be on the pilgrim route but at least they know how to cater to the wayfarer.

The pleasant modest country town of Cacabelos lies in wine-making country some twelve kilometres to the north-west. We arrived to find it in *feria* with a huge street market, and a horse fair. Once Cacabelos had been home to no less than five pilgrim hospices. All of them have long since vanished but the tradition of hospitality for pilgrims survives in a *bodega*, the Moncloa, at the town's entrance, where a pretty young woman gave us wine and thick slices of pie and then kisses as we left.

We wandered the thronged market.

I bought a canvas hat from a merchant who came from the Picos de Europa, a wooden cup, some of the season's first salty olives, a bagful of *churros* filled with delicious custard, thick and yellow, and a little brass goat's bell for my staff.

Hilary, a musical expert who spends many of her days at Glyndebourne or Covent Garden, complained the bell was out of tune, it was A flat sharp or sharp flat A or B-minus or something – the poor little object might have been being graded for an exam and miserably failed to pass. To me it just sounded jolly and familiar, a robust chime of the countryside, but she refused to walk with me unless I removed it. Which of course I did.

As I'd learned and have mentioned before, Hilary is not someone to be argued with – whether over God or bells.

It was three o'clock, we were hungry, and there were *pulpos*, squid. To me, it was one of the great gastronomic experiences of the journey – not just for the taste, although it was magnificent, but for the whole street-theatre of their preparation. Fierce muscular women, bawling and cursing each other, had lit charcoal fires on the cobbles. Great blackened copper cauldrons were filled with water and heated until the water boiled.

The squid were tossed in. When ready, they were lifted out with tongs, scissored into chunks, tipped onto wooden or pottery platters, splashed with olive oil, salt and scarlet *pimentón*, and then shoved at the customers – accompanied by rough country bread and carafes of even rougher Moncloa wine.

We didn't just eat that day. We feasted in the company of the good citizens of Cacabelos.

We left as the rain set in, tramping upwards under dark turbulent skies with the wind in our faces and storms coiling above us. The Pilgrim Way led through lanes of red clay, frothy and foaming with water and overhung with dripping hawthorn, the white sprays of blossom gleaming in their spring flowering. Late in the afternoon Hilary and I – Priscilla was struggling a little behind us – reached the small town of Villafranca de Bierzo.

We followed the signs to the pilgrim *hostal*. It turned out to be a plastic greenhouse that smelt of cat's pee and otter droppings. A few youths were strumming guitars and smoking marijuana in the little bar that appeared to be part of the establishment. We were so tired and wet we were prepared to accept it. Then Priscilla appeared.

She took a quick look round. 'No,' she snapped. 'Over my dead body.'

An hour later she'd installed us in the oak-floored Hotel Commercio with a hip-bath down the landing, and fire-escape arrangements which would have chilled the blood of any British safety inspector. None of us smoked. We ate in the town, slept well, and survived the night.

Early in the morning – we'd paid our bill the evening before – we were on our way again before anyone else was up. We'd climbed and descended before. Now we were truly heading up into the mountains.

For me it was one of the journey's hardest days. The fault was entirely mine. Tiring towards midday, I let the other two – eager as always to press forward – go on while I lingered in a little roadside café. A local van-driver came in. It was his birthday and his mother had made him a cassoulet, which we heated over the stove, and a wonderful *tarte aux fraises*. Of course, I was invited to share the feast and the wine that went with it, and discuss a whole raft of the valley's concerns. I left a good two hours later than I'd intended.

Several hours afterwards I lost my way. I knew the day was going to be demanding, but the road that wound up through the mountains seemed easy enough to follow. I was already weary and I became idle. I missed the crucial turn-off track to our night's destination.

Eventually I realized something was wrong and found a farmer who set me right. I'd way overshot the mark. I could either retrace my steps or take a tortuous route through the valleys and over the uplands. In both cases ten or more kilometres would be added to the day's journey. I opted for the valleys and uplands. The weather changed. The sun of the morning vanished behind storm clouds, rain fell and turned to stinging hail which beat painfully against my face.

Cursing, I struggled on.

By the time I reached the pinnacle village of O Cebreiro, our destination on the heights, I was sodden, bone-chilled, and once more bone-weary. I found Hilary who, bless her for this eternally, took one look at me and knew there was only one answer on the bitter mountain top: strong drink. She ran to the bar and began to top me up. The sugar and the alcohol did the trick. Within half an hour the cold tremors had stopped and I was beginning to make sense again.

Some sense, but not much. The long, strenuous climb had sucked the marrow and much of the heart out of me. It came after other climbs, other blasts of bitter upland wind, other laboured trudges over rock and through thorn. The journey had, for me, become an exhausting tramp, a catalogue in my diary of barely noticed one-night stops.

Where were the moustachioed lady cyclists from the Swiss Inland Revenue? Where was Dutch Robert from Gouda with tail-wagging Fanny? Where were little stocky Jean-Paul, with his house on his back, and the handsome swift-striding Eduardo who'd given me the *concha*, the pilgrim shell? Where were the engaging Primi and his feast, the ageing Franciscan monks with their learning and smiles, Mme Astruc and her son in the Auvergne snows?

They belonged to the past.

I was reminded of my days as a soldier, and those long arduous route-marches. Foot-soldiers don't make many friends while they're route-marching. They're too tired and too busy looking after their packs and rifles. Pilgrims aren't much different.

26

O Cebreiro – the very name with its Portugese cadences is an indicator of how far we'd travelled north-west from the Castilian heart of Spain – is a strange little place, more of a hamlet even than a village.

It sits some 4,500 feet high like an eagle's nest on a hog's back, well above the snow line. Snow lay all round the tiny group of houses and the evening air was bitterly cold. The intelligence officers of the Roman empire sensibly built a fort there – from the ridge you could see the approach of an enemy convoy for fifty miles in every direction.

The Romans retreated when their empire crumbled, the Dark Ages passed, and in the tenth century Carthusian monks re-colonized the eyrie. They built one of the loveliest little churches we saw on the whole journey. Simple and plain, sweet-smelling and wholesome, it adorns the mountains. Inevitably, after a thousand years, it has garnered its fair crop of legends.

A German monk, a pilgrim, lost and on the point of dying in the snow and mists below, heard the sound of bagpipes. He struggled to his feet and followed the music upwards. It was a shepherd boy playing his pipes for his sheep. The monk survived and in gratitude for his deliverance, he devoted his life to building O Cebreiro's first pilgrim *hostal*.

I doubt he'd have recognized the one we slept in. It had plate-glass windows over the valleys, a vast kitchen equipped with washing-machines, hot showers and comfortable bunks. We passed a fine night.

Next day we followed the ridge for hours, still high above the snow line, and then began to descend.

Several years earlier in South Africa's province of Natal I'd watched the great Comrades' marathon, in fact a double-marathon of more than fifty-two miles over the infamous Shaka's Zulu land of the one thousand hills. Talking to one of the successful competitors at the end of the race, he told me: 'It's not the upward slopes that hurt, it's the ones going down. Man, that's where it really gets to you.'

I knew exactly what he meant.

The knees jar and buckle. The heels bruise. The strain comes on the hips and shoulders. It happened to us that morning, and the pressure was compounded by the weight of our packs. At the start it was icily cold. We tramped through snow-patched rocky lanes with spring flowers starting to appear through the frost covering. Once or twice we had to step aside on the narrow path and let the first transhumance herds of cattle pass through on their way up to the spring pastures.

We reached the village of Triacastela at the foot of the pass and lunched with our latest platoon of companions. They had had enough for the day but our schedule was more demanding. We were heading on for Samos and evening mass at the monastery.

We walked there through an afternoon of glorious golden sunlight. We attended mass. It was badly sung by some amiable young monks and a few hoarse and crusty old codgers from the ecclesiastical community. Once there would have been a presence of two hundred, now it was down to fifteen – and that included the three of us. Priscilla and I were almost asleep on our feet.

The monastery's pilgrim *refugio* could have accommodated an army on its ranks of bunks, but we had the cavernous hall to ourselves. We left at dawn and walked across green and gently rolling countryside filled with rivers and little meadows – the landscape reminded me of Hardy's Wessex in high summer – to the town of Sarriá. We found our band of companions – or, uncannily, they found us – and lunched with them in a bar on the hill above the town, drinking dry white wine out of tiny brown pottery bowls.

Afterwards Priscilla and Hilary strode off with the keen fierce determination in their eyes I'd come to know so well. For me, however, the journey had become something of an amble, an adventure, a chance to dawdle, to talk to people and see the way they lived. Also, in all truth, I was tired. I roamed the old town and found my way into the church – by chance the priest arrived to unlock the door just as I arrived there.

He showed me round and told me its history. I thanked him, left, and headed for the bus station. An hour or so in a bus would win me a dozen kilometres, and save my legs. It was a Sunday and the last bus had just left. However, the station's manager had a brother-in-law who owned a taxi and, most remarkably for a hot and sleepy afternoon, happened to be available.

The taxi arrived and we set off. I told the driver where I wanted to end up, but added that I fancied a little tour of the countryside first. He could do better than that, he replied, he'd take me to visit some of his relations who lived in the area.

We had a wonderful time.

He took me first to the farm of a cousin who was the local charcuterie or, as it's known in Spanish, *chorizo* expert. The man had inherited a remarkable collection of old peasant sausage-making equipment — brass and steel pipes, rollers and mincers and funnels — which he still used. He couldn't demonstrate them to me, the pigs weren't slaughtered until the autumn, but if I came back then he promised he'd show me how everything worked.

We went on. A niece of the driver's sister was getting married that day. We headed for the church — I was starting to suspect a private spin had been put on our journey, but I was being plied with wine and it didn't matter. We missed the ceremony but arrived in time to drink her health on the church steps. Then we made our last stop at a farm owned by another of the driver's cousins.

The cousin had agreed to loan his mule to a neighbouring farmer, and the saddled-up animal was waiting in the yard. I was asked if I'd like to ride the creature — the neighbouring farm was in our direction. I heaved myself up and we set off with the farmer at the halter and the taxi trundling behind. Like the afternoon before, the day was glorious. Warm and sun filled, blending cloud and shadow, full of the scent of wild flowers and the smells of the thickening grass meadows.

The cousin didn't speak, he merely smiled companionably. The taxi rumbled. I felt like Christ riding into Jerusalem — pilgrims, of course, have always used donkeys or mules. And later, at the end of the day, Hilary was enraged. She questioned me, interrogated me, checked my timings of my afternoon's experiences, asking me to account for them almost minute by minute. To be honest, I think she was cross that I had had such fun while she and Priscilla had soldiered on.

Life isn't fair but it can be fun, and the fun continued.

We left the mule at the farm. The taxi took me on to where I wanted to be dropped off, a small *pensión* several hours from our night's rendezvous at Portomarín. Sitting outside, finishing a very late lunch, were Wolfgang and Atti, the two middle-aged German men we'd met briefly in León, one an academic, the other a businessman, and both fellow-pilgrims. We agreed to walk together for the fifteen kilometres ahead of us.

They were delightful, sensitive, funny, and they spoke fluent English. They had walked together for years and they had two abiding passions – poetry, not least English poetry, and music. Wolfgang quoted Eliot to me and asked me to fill in the gaps. I did. Atti did the same with Dylan Thomas and asked me again to complete the verses. Which again I did.

'Right,' I said, 'now what are you going to do for me?'

'We'll sing for you,' Wolfgang or Atti replied.

And they did. They sang me *lieder*.

They weren't very good as singers, their voices more vigorous than tuneful, but there was passion and conviction in what they sang. They were scholars and knowledgeable. They sang the works of Schumann and a wonderful lyric by Eisendorf that I didn't know. I later asked Atti to write down the words for me.

Thus it was that a former British special forces soldier and two former members of the Hitler-*jugend* – both of them admitted to that – found themselves tramping across the Galician landscape on pilgrimage alternately quoting T. S. Eliot and Dylan Thomas, and singing romantic German *lieder*.

We reached Portomarín and parted. Late in the evening Priscilla and Hilary limped in. They were both desperately tired. We ate and fell into our beds.

The next day's journey was slightly easier, but the relief of crossing a gentler countryside was offset by the weariness that was accumulating in all of us.

We walked for most of the way along roads with yellow gorse on every side. The air was sultry and humid, and clouds were gathering. Hungry at midday, the only bar I could find was closed. I knocked and rang the bell and outfaced a snarling dog. A man eventually appeared with his wife peering over his shoulder. The owner, the man explained, was in hospital and the bar would be shut for the rest of the year.

I pleaded, cajoled, smiled, almost begged them to give me something to eat and drink. Warily they agreed – how could they refuse a pilgrim? I dumped my pack and staff, with my hat on top, outside as a marker for the others, and went in. One by one they straggled in too, Priscilla, the Germans, Jorge and Paco. We sat in the kitchen, drinking beer and eating a classic Spanish *tortilla con chorizo*. We talked, Priscilla and I translated for Wolfgang and Atti, and we had a wonderful impromptu party. Then we headed on.

Our night's stop was the little hill town of Palas de Rei. The climb up towards it was long and steep. The journey was approaching its close and Priscilla, with the end in sight, had refound her energy. Telling her and Priscilla to go on ahead, I lay down and slept for an hour in a meadow with my head on my pack. I joined the two of them at the *refugio* in a drizzling dusk.

'This is a day for angels to walk,' Wolfgang said next morning, a couple of hours after we had set out.

He was right.

The sky was clear, the sunlight soft and warm, the winding lanes patterned with shadow, the air fresh and scented. There was a whole procession, a caravan of us now, tramping the Way. Two delightful young French girls had joined us. Some handsome Barcelonan Spaniards were there, stubbly-bearded little Luis, the girls from Brussels, Jorge and Paco, the Germans, a dozen more.

We all stopped at eleven o'clock and breakfasted off peaches, home-baked bread, and *copas* of chill white wine. Two hours later we reached the somewhat dreary town of Melide. I left the group, bought several Spanish newspapers, and read them over a bowl of *pulpos*, the same pepper-dressed squid we'd eaten in Cacabelos a week earlier. Then I went to the restaurant's bar.

'I'm heading for Ribadiso,' I said. 'Can you call a taxi to take me part of the way?'

Before the barman could answer, a burly grey-haired man intervened.

'That's my direction,' he said. 'I'll run you out there in my truck.'

He was called Diego. He worked for a transport company that made deliveries all over Spain. That day his assignment was close to home – he lived in La Coruña – and he was delivering cattle food to local farms. We made a couple of farm visits where I helped him and the farmers lift off the sacks, then we drove towards Ribadiso de Baixo. He dropped me off on the highway a couple of hundred yards from the village.

'*Suerte*, luck, for the journey's end,' Diego said. 'Come back soon. The *pulpos* in Melide aren't bad, but they can't compare with the seafood we'll give you in La Coruña.'

I waved and he drove away.

I walked down into Ribadiso. An old woman was fishing from the bridge over the river that ran beside the hamlet. She wanted a couple of trout for her supper and she hadn't landed anything. I examined her tackle. The leader was a crude bundle of badly tied knots. I cut the whole thing off, re-threaded the catgut, kicked over a cowpat, found a plump worm – she'd been using soggy scraps of bread as a lure – and attached it to the hook. Within minutes she pulled in her first fish.

'*Gracias, señor*,' she said, smiling in delight and amazement.

'*De nada, señora*,' I replied, raising my hat.

In truth, although I can hold my own on the water, I'm not much of a fisherman. Compared to some of my friends, who whip their rods and throw their lines out with all the skill and elegance of a ballerina, I'm a journeyman angler. But as a Hebridean I'm expected to fish, I know the value of a meal, and it's a duty bound-in-the-soul to help others secure it.

The night was dark. There were storms and rain and no moon, no stars, no owls calling. I slept fitfully. Early in the morning, with mist lying heavily in the valleys, we set off on what was effectively our last day.

27

It was almost the last day of the journey and one of the longest, almost forty kilometres.

As so often Priscilla and Hilary were determined to make an early start, and left well before me. I rose late at 6.30 and set off in their wake. The track through the now gently rolling green Galician countryside was tree-shadowed, soft and gentle underfoot, warm and friendly. My pack weighed heavily but I made good speed. At eleven o'clock, I found a bar and stopped for breakfast.

The only other customers at the bar's counter were two handsome young Spaniards, brothers, it emerged, on the Pilgrim Way. They eyed me and then approached me.

'Are you by any chance Nicholas, the brother of Priscilla?' one of them asked.

'Yes.'

'We have a message for you. Your sister and your friend, Hilaria, have changed their plans. They are heading on to spend the night at the big *hostal* of Monte do Gozo just outside Santiago. They will meet you there.'

The brothers came from Barcelona. They were delightful. They had lovely olive skins, shining black eyes, quick minds and professional careers. They were quintessentially successful young Catalans and both their lives were in a mess. They'd embarked on the *Camino* in an attempt to come to terms with a divorce in the case of the older of the two, and the end of a love affair for the younger.

The Way of St James, they thought, might be the answer.

We bought each other drinks. I thanked them and embraced them as I left. I doubted St James would solve their problems, but I liked their spirit and their laughter.

I went on.

I overtook Priscilla and Hilary, but I didn't tarry with them. I was exhausted and so were they. I was happy to be on my own. For the moment the bonds that held our little group together were frayed and creaking. The three of us were grating on each other, complaining about each other, imagining slights and insults and betrayals. The easy comradeship of the early stages of the great journey had gone.

I could say it was Priscilla's fault or Hilary's or even mine – perish the thought of the last, benign and patient and accommodating man as I am. Of course, the overwhelming blame lay with me but not entirely. The truth is almost certainly more simple. Wind and weather and fatigue. They were affecting us all, and there are few more powerful solvents of human relationships than mountains, sore feet and sheer weariness.

We met up again by chance late in the afternoon.

Not far from Monte do Gozo, the hill town that overlooks Santiago, I saw a sinewy little Galician roadmender. Dark cumulus clouds were gathering, I didn't need to be a Hebridean to know storms and rain were close, and I thought he might tell me where I could find a bus to carry me the last few kilometres through the approaching downpour. We sat and chatted for a while beside his pile of gravel. As the first drops fell I followed his directions and headed for the bus-stop.

I was standing there when I was hailed from a nearby roadhouse. I'd been spotted by one of the handsome young Barcelonan brothers. They too had caught up with Priscilla and Hilary, and all four of them had decided to have a lavish late lunch in the roadhouse. I joined them for a *copa* of wine. They set off in what by now was a black, brass-rods-and-rails, screaming-cats-and-howling-dogs-deluge, with rolling thunder and crackling lightning.

I watched them splash away, soaked and huddled. I waited. I had another glass of wine. The storm grew fiercer still.

'I have to go into Santiago in the van for tomorrow's fruit and vegetables,' the owner of the roadhouse said. 'Perhaps I can give the *señor* a lift.'

'If you're going by ox-waggon,' I replied, 'I'd be delighted.'

'*Perdon?*' He looked at me puzzled.

'Never mind,' I said. 'Let's just go there. Although I'll have to rebaptize the van first.'

We waded through the rising puddles outside. I drew the sign of the cross on the van's hood, declared it a cart, renamed it Santa Teresa, then we set off.

The *hostal* at Monte do Gozo proudly proclaims it's the biggest in Europe.

It was built to house some of the multitude of pilgrims who gathered at Santiago to see and honour Pope John Paul on his visit to the city in the holy year of 1992. While in many ways excellent – its endless barrack-blocks with their tiered bunks are clean and well lit and the cost of sleeping there is nominal – its general appearance and design belongs to the world of the *gulag*, of one of Stalin's architects' fantasies.

The blocks march and line with each other to a measured inch. The tiled corridors echo and clatter. Framed sets of rules of behaviour dominate every entrance. Someone, an escaped inmate perhaps, has planted a few roses outside, but even they seem to know they're unwelcome, and they struggle to survive.

I signed in. I threw myself down on my bunk, waiting for Priscilla and Hilaria to arrive. After eating, we went to sleep to the sound of cascading rain.

In the early hours of the morning I woke and although I was exhausted I couldn't get back to sleep again. I was restless and uneasy. I tossed and turned. Eventually I slipped from my bunk and went outside. When, immensely reluctantly, I gloomily agreed to move from the Isle of Mull to the edge of the Cambrian mountains in Wales, where my godmother had left me what the rest of the family thought was a far more accessible little estate, my wife, trying to cheer me up, observed: 'Celts, sheep, beautiful wild landscapes and buckets of rain – you won't notice the difference.'

She was largely right, although the heart never quite cuts the anchor ropes to its true harbour and home. Galicia was much the same as Mull and the Cambrian mountains. A Celtic nation tending their flocks in lovely countryside under an almost constant downpour. I sat beneath the canopied porch listening to the storm's tumult, and gazing through the screen of falling water at the blurred lights of Santiago below. I considered Francesca. And then something remarkable happened, echoing the past, anticipating the future.

Compostela means, of course, the Field of the Star. For a few short moments, a tiny window opened in the sky's dark and dense cloud cover, and the stars shone down over the city. I could even see the distant towers of the cathedral, luminous in the fragile light. Almost instantly they were gone. The storm swept back and afterwards there was nothing except the falling rain.

The clouds had parted too when we buried the girl in the Sussex graveyard on that dark December day. Briefly at the heart of the service, sunlight had shone through the emerald panels of glass in the old east window. Candlelight became her, the sun even more.

I went back to bed and fell asleep immediately.

It was a dour, grey and clammy dawn.

We set out early for the last couple of hours which would complete the Way. We should have been eager and buoyant, filled with excitement and anticipation as we'd been when we started. I doubt any of us were that morning. The *Camino*, its heat and snow, mountains and winds, the wounds it had inflicted, physical and psychological, hadn't defeated us but it had certainly stretched us to the limits.

We were halt by now, stumbling and drained.

We made our way through the long and drear urban approaches to Santiago, through the suburbs and past the factories. The sky grew heavier. Once again there was the smell of rain in the air. Several times we lost our direction and had to ask where we were. Finally we found the great cathedral at the city's heart, climbed its steps and limped inside.

I dropped to my knees, too tired even to offload my pack, and made a cat's cradle of my staff and my wrists on which I could rest my chin.

All I could register at first was music. We'd arrived by chance in the middle of the early morning sung mass. Voices soared above the magnificent resonances of the great organ. I glimpsed the moving figures of the cathedral's priests round the altar, black-robed and with the dramatic scarlet sword of the Order of Santiago embroidered across their chests.

I closed my eyes and prayed for my daughter, for her peace and safety. Her mother and sister had taken her across the river, and handed her into much stronger arms than mine.

Sleep well, child, I whispered. Rest in the arms of the carpenter's son. And then I asked for health and true solid well-being for the rest of the clan, mother, brother, sisters, friends, and the whole damn crew of them who loved the girl so much.

No, it wasn't a particularly satisfactory prayer. At the end of a thousand miles it should have been much more considered and eloquent. Something to be framed and held in the mind. It wasn't, just a few tired words. With the cuts and bruises, blisters, weariness and damp, it was all I could muster. Yet I find, however inadequate they were at the time, I can live with them now. The words didn't add up to much, but there was passion behind them.

I heard the tap of footsteps approaching me. The steps went away and then returned. It was one of the priests, an old man with dark deep-set eyes and a white beard who might have been painted by El Greco. He'd dipped his hand in the holy water and he made, smiling, the sign of the cross on my forehead.

'In the name of the Father and His Son, I bless you,' he said. '*Felicidades, peregrino.* Congratulations, pilgrim.'

'*Gracias, padre,*' I replied.

The music rose again. I wept.

Some time later, I've no idea how long, I heaved myself up and found Priscilla and Hilary sitting in the nave. I joined them and together we studied the cathedral.

It needs no description, although it has often been written about. It's enough to say that it's a noble and magnificent monument to the Christian faith — vast and bare and clean with its lime-white vaults overhead, its extraordinary internal 'gateway' at the west door, one of the finest and most intricately carved medieval artefacts I've seen, and its somewhat over-embellished altar clutter.

The last, for all its associations with St James, is only a minor blemish. The whole is a triumph — a mighty statement in stone to the spirit of man and his God, and a fitting end to the pilgrimage road.

Across a thousand years millions of people have striven to reach it. Many died on the road, drowning if they came by sea, starving or felled by illness, eaten by wolves or murdered by bandits if they chose the land routes. But those who got here won't have been disappointed.

We went out. We found a small cheap hotel. Then we returned to the cathedral for the daily pilgrims' mass.

The three of us sat together. As I've said, Hilary is a defiant and articulate agnostic. Priscilla and I are Christians, although with rather different perspectives on our faith. Priscilla is austere, hardline. I, in spite of coming from Huguenot stock, tend to be more flamboyant – I rather enjoy bells and smells.

The service began.

The famous *butifera*, the massive silver-plated censer the size of a great bell, was swung from the rafters. Smoke and incense billowed over us as the team of ten sturdy men hauled on the ropes, and the censer rose and plunged like some vast swallow lifting and dipping in flight. The sacrament was offered. I nudged Priscilla and got to my feet. There was no point in nudging Hilary, she did not accept the sacrament of the flesh and blood and would, I knew, have no truck with it.

Priscilla followed me. For the first time in both our lives we stood in line to take the sacrament at a service of the Roman Church. The sky above the cathedral was grim and dark with Galicia's infamous rain-bearing clouds, clouds we were beginning to know so well. The air inside was murky. If you visit Santiago, its citizens say with a certain defiant pride, you must always carry an umbrella.

We reached the altar and it happened again.

The lights were suddenly turned on and the whole nave blazed. Or so, for an instant, we thought. And then we realized it wasn't electricity. No one had touched a switch. Another window had opened in the clouds above, the cathedral was flooded with sunshine, the great stone edifice glowed. Shafts of brilliance were rippling through the windows of every side-chapel, and the scarlet swords on the priests' chests seemed to be on fire.

Priscilla and I looked at each other in astonishment.

We both knew. Priscilla, too, had been in the church at Ripe when the girl was buried, and the same light had momentarily flared through the old panes of clear and emerald glass. Francesca was about her irradiating business again.

We took the bread and the wine. The clouds closed in. The nave darkened. We collected Hilary and left.

One can make of it what one will. Perhaps I have spent too much time with the oldest, and in my view the wisest, people in the world, the hunter-gatherer clans of the Kalahari Bushmen, the San. They believe in signs and portents, but of course they've been there far longer than the rest of us to consider matters. They would have considered the sun's appearance in celebration both of a journey's end and of a girl who, for me, had inspired it entirely natural.

I wasn't remotely surprised a year later at the launch of the Francesca Friendship Trust, where half a thousand people gathered to celebrate her – an extraordinary tribute to a young woman of only twenty-nine – to be called out onto the street and told to look at the sky. Not one but two vivid rainbows were bending down over the gallery where her paintings were being shown.

Of course.

The black-eyed girl is going to be digging her shovel into my stores and my heart for the rest of my life. And the only coinage she's going to pay me back in is rainbows. Where, Francesca, am I going to spend them?

There were some odds and ends to be tidied up.

We went to the pilgrims' office to show our stamped passports, and collect the official certificates with our names recorded in medieval Latin showing we'd duly and properly completed the *Camino*. There are two different certificates: one for those who've walked the Way in its traditional form for spiritual reasons, and another shorter and simpler one, a crisp secular version for those who'd travelled out of cultural and historical interest.

We dealt with the formalities. As best we could we rested, the three of us packed once more head-to-tail like canned sardines in a single room. We roamed the little streets at Santiago's centre searching like tourists from a thousand years ago for souvenirs. Among the tawdry clutter I found a few elegant silver scallop shells. I bought several of them. I gave one to Priscilla and kept the others to be handed out when I got back.

Our last group of companions on the road trickled in. We bought each other drinks and exchanged stories and addresses. The Germans, bless them for behaving so true to type, sang Bavarian marching songs. Jorge promised us free meals for ever at his Majorquin restaurant. Paco offered to patch and caulk my yacht (not that I have one, although it seemed ungracious to say so – British gentlemen are always assumed in the Mediterranean to own yachts) if ever I put in there. And so it went on.

We left for the airport exhausted and somewhat dizzy from the farewell celebrations. I was booked on a direct flight back to London. Priscilla and Hilary had a long and complicated itinerary that routed them through Madrid. On impulse Hilary leant over the check-in counter.

'Is there any way we could travel with our companion?' she asked.

'You are pilgrims, no?'

She nodded. It was obvious from our staffs and packs, the dust on our clothes, the general air of triumph and weariness that enveloped us. The booking clerk ran his fingers over his computer keyboard. He glanced up.

'It's against all IATA rules,' he said, 'but I've transferred you to the same direct flight.'

Hilary blew him a kiss. 'Bless you.'

The young man smiled. 'Don't thank me. Thank Santiago. Just consider it another of his miracles.'

The three of us boarded the plane. After more than three years and something approaching a thousand miles, the journey was over. Well, almost over. But before that, what had I made of it all?

Was it a great spiritual experience? Not in terms of providing sudden searing flashes of illumination, those windows of perception hurled open which change one's life because of a new view beyond. I embarked on the Way with a thoroughly unfashionable belief in this secular age in God and His boy, the carpenter's son. Over the thirty-five years of my adulthood, that belief has increasingly been subjected to assault and battery. Grievous spiritual harm had been visited on the Anglican faith.

The nature, style and rituals of the Church of England have been dislocated, wrenched out of joint almost beyond recognition. The cadences and simple flinty poetry of the King James bible has been jettisoned as 'inaccessible'. Forty per cent of all new ordinands, a member of the Church's Synod told me recently, were practising male homosexuals. Women have been admitted to the priesthood. Electric guitars are replacing organ music, pop doggerel the ancient hymns, crispy wafers stand in for wheat bread in the sacrament, non-alcopop cordials are being offered instead of wine.

I can live with many of the changes and positively welcome others. I have never seen why male pederasts couldn't function effectively and compassionately as pastors, and the arrival of women in the curacy was perhaps the most overdue reform since the crucifixion. Eve and Mary, not Adam and Paul, bear, nurture and rear us. We charge them with our beginnings. If we cannot trust them with the direction that points towards our endings, if we cannot draw on their wisdom, then who on earth can we trust?

I bitterly regret the loss of the old Bible, but until the Church starts withdrawing and even burning the books – in the current climate not as far-fetched a notion as it may sound – I can still read Genesis, Solomon and the New Testament in the old, right and proper version at home. I regret, too, that one often has to search for churches which still include the great hymnal songs, with their lyrics by poets of the likes of Herrick and Blake, and the soaring melodies that accompany them. I prefer bread and wine to cordial and crisps.

What I cannot tolerate, what lies at the core of the present uncertain and fumbling mess, is the abandonment of conviction, the laziness and timidity of the Church's hierarchy, the hapless drift into winsome acceptable secularism where bishops abandon the divine to bicker with politicians over issues of social security.

Faith isn't safe.

In its fierce way it can be comforting, of course, bridging now and eternity and all the way-stations between the blood-stained birthplace and the stars. But it's dark and austere, dangerous and challenging. It isn't much fun. From the earliest worship of the pagan gods – from the wild flowers buried in necklaces round the bones of slain neolithic bears to the nails hammered into the hands and feet of the young man from Galilee – humanity has never wanted it to be anything else.

Faith is the only, the inevitable and necessary, conclusion. Faith is the candle in the dark that the night winds cannot blow out. Faith makes the unendurable endurable. And of its nature it can only be wild, inexplicable, transcendent.

I ended the *Camino* with that belief, reinforced unquestionably, but essentially unchanged. On the dusty road, drenched with the sweat of summer tiredness or chilled to the stomach's pit in the snow and winds, looking at mountains and landscapes, watching horses, birds, deer and the rising trout in the Navarran rivers, talking to the inhabitants of the countryside – the innkeepers, priests, farmers and wandering thieves – drinking the black wine and eating the wild fruit, kneeling and asking for peace in the wayside chapels, I felt at ease. It seemed natural to consider, speculate and dream, much more natural than in a rooted place.

Pilgrimage demands thought and I did my best – in prayer and with lighted candles. I arrived at no fine perceptions, no new deep and penetrating insights into the meaning of life. Instead, a few at first tentative conclusions which later turned to certainties. They are so old, so obvious, they shouldn't need the telling, but for me the closet that held them needed unlocking and Francesca was the key.

Love, funnily enough, *is* enough.

It's all that matters. Not as some vague romantic concept but the laughter in the greeting embrace at the door, and the beans-and-bones reality of the smell from the stew on the stove beyond. Forgiveness accompanies it. To forgive means little more than to tolerate, to accept and understand, both the faults and flaws in others and, most importantly, in oneself. A feud with oneself is unlikely to help in making peace with the greater and much more interesting gathering and alliance, the companionship of one's family and friends.

The *Camino* led me in the right direction.

There was something else, something harder but necessary. I searched for a definition and recalled it, or at least an approximation to it, in some lines in a poem by A. E. Housman entitled *Epitaph on an Army of Mercenaries*:*

> *These in the day when heaven was falling,*
> *The hour when earth's foundations fled,*
> *Followed their mercenary calling,*
> *And took their wages and are dead.*
>
> *Their shoulders held the sky suspended,*
> *They stood and earth's foundations stay.*
> *What God abandoned, they defended,*
> *And saved the sum of things for pay.*

Love and forgiveness aren't quite enough. They need to be threaded together with vigour and toughness. Like Homer, God occasionally nods – He was certainly taking a siesta when the illness invaded my daughter. We need to keep a constant watch on the battlements. Good commanding officers are nothing without brave and vigilant sentries. That is the message and task for the pilgrim.

The sum of things remains to be fought for and saved for pay.

Was I enriched by the journey? Yes, beyond any doubt. It was one of the most rewarding experiences of my life. Did it change me? Probably, although I cannot measure the ways and degrees. We tend to remain what we are, prisoners of our pasts and carrying the chains of memory and habit shackled to us in our childhoods. I set out difficult, truculent, combative and, in the words of my sister at some moment of collision, deeply selfish. I fear she was right and I fear I finished the same, although perhaps a little tempered, harder but perhaps a little less abrasive.

Pilgrimage is not a cure-all for the pilgrim's faults – although, sceptical as my family, companions and friends may be, I shall work on them.

Would I recommend others to take to the path? Given care and thought before they start, given a proper acknowledgement of the

* Reproduced by permission of The Society of Authors as the Literary Representative of the Estate of A. E. Housman.

hardships involved, given seriousness and dedication, my answer would unhesitatingly be, yes. Once again I go back to Matsuo Bashō: 'The journey itself is home.' In the street jargon of Francesca's generation while she was still a teenager, Bashō's message would translate as: 'Just once round the block, mister, that's all you've got.'

Pilgrimage, the journey, is all we've got and the road to Santiago is a fine way to travel it.

Letters to Francesca: 13

And that, Francesca, is virtually the end of the story I'd hoped to be able to tell you myself.

If my hat's not on the ground for you to throw a penny into, or even — should I be so lucky — one of your accusing £1 notes, then at least it's done. Much more fun, of course, if we'd been able to talk it through, to explore and examine it, face to face. The best stories are the old and epic ones, and they slowly acquire a resonance by their re-telling.

My journey to Santiago was hardly Homeric — Odysseus would probably have done it at a quick hand-canter — but to me it was in a way a personal epic. Over the four years, I walked nearly a thousand miles across mountains and plains, through wind and snow and sun. Each day I lit candles for you. Each night I thought of you, tried to measure you in my mind.

It's seductively easy to mythologize someone who's died. Convenient and comforting to turn them into something they weren't, something neat and tidy and, in the case of a daughter, pretty. Prettiness sits neatly and comfortably in the memory like a carefully posed photograph. We, the survivors, can live with that. You are far more demanding. I have photographs of you and there is, metaphorically, blood over every one of them — blood and anger, laughter and challenge. You had talons, you had bells, you called to the wind like one of the wounded falcons we housed.

Sentimentality at least was never a threat. You'd have knocked that one on the head as swiftly and expertly as you broke the necks of the rabbits and game birds I shot for the pot. When you chose, you could wield your hand like an axe.

And although scrupulously fastidious in the conduct of your life, you weren't neat or tidy in the sense I mean and you weren't conventionally pretty — you were either dark and sulky or, if you chose, a blazing beauty, the swan whose entrance could silence a room. Prettiness wasn't part of your personal vocabulary.

So who were you, who are you?

We left the hotel at 8.00 a.m. It was 23 April, St George's Day, a good omen, I thought, for a trio of English pilgrims to set out. The spring morning was bright and clear and chill. The skies over the town shone the pale translucent blue of a clutch of eggs in a blackbird's nest and the early sun was golden, but there was the promise of rain in the damp air. We climbed upwards to the traditonal departure point, Le Puy's cathedral, our boots and staffs tapping on the cobblestones.

Small children waiting for school to open, the girls in neat pinafores, the boys in carefully pressed shorts, each of them clutching a little metal canteen holding the hot midday meal. They perched like swallows on the walls on either side of the school gates, chattering and giggling. We stopped and spoke to them.

What were we doing, they asked, and where were we going?

We were pilgrims, we said, we were following the Chemin de St Jacques to the city of Santiago in Spain. Did they know about St Jacques? They shook their heads. They had never heard of the Pilgrim Way or the city at its end. Five centuries earlier, when hundreds of pilgrims left Le Puy every week, they'd have known about little else. Today it was a mystery.

A bell rang, the gates rattled open, and the children vanished as abruptly as the tiny migrant birds they so much resembled.

We went into the cathedral. Above the altar is an exquisite black madonna, thoughtful and serene and clothed in an alabaster cloak decorated with gold flowers. I studied her. She reminded me of the black St Sara in the little fortress church of Saintes-Maries-de-la-Mer in the Camargue, but somehow gentler and more generous – the Camargue lady's features and no doubt her spirit, too, are as tough as teak.

Le Puy's lady, I discovered, isn't the original. She was hacked to pieces and then burned in the obscene and infamous event known as the French Revolution. By great good luck, just before the carnage erupted and left its lasting brutalizing stain on France's soul, a geologist, who was also an artist, happened to be in Le Puy studying volcanoes – the region is a famous volcanic area. He fell in love with the madonna, and got the church's permission to make detailed drawings of her.

After a measure of sanity returned to the country, his drawings were used to recreate her. Whether the peace in her face comes from him or from her first incarnation no one now knows and it doesn't matter. I committed Le Puy's black virgin to my memory. She looked like a good companion for the journey – and I needed good companions.

I lit a candle and looked round for the other two. Priscilla and Hilary had vanished. I went outside, sat down on one of the walls where the swallows had gathered, and waited for them. I knew what they were doing.

They had gone to have their passports stamped.

It's often cynically claimed there's no such thing as a free lunch. In fact, as human nature is capable of being infinitely benign and generous as well as infinitely malign, there are not only free lunches available in life but free shelter and medical care too – to the wayfarer, the destitute, the beggar, the holy man and, above all, the pilgrim.

If we read the formidable intelligence of dolphins correctly, we're not unlike them – social creatures programmed not just to look after and nurture each other, including utter strangers, but different species too. We also know, and here dolphins seem to be more innocent and trusting than we are, that our freely given bounty, our generosity, is a magnet for exploitation by rogues, thieves and ruffians.

When the pilgrim roads began to thread across Europe, a vast support system evolved to help and care for the traveller. Religious faith played a major part but the motive for much of it was bluntly commercial. There was money to be made, large sums of money, out of the pilgrim trade; from ferries, inns, shops, vineyards, waggon hire, candle-selling, prostitution, blacksmithery and cobbling, so much more. Yet there was altruism too.

Pilgrims travelling the Way were on God's business. People on God's business deserved to be looked after. Military orders developed to protect them. The problem was to distinguish the charlatan determined to dig his shovel into the stores of generosity available to the true pilgrim, from the true pilgrim himself.

The answer was the pilgrim's passport.

The original passports were blank rolls of parchment. At every staging-post along the way, the pilgrim would have it stamped and dated by the local priest. Arriving at his next destination, the traveller

I hoped to find out. The child who played chess for the Foreign Legion and then for England? The clever scientist? The Vogue model? The dazzling mini-skirted party-goer and music-lover? The trilingual journalist, the writer and the painter? The girl who became a beacon-star to her generation? Or the angry young woman who, tellingly and perceptively, so often criticized my writing and even more often stormed in a rage from the house?

How many times have I raced after you, apologizing for arguments that had nothing to do with me and begging you to return? Do you remember the time when, to my deep embarrassment, you telephoned every hotel on Mull trying to book a room and get away from me and your mother?

Damn you, Francesca, damn you again. Why does life throw troublesome comets of people like you at nice people like me?

Except – I can only be thankful life tossed you my way.

It's not just that I'd have been impoverished for not knowing you, that life would have been thinner. Everyone, as so many vividly and eloquently expressed in the words of their grief, would have been poorer without you. Nor would I miss you for the singular, extraordinary qualities you had. Nor even, in spite of all your rages and tantrums, because of the deprivation I'd have felt if I hadn't witnessed your gift for friendship, your love of your companions, the way you could change lives, calm weeping children, still frightened animals. Nor for your gaiety and unflinching courage as the end approached. Least of all perhaps for the Lagioule-bladed sharpness of your intellect.

No, I think in the end I'm glad for something much simpler, much older.

Once as a very small child you were photographed naked alongside a smouldering sparkling 'bomb' for an anarchist poster devised by your sister's godfather, the poet Christopher Logue. You handled the long photographic session with calm and aplomb. But once, unsettled by the constantly popping flash bulbs, you felt you needed a break.

You came over to me – I was squatting on the floor watching – and for an instant rested your cheek against mine. Then you smiled and walked back into the glare of the arc-lamps.

You were my daughter, Francesca, my eldest daughter, and even wayward absent fathers love daughters with a passion words cannot encompass or define. For all our furious disputes, our silences, you were the heart of my heart, myself, my hold on the future. You were inseparable from me. I think now that I probably 'designed' you in my mind to shore me up and carry me forward, and you, being you, decided the design didn't fit.

The hell with it, you said. You threw it all off and stitched something quite else for yourself.

The embroidery was of course far more interesting, more intricate and densely woven, than anything I'd planned. My immense good fortune was your generosity, that you didn't toss me away too. You grew up as a member of a clan, you kept your deep and passionate allegiance to the clan members, even to me, the most difficult of them all. Months after you died I was fretfully discussing the relationship between us with your sister, Honey.

'Forget it, Nicholas,' she said. 'You were with her when the T-cell diagnosis was made. That was the worst. If she'd wanted someone else — Amy or Marielle or whoever — she'd have asked for them. She didn't. She wanted you with her.'

I remembered you in your tattered jeans that terrible day, your eyes blazing with defiance, and the Trafalgar Square car park and the Chinese restaurant and then the falling October leaves whirling round us as we walked back. Yes, of course, I was there. Not so much at your request as at your order. Honey's reminder was the most comforting reassurance I've ever been given.

I wanted a reconciliation.

The long walk to Santiago was intended to provide it, but of course I didn't get it. Death and truculent daughters and difficult fathers combine to make a combustible mix, much like a haystack drenched by the spring rains and then half dried out in the summer's sun. The stack can ignite and flare.

Much I guess, Francesca, like you and me. There's no reconciliation with a still burning fire. It hurts if one is unwise enough to stick one's fingers into it. It leaves you with blisters and blood.

So we'll have to go on living warily together as this thing continues to smoulder — and it will for my lifetime. Haystack fires can burn for years. Neither coming too close to each other — we both need our privacy — nor staying too far apart, even if for a while we're physically separated. You in your favourite Caribbean — in the mind's eye I can see your shadow still on the white beaches there — me in Wales, Scotland, Africa, the Himalaya, wherever my travels take me. Your portrait hangs on the wall. Your corrida sketches line my study. Your boots, the ones you wore on our snowy climb towards Tibet, sit perched on a shelf above my reference books alongside the flint from your Sussex grave. Your presence is everywhere.

The shining flint from your grave, with the sunlight refracted from it in shafts of storm-grey and honed steel, represents you best.

I can't even claim it as my own stone either. I have to share it with so many, not just the extended clan but increasingly with others, with complete strangers. They've heard or read about you, they make their own pilgrimages to your grave at Ripe to look at the white dove carved on your headstone, to lay their flowers, and think about you and themselves, and then they write to us.

God knows what you would have made of it.

I can see your eyes, those unfathomably dark eyes sidling downwards, ranging, speculative and bemused.

'Let me be.'

And then you'd lift your head, the white neck arching and the black hair tossed back and something flashing silver or amethyst at your wrist, and you'd laugh and talk to them. Which is what they want.

Because you weren't just a girl who died of AIDS, Fran.

You knew that yourself. As I've quoted, you wrote in your journal: 'I am unremarkable except for the fact that I believe myself to be truly remarkable.' You were. You had the absolute sureness to see it. And you used it to teach us who were afraid, deeply afraid, not to be afraid. Death had no dangerous claim on you. You withered, your sparrow-bones poked through your dusty flaking skin, you became a hoarse and blind chestnut-brown and goldfinch-yellow little husk of a thing, a wind-blown maple leaf, and none of it mattered. You outfaced it all.

'No grim reaper tonight,' you'd say in that last week before dismissing us with a smile for the night. 'Let's see what's for breakfast.'

Contentedly I'd leave you and have a late-evening pint at the Florence Nightingale across the road. I asked your brother in those confused and anguished moments after you died if you'd been safe. A mindless question. Of course, you were safe. Much deeper and more lasting was what you quite consciously and deliberately did.

You made the rest of us safe.

'Look after your man, ma. He needs you.'

'Get a life, Nicholas, and make sure your speech for Laurens measures up.'

'Hullo, big bro. What of the bulls at Pamplona this year?'

'Tell little sis I love her — and will she please remember to keep breathing through her mask while she's under water.'

And then:

'My white skirt, please, Pops, the one I love, and the lacy white shirt to go with it.'

Such simple injunctions. Fragments from the final hours but considered fragments, fragments with passion and purpose. To give us reassurance. To confer safety. That's why the strangers come to your grave. They want to be in the presence of a spirit that lacked all fear, and had both the conviction and the generosity to make others understand fear is needless too.

Like all fathers everywhere I thought I was rather grand and important, a figure of wisdom and authority. You taught me otherwise. Kindly and without pressing the point, you taught me I was merely a spear-carrier at the edge of a much larger firework-strewn parade. The parade was yours. The drums and trumpets played for you.

God help fathers and daughters.

May He guard you well, Francesca Susan Luz de Beauregard Baron, dark-eyed first lady of my heart and my sweet love. You never thought you'd hear me say that, did you? Well, you have now.

It's almost the end but, as I've said, not quite.

28

The little Andalusian *pueblo* of Gaucin lies on the mountain road that leads upwards from the coast to the sierra town of Ronda. It was a road we'd all travelled often during our years in Spain.

In winter, the two winds that sweep the mouth of the Mediterranean – the westerly *poniente*, named for the sun's setting, and the much fiercer easterly *levante*, the equivalent of France's arid *mistral* – rage across the upland valleys. In summer, the earth beneath the cork oaks is burned and glazed with the translucent stems of the dry grass. In a green spring, the verges briefly cascade one of the richest wild-flower fountains in Europe.

Orchids star the roadside banks. Gentian-blue anchusa, wild lupins, incandescent scarlet poppies, white and pink bowls of cistus, stiffly erect sierra snap-dragons, drifts of buttercup and the tangled mountain sweet-peas, all of them and a hundred species more spill across the winding rutted track or rise to form a tunnel above it.

Driving to Ronda then, particularly at dawn or returning in the evening as the sun dips over the Atlantic beyond, is to drive through an arching scented rainbow.

I took the Ronda road again very shortly after leaving Santiago. In between I'd returned to London, flown to Scotland to chair a conservation conference, and gone back to Spain. Elisabeth was giving a course on Andalusian food and culture based in Gaucín. She'd asked me to join her.

It was the first time I'd been there in fifteen years. As I drove into the village towards midnight, I remembered the last occasion. The six of us had been heading up to explore the sierras beyond Ronda. We stopped at an inn in Gaucín, the Posada Ingles, for a break. I asked the inn-keeper's wife why it was called the Posada Ingles – the 'English Stable'.

She explained that British officers from Gibraltar once used it as a midway point to stable their horses and sleep on their way up to

Ronda – drawn to the dramatic gorge-straddling town in the wake of Wordsworth's 'Romantic revolution'. Proudly, she produced the visitors' book in which the guests had written their comments from the 1840s onwards.

On the third page, after an entry in Arabic by Sir Richard Burton, were some cautiously friendly but acerbic comments – 'tolerably acceptable welcome and at least fewer fleas, better than those damnable Spanish inns we've become used to' – by a certain Captain Luard, Coldstream Guards.

The Luards are a small family with a long military tradition, and the Coldstream the regiment in which many have served. In 1815 three of them died defending the little farm of La Haye Sainte at the centre of the field of Waterloo. The farm was the key to the battle, and the fight to hold it desperate. Again and again Napoleon threw his Imperial Guards at it, again and again the Coldstreamers beat them back.

Like Rorke's Drift in the Zulu wars, the defence of La Haye Sainte is part of the mythology of British military history. A former Coldstreamer myself, I was intrigued to know which of my ancestors this Captain Luard was. I wrote to the family genealogist, my great-uncle Percy, a scholarly canon who had christened me, to find out. A couple of months later I had a long letter back giving me the information I wanted.

Written in a beautifully clear and elegant hand, the letter ended:

'I'm sorry it's taken some time to reply. At the age of 103 I find it takes me rather longer than before to deal with my correspondence. At least the fact I can still tackle it with enjoyment confirms we Luards come of hardy stock!'

I parked the car and rang the bell of the rambling *hacienda* below the village where Elisabeth was staying.

I remembered the seven-year-old Francesca in a T-shirt and ragged jeans, nut-brown and as lithe as an eel, skipping across the little square above as she played the Spanish version of hopscotch. She was hardy, I thought as I stood in the darkness. She'd have made a fine companion-in-arms at La Haye Sainte or at Rorke's Drift, come to that.

Hardy, certainly. Just not hardy enough to withstand what had been thrown at her. Although if disease broke her body, it couldn't make its way through to her spirit. That remained robust and intact – utterly invulnerable.

We stayed a week in Gaucin.

Spent by the Santiago journey, I rested and slept. At the end of the week the organizers of the course decided to give a *fiesta*, a party, to celebrate its completion. They borrowed a little local barn, lit it with candles, hired a couple of *flamenco* guitarists from a nearby village, asked some of the local girls to dance, bought some excellent country wine and, naturally, got Elisabeth to orchestrate the food.

I still wasn't in the mood for 'partying', to use one of Francesca's favourite phrases, but I was persuaded to go. It turned out to be a lovely evening, funny and convivial with perhaps sixty or seventy of the local community, Andalusians and foreigners, drifting in and out. At about midnight the guitarists started to play and the girls to dance – and instantly something locked into place.

The music and the girls.

The harsh staccato sounds and rhythms of the *cante jondo* with its plaintive cries I'd heard time and again all over Andalucía, from the summer meadows where we'd gathered for picnics to the winter nights in the waterfront whorehouses of Algeciras. My beloved daughters who came there so often with us, I sometimes laughingly say, at least grew up as equals under the skin with their Andalusian bordello sisters.

The girls that night danced well although they didn't dance anything like as well as Francesca. They lacked her *gracia*, her fluency, her instinctive understanding of the music and the tapping beat of the guitarists, the elegance of the way she wove patterns with her wrists, lifted her neck, stamped her feet, held her head, cast down her eyes or boldly raised them with a challenging mocking smile. The girls were pure-bred Andalusian hill-folk, but she was even more Andalusian than they.

She had the *duende*, the soul and spirit of Spain's heartland, and I could see her turning and spinning in the shadows much more clearly than I saw them. It was too much for me to watch. I walked out into the night and walked through the woods back to the house. Inevitably owls were calling. Owls always called when she came to mind.

Somehow I had found Francesca in the dance more vividly than on the entire journey to Santiago.

'I offer you no comfort,' Priscilla wrote to me after the girl's death, 'nor will time, because there can be no comfort in the loss of a girl like that. Not now, not ever.' It was a bleak but wise assessment, infinitely more truthful – and, paradoxically because of that, more comforting – than the anodyne and pious messages of others. Truth needs the telling. This thing's final and time's no healer.

What time's passage can do is to serve as an accommodator. It may in the end make the pain bearable.

It was a cross and a delight to have a daughter of such shining brilliance. A cross and delight to have grown up in her company as she too grew up in mine. A cross, certainly, for her rages, her inability to compromise, the fearsome bleakness of her approach to the world's niceties. But a delight, yes, that above all was the abiding warming touch, a touch of fire – memory is far too weak a word – of her presence. Her sweetness, her beauty, her smile, her towering intellect that was frightening in the perceptions it led her to, the passion in her loyalty to her friends. All of that and her grace as a dancer.

I had seen her dancing again that night.

She had always danced everywhere. By the fires in the dusty glades of the Rocio pilgrimage. With the prostitutes in Andalusian cat-houses and the gypsies at the starlit annual Spanish *ferias*. Across the chill and wintry Languedoc and Provence with her friendly Legionnaires, spinning round them as the hulking bull-shouldered men clumsily tried to follow the child. At grand balls and teenage London nightclubs. In Switzerland, Cuba and Jamaica. Paris, New York and Madrid. Even one night, I remember, in Kathmandu after our return from the Himalaya.

Best of all for me to the bagpipes on my home island, the Hebridean island of Mull, that she loved too. There among her own clan she was briefly safe.

> *Beanntaichean arda is aillidh leacainnean,*
> *Sluagh ann an comhnuidh is coire cleachdainnean.*
> *'S aotrom mo cheum a' leum g'an fhaicinn,*
> *Is fanaidh mi tacan le deoin.*

The lines in Gaelic by the poet, John Cameron, were sent to me after the girl died by the scholarly Chrissie Macdonald, to whose little croft on Mull, looking out towards the Atlantic over Loch Tuath with its seals and storms, its sunsets, otters and gannets, Francesca loved to walk to collect the brown-shelled eggs with their rich clean orange yolks from Chrissie's hens. The lines translate roughly as follows:

> *Tall mountains and beautiful glades,*
> *My people gathered, kind, familiar.*
> *My step is light, skipping when I see them,*
> *I shall stay with them a short while, with their permission.*

Too short, Francesca, far too short, but none of us will ever forget the skipping.

Give her a hearty welcome, Santiago, St Jacques, St James — she likes champagne and developed a fondness for caviar and truffles. As welcoming presents a really stylish frock, a *flamenco* or *cante jondo* air to greet her at the gate, and the latest work on philosophy or physics, a book of poems or a South American novel in Spanish — all would go down well.

Good paste jewellery from Bond Street — it doesn't have to be expensive — would not come amiss. A stack of high-fashion magazines, the day's newspapers in several languages — she'll clip the bullfight reviews from *El País* for her brother — a pack of cigarettes (yes, I'm afraid she smokes, black French Gauloises or Gitanes will do), a flask of Guerlain's *L'Heure Bleu* scent, a *tarte aux fraises* from Revel's medieval market in the Cathar country, and a full set of London's telephone directories. She'll set about using them before you have time to say *matamoros*.

And to complete the list, a Legionnaire's *képi blanc* to be worn at a jaunty angle, Pamplona's scarlet cotton sash for her waist, and a chessboard furnished with proper wooden Staunton pieces.

Just look after the girl, would you?

Meanwhile, thank you, Santiago, traveller in stone boats, green man, giant, pagan, Christian, diviner of streams and waters, gentleman and blackamoor slayer, for seeing us safely on our way along the long

Camino. We'll continue to light candles to you and, of course, to the bonny girl.

What have we all got except children for our legacy of blood, bone and heart, saints for hope of something more, legends to knot and bind them both?

Sleep well, the two of you, saint and girl, and tell each other the stories I never quite got round to finishing. And keep a firm eye on Malcolm Lowry in that churchyard at Ripe. He can be a devil if he gets to the whisky. But then you can handle that, Fran, as resolutely as you handled me and everything else.

Appendix

More and more people, and I'm glad it's so, are setting out on pilgrimage journeys, particularly to Santiago.

Speculatively, wonderingly, they are exploring their own lives and looking for an experience that will change and illuminate them. Some will think they find it on the Way. Most will not. All of them will discover, perhaps years later, that it doesn't matter at all. All that matters is the journey itself: *that* and its latent coded messages is the experience.

Several people, I know at first hand, have decided to embark on the Way after listening to my own stories of our travels to Compostela. Others, perhaps, after reading this will make the same decision. To those who are thinking about it I would, as a hardened traveller in some of the most remote parts of the world, say this.

The entire traditional *Camino* to Santiago is, of course, perfectly possible to complete, but it's long and demanding – much more demanding than it appears on the maps. One thousand miles across often mountainous country isn't something to be undertaken on some romantic whim; it needs careful thought, and a number of searching personal decisions, before one starts. The best method, the most interesting and rewarding method of tackling it, is on foot.

Foot of course means feet, and feet are the key.

Give your feet tender loving care both before you begin and along the Way. The soles, the heels and front pads don't need to be hard. Paradoxically as it may seem, hard feet on a long tramp are a hazard – the skin tends to crack and bleed. What one needs is an underpinning of skin that is soft and supple, that can bend with the rocks and absorb their impact. The best way to achieve it is with lavish applications of a good lanolin cream.

Acquire a pair of good strong walking boots, and wear them in for at least a month before you start. Use them every day. Walk up and down the stairs in them. They'll get to know your feet and shape themselves to their contours. Oil or wax them every week: nothing's worse at the end of a long day's tramp than damp leaking leather, and blisters from sodden socks.

If you don't have a rucksack or backpack, buy or borrow one. If it is new, soak it in a tub or water-butt for a couple of days, then bring it inside and let it dry out. It will soften and unstiffen. Put four bricks in it and go for a two-hour walk. It will give you an idea of what you'll be carrying. Then soak it and dry it again.

Lay out on your bed everything you think you'll need – and then tip at the very least half of it onto the floor. You'll want nothing like what you imagine. Most of what you discard may look interesting and attractive, but on a pilgrim road it will prove to be weighty junk. If you are missing anything, you should be able to get it as you travel. Many people, particularly the older generations, forget how much the world has changed. Whereas I can now buy torch batteries in the most distant Kalahari bush camps, a year ago I found my mother on the eve of her departure to Sydney, rushing out in something of a panic to buy a spare tube of toothpaste. I gently had to explain that even the Australians brush their teeth now, and that Sydney has more pharmacies than Kensington.

For clothing, use the layer principle. Four T-shirts are lighter, warmer and more adaptable than one heavy sweater. I personally favour silk – the lightest material of all – but a good pure cotton-weave is probably even warmer. Many veteran Scottish hill-walkers, the dedicated climbers of the high tops, like changing their socks halfway through the day. It's an excellent practice, cutting down on the risk of blisters.

For myself, I like a complete change of clothes when the day's tramp is over. I unpeel everything, hang it out to dry – wherever that's possible – shower if I can, have a wash at the least although certainly not in the cold water basin in the goat-roaming slurry-stenched lodging on the Meseta, and pull on a polo-neck. Then, having lit candles in the church, I'm ready for music, champagne, dancing girls and the ball.

A good torch. A compass. A folding knife – endlessly useful. Good maps in a waterproof case. The London-based Confraternity of St James

[1st floor, Talbot Yard, Borough High Street, London SE1 1YP – tel. 0171-403 4500, fax 0171-620 4356], a quaint but splendid charitable organization with a multitude of addresses, will give advice on maps and books. We used the famed *Topo-Guides* in France – excellent in many ways but variable in their reliability, and needing navigational skills and experience to get the best out of. In the deep snow and moonless darkness of a thick Auvergne pine forest, a compass and a good nose are much more use than any map.

The pilgrim should have a careful pedicure before setting out; we are back on the subject of feet again, but it is vital. The condition of one's toenails, mundane as it may seem, is a key to contentment on the journey. Treat them like Bahrain pearls. Polish them, oil them, shape them, balance them, get them right, and the pilgrim is saved endless misery.

A flask of whisky for cheer in those moments of darkness and distress. A book of poetry or whatever one likes to read for consolation. A strong staff, a gruff voice to see off dogs, wolves and dragons, a cloak against the rain and snow, the pilgrim's scrip, for his most valued possessions.

That is all the pilgrim needs.

That and a measure of hope and faith, physical strength and mental tenacity, an inquiring mind, an observant eye, ideally languages (to me, at least half the joys and rewards of the journey would have been forfeit if the three of us hadn't been able to speak fluently in the common languages used along the Way) and, of course, song and laughter.

Finally, a box of matches with which to light the candles. The ignition systems in the churches of Rome seldom work. They must have been designed by a subversive Protestant.

Probably by my daughter.

'Index'

What follows is, I fear, a little unorthodox – a list of the full names of those I mention in the story of the long journey, and the places where I and my companions stayed along the Way.

I have divided it into two parts: the people first and then the places. I do not name the pilgrims we met on the Way, simply because on pilgrimage first names are enough and those are what I have used in the book. Robert from Gouda will always be for me Robert from Gouda. He was a fine, decent, jovial man, and his identification as such is enough.

My companions were my sister, Priscilla Wintringham-White, and Hilary Hugh-Jones. The other two Camberwell beauties who joined us for part of the journey were Angela Bebb and Elizabeth Capon. Caspar Luard, Dr Charles Knight, James Fergusson, and Nicholas Sole accompanied me through the Pyrénées to Pamplona.

Sir Laurens van der Post was an abiding presence. Elspeth Vernon chose the Ethiopian crosses for my companions to wear. Venetia Parkes' Dorset rectory was a sanctuary and safe-house during the last weeks of Francesca's life.

Among Francesca's throng of friends I have mentioned Amy Baker, the brilliant young lawyer who set up the Francesca Friendship Trust in the girl's memory; Peter Nash, the music impresario and her constant loyal companion; Marielle Wyse, the television and film producer, and another staunch friend of her heart; her flat-mate, the drummer Joe Crisp. I could add hundreds of names to the list. Those four will have to stand for them all.

The company, on the walk itself or standing in support, was eclectic and distinguished. With Francesca as the focus it was never likely to be anything else.

*

Then the places. Pilgrimage is essentially a movable wandering feast – one of its great delights. Where we stopped for the night will not necessarily fit the plans and routes of others, even if the path is broadly the same. We occasionally made detours, but all appear on the pilgrim maps and are places at which most pilgrims would stay.

The spelling of place names in remote France and Spain is always a problem. A village or hamlet can have two or three variants of its name. By and large I have followed the Serie Verte maps for France, and the Sampedro book of the *Camino* for Spain, although they may differ from the versions in, say, the Michelin maps. As I said at the start, this is not a guide or gazetteer. For me, the internal journey was perhaps even more important than the one on the ground, but here for what it is worth were our resting places.

The names of the overnight stops are listed in order, and in groups which indicate the six stages of my journey. Those *asterisked are places where my companions stayed on the few occasions when I could not be with them. I did not actually stay in those places within square brackets but they are included since they were staging posts.

Stage I: April 1993
Le Puy 15
St-Privat-d'Allier 26
Sauges 39
La Roche 44
Aumont-Aubrac 46
Montgros 50
St-Chély-d'Aubrac 53
Espalion 56
Estaing 58
Espeyrac 60
Conques 60
*Livinhac-le-Haut 61
*Figeac 61

Stage II: October 1993
Figeac 69

Cajarc 72
Limogne-en-Quercy 74
Mas de Vers 75
Cahors 76
Montcuq 78
Dufort-Lacapelette 81
Moissac 82

Stage III: April 1994
*Moissac 96
*Angeville
*St-Antoine
*Ste-Mère
*La Romieu
Condom 96
Montréal 98
Manciet 101